Resisting Asian American Invisibility

The Politics of Race and Education

Stacey J. Lee

TEACHERS COLLEGE PRESS

TEACHERS COLLEGE | COLUMBIA UNIVERSITY
NEW YORK AND LONDON

Published by Teachers College Press,® 1234 Amsterdam Avenue, New York, NY 10027

Copyright © 2022 by Teachers College, Columbia University

Library of Congress Cataloging-in-Publication Data is available at loc.gov

ISBN 978-0-8077-6744-3 (paper)
ISBN 978-0-8077-6745-0 (hardcover)
ISBN 978-0-8077-8127-2 (ebook)

Printed on acid-free paper
Manufactured in the United States of America

Contents

Acknowledgments   v

1. **The Problem of Asian American Invisibility**   1

    The Harm of Invisibility and Hypervisibility   4

    Anti-Asian Racism   5

    Resisting Anti-Asian Racism: The Politics of Being the Model Minority   8

    Resisting Anti-Asian Racism: Panethnicity and Cross-Racial Coalitions   10

    Community-Based Education as Resilience and Resistance   12

    Road Map for the Book   13

2. **Hmong Americans in Lakeview**   15

    Team Approach to Multi-Sited Ethnography   18

    Researcher Politics, Ethics, and Positionality   21

3. **Invisibility and Hypervisibility at UHS**   29
    Stacey J. Lee and Linda M. Pheng

    The Academic World of Hmong American Students at UHS   31

    Trapped in ESL   34

    College Readiness Programs   41

    Beyond Academics: Hmong American Students' Social Worlds   45

    Conclusion   52

4. **Middle-Class Hmong Leadership and the Push for Inclusion**   56
    Stacey J. Lee and Mai Neng Vang

    Hmong Education Advocates (HEA)   59

    Disaggregating Hmong Data   61

Concerns Regarding ESL   66

Calls for Culturally Relevant Pedagogy and Hmong Staff   70

Community-Based Education: The Hmong Meskas Summer Camp   73

Program Funding and Support   76

Youth Voices   78

Conclusion   80

5. **Solidarity Holds Our Unity Together (SHOUT):**
    Education for Liberation   **84**
    Stacey J. Lee and Choua Xiong

Community-Based Education at SHOUT   87

Challenging Anti-Blackness   88

Culturally Specific Programming   94

Critical Approaches and Radical Healing   100

Conclusion   103

6. **Disrupting Invisibility**   **107**

Disrupting Invisibility Through Culturally Sustaining Pedagogy   111

References   **115**

Index   **129**

About the Authors   **137**

Acknowledgments

This book was a team effort from the initial conceptualization of the research project to the final edits on the page. The book would never have been possible without the insights and labor of my co-researchers—Linda Pheng, Choua Xiong, and Mai Neng Vang. I truly appreciate the way the three of you stuck with the project as you balanced your own research and personal lives. I learned a lot about the benefits of team-based ethnographic research, including the value of diverse perspectives. Thank you. Our research team owes a huge debt of gratitude to the people at the three research sites—University Heights High, Hmong Education Advocates (HEA) and Solidarity Holds Our Unity Together (SHOUT). Thank you for letting us learn from you. I hope we've done justice to your stories. The initial research was generously funded by a Vilas Mid-Career Investigator Award at the University of Wisconsin in 2015.

I'd like to thank the following colleagues for listening and giving feedback, commenting on drafts, and/or pointing me to relevant cites: Bianca Baldridge, Lesley Bartlett, Nancy Kendall, Adam Nelson, Linn Posey-Maddox, Erica Turner, Maggie Hawkins, Diana Hess, Lois Weis, Xue Lan Rong, A. Lin Goodwin, Gilberto Conchas, Deoksoon Kim, Rebecca Lowenhaupt, Stanton Wortham, Kevin Kumashiro, Shuning Liu, Bic Ngo, Sabina Vaught, Danny Walsh, Reva Jaffe-Walter, Stefanie Wong, Julissa Ventura and Eujin Park. Thanks also to my many current and former students for inspiring me every day. I've had the opportunity to share aspects of this research with audiences at the following institutions—Boston College, University at Buffalo, UC-Irvine, University of Kentucky, and the University of Pennsylvania—and with audiences at various conferences—AERA, Asian American Studies Association and the Southeast Asian American Studies Conference.

Thanks to the anonymous reviewers for asking tough questions on an early draft of the manuscript. Thanks to Brian Ellerbeck and the entire team at Teachers College Press.

And finally, thanks to Lisa Konoplisky for providing critical feedback on this and all my other research projects since my dissertation, and for being my anchor.

CHAPTER 1

The Problem of Asian American Invisibility

The first time Stacey met Kendall was in February 2016 at a community event for Black History Month. At 13, Kendall was the leader of SHOUT's Hmong girls' dance troupe. SHOUT (Solidarity Holds Our Unity Together) is a community-based organization that serves the low-income Southeast Asian American and Black communities in Lakeview, Wisconsin. Speaking in a mix of English and Hmong, Kendall directed her fellow dancers to practice before going on stage. In Stacey's fieldnotes for that day, she described Kendall as "sassy and confident." The second time Stacey saw Kendall was at a meeting for SHOUT's Hmong girls' discussion group in April 2016, where Kendall led a discussion on girls' body image and self-confidence. While she expressed some insecurities about her appearance, Kendall was articulate, confident, and critical in identifying the role of popular culture in girls' body dysmorphia. When our research team learned that Kendall would be attending high school in the fall of 2016, we looked forward to seeing her challenge social injustices at University Heights High. During our first few weeks at University Heights High in 2016, however, we had a very difficult time locating Kendall, and when we did finally find her, she was sitting with one other Hmong girl in a dark corner of a hallway during lunch. Unlike the bright, critical, and exuberant youth we'd seen at SHOUT, Kendall appeared withdrawn, isolated, and nearly invisible at University Heights High.

Over time, we learned that Kendall was academically and socially marginalized and adrift at University Heights High. Like the majority of Hmong students at the school, Kendall was still labeled an English learner despite the fact that she was born and entirely educated in the United States. Like many of her Hmong peers, she received sporadic ESL services but had little understanding of why she was still labeled an English learner. Over the course of our ethnographic fieldwork at University Heights High, members of the research team often found Kendall cutting classes, and when she was in class, she was silent and disengaged. Similar to most of the Hmong youth we spoke with in our study, Kendall had experienced racism in and out of school; she did not feel as if any adults at the school would advocate for her. Kendall often discussed feeling alienated by a school that did not know or care about her or Hmong people. When asked who she would go to if she experienced problems at school, Kendall shrugged and said "Well, I can't go to anyone at school because I don't feel comfortable around them."

The feelings of isolation and invisibility experienced by Kendall were all too common among the Hmong American youth we encountered. Indeed, invisibility—the state of being unseen, unknown, unrecognized—has become a central trope in describing Southeast Asian American educational experiences, including Hmong Americans. The Hmong youth we met complained that most of their non-Hmong classmates and teachers don't know who Hmong people are or how they came to live in the United States. In fact, all our Hmong participants, including both youth and adults, expressed concern about the relative invisibility of Hmong Americans. Wisconsin has the third largest Hmong population in the country, and the last significant group of Hmong refugees was resettled in the United States in 2005, but most non-Hmong students and many educators know little about Hmong people or their refugee history. For many educators, 2005 seemed like a long time ago and the Vietnam War that turned Hmong people into refugees seemed like ancient history. The busy and often overwhelmed teachers we met had turned their attention to newer groups such as refugees from Burma, and to the Black and White achievement gap.

Because they are lumped into the Asian American racial category, the specific history, culture, and experiences of the Hmong people are rendered invisible. Hmong American youth and adults regularly remarked that "people don't know who Hmong are" or "they [non-Hmong] think we are Chinese or something." Like most other school districts in the United States, the Lakeview School District where we conducted research relied on aggregate data on Asian Americans for years. As scholars have long argued, aggregate data on Asian Americans masks the educational experiences, concerns, and challenges of smaller Asian ethnic groups and perpetuates the stereotype that Asian American students are high achieving "model minorities" (Lee 2009). The disaggregated data on Hmong students in Lakeview (discussed in Chapter 4) revealed that nearly all Hmong students are classified as English learners when they enroll in Lakeview schools, and many remain in ESL when they enter high school. The academic issues faced by Hmong youth, including being labeled long-term English learners led some Lakeview educators and students to view Hmong people as "failed" model minorities. Indeed, many of the Hmong youth in our study were afraid that there is a stigma associated with being Hmong. Although all our Hmong participants are concerned about the invisibility of the Hmong American community and the racism directed at the Hmong American community, they did not express a common response to the problem of invisibility. As we will show, our participants' responses to invisibility and racism reflected their various social positions, their aspirations, and their understandings of race and inequality.

Resisting Asian American Invisibility focuses on the problem of invisibility, and the related problem of hypervisibility, faced by Hmong American youth in a Midwestern city we call Lakeview, and the responses of the Hmong American community to their invisibility. The theme of Hmong invisibility emerged from the data early in our fieldwork and from this initial theme we developed the following guiding research questions: How are Hmong youth rendered invisible in schools and through dominant discourses regarding race and racism? How are Hmong

American communities challenging their invisibility? What role do community-based educational spaces play in community resistance? In this book we examine the ways Hmong youth are marginalized and rendered invisible by educational policies, practices, and discourses, by dominant Black-and-White understandings of race and racism, and by the Asian American panethnic category that advances the model minority stereotype. We also explore the ways Hmong American leaders, parents, and youth understand, negotiate, and challenge invisibility and hypervisibility through educational advocacy and community-based education.

Our participants generally chose one of two strategies for challenging the invisibility and concomitant hypervisibility faced by Hmong American youth, which harken back to the strategies used by other Asian Americans. On the one hand, the growing number of college-educated Hmong professionals are working within the dominant system for inclusion and recognition. These middle-class professionals are deeply invested in maintaining a distinct Hmong identity and engage in strategic essentialism in their efforts to work with the dominant society (Ngo, 2013). As individuals who have successfully used formal education to achieve social mobility, these leaders believe that formal education is key to the social mobility of Hmong American youth and the larger Hmong community. These individuals were particularly concerned about the opportunity gaps faced by Hmong youth, including the relative absence of Hmong perspectives in educational debates that they argued were dominated by the Black-and-White racial paradigm. They sought recognition from schools in the form of culturally responsive pedagogy, bilingual education, and the hiring of Hmong staff. By cultivating relationships with institutional agents associated with dominant institutions, including school leaders, Hmong professionals were recognized by district leaders as the voice of the Hmong community. In addition to working within the public school system, Hmong professionals developed community-based educational programming that aimed to teach Hmong youth about Hmong culture, history, and language.

In contrast, low-income, politically progressive Hmong leaders are building cross-racial coalitions with Black communities to challenge anti-Black racism, and to fight for the redistribution of power. These politically progressive Hmong community activists rejected the dominant narrative of social mobility, and actively resisted and challenged the authority of dominant institutions, including public schools. These Hmong American leaders had roots in low-income Southeast Asian American communities and remained committed to the concerns facing the poorest and most marginalized Southeast Asians, which they argued have been left behind by their middle-class co-ethnics. Significantly, through grassroots organizing and community-based education, they encouraged Hmong and other Southeast Asian American youth to build cross-racial coalitions with Black communities to fight for the redistribution of material resources and for a form of recognition that addressed status inequalities. In contrast to Hmong middle-class professionals who were concerned with culturally responsive educational programming, politically progressive Hmong activists were involved in educational campaigns for "police-free schools." Finally, while Hmong professionals focused exclusively on advocating for the Hmong community, progressive activists were committed to challenging anti-Blackness as a route to freedom for all minoritized communities. We argue that the strategies employed by the Hmong American community leaders reflected their respective understandings of race and racism, their aspirations for the future of their communities and their understanding of the role of education in achieving their aspirations.

While this book focuses on the experiences, perspectives, and actions of Hmong American youth and adults in one city in Wisconsin, it is not *just* a story of these individuals or even of Hmong Americans more generally. In the tradition of critical ethnography, we argue that the story of invisibility/hypervisibility and educational advocacy among Hmong Americans in Lakeview is an illustrative one that reveals the way educational policies and existing racial discourses influence the options that Asian Americans, and Hmong Americans in particular, have for challenging inequality.

THE HARM OF INVISIBILITY AND HYPERVISIBILITY

Marginalized and minoritized groups, including groups of color, too often suffer from *invisibility* in dominant institutions that reflect and value White, middle-class norms. In schools, for example, the perspectives, histories, and concerns of non-White students are often rendered invisible—they are erased, silenced, excluded. In addition to invisibility, marginalized groups can also be subjected to *hypervisibility*, whereby their experiences and identities are essentialized, demonized, stereotyped and/or viewed from deficit perspectives (Lee et al., 2017; N. Nguyen, 2019; Truong-Vu, 2022). The experiences of Black and Muslim students subjected to heightened surveillance in schools demonstrate the ways hypervisibility operates (Brown & Donnor, 2011; Dumas, 2016; Ferguson, 2000; Morris, 2016; N. Nguyen, 2019; Vaught, 2017; Wun, 2016). Students categorized as English learners are faced with assimilationist language policies that render their linguistic practices both invisible and hypervisible. While seemingly different, both invisibility and hypervisibility deny members of marginalized groups full humanity, including the right to be seen both as members of groups and as individuals. Both invisibility and hypervisibility are the result of power and inequality, and therefore are not natural states, but ones produced by violence and neglect.

The scholarship on recognition (i.e., respect for cultural differences) and misrecognition (i.e., erasure or denigration of cultural differences) offers important insights into the harm experienced by groups who are rendered invisible and/or hypervisible. Advocates for the politics of recognition argue that social justice requires the recognition of cultural differences, and that misrecognition is the central social injustice for marginalized groups (Taylor, 1994; Taylor & Gutmann, 1997). According to this perspective, identities are produced through social interactions in both private and public realms, and misrecognition or lack of recognition in the public realm causes psychic harm to members of marginalized groups. Self-hatred, such as internalized racism or internalized homophobia, is understood to be a core harm that denies marginalized groups full humanity. Thus, freedom for marginalized and minoritized groups requires being freed from the harmful and deficit images cast upon them by dominant groups (Fanon, 2008; Taylor & Gutmann, 1997). Expanding on the debates surrounding the politics of recognition, Fraser, Honneth, and Golb (2003) argues for the importance of going beyond social and cultural appreciation to include equal legal recognition that allows groups to fight for social rights. Thus, the fight for "a politics of equal recognition" calls for differences to be acknowledged and accorded equal status (Taylor & Gutmann, 1997). Overall, proponents of a politics of recognition support actions that lead to visibility and recognition, such as those associated with identity politics.

While Taylor and Honneth view misrecognition as the central harm facing marginalized groups that must be addressed to achieve justice, Fraser et al. (2003) argue that recognition is "one crucial but limited dimension of social justice" (p. 199). In making her argument about the nature of misrecognition, Fraser fuses the harm done by misrecognition with the harm done by economic inequality or mal-distribution. Furthermore, in contrast to arguments that the harm done by misrecognition is centrally about the lack of affirmation, Fraser argues that the harm done by misrecognition is centrally about a lack of *status*. Specifically, Fraser asserts that a lack of recognition results in a status inequality that prevents marginalized groups from full and equal participation in social realms, including the economy (2003, p. 29). To the discussion of recognition and redistribution, Fraser (2009) adds the political dimension of justice, which she argues "specifies the reach of those other dimensions: it tells us who is included, and who excluded, from the circle of those entitled to a just distribution and reciprocal recognition" (p. 20).

Within the current historical moment that is characterized by growing economic inequality, heightened racism and xenophobia, and the ongoing pandemic, low-income immigrant communities suffer from misrecognition, economic precarity, and political harm in ways that highlight the ways injustices overlap. Educational inequalities reflect economic injustice, cultural misrecognition, and lack of representation. As education scholar Amanda Keddie (2012) argues, "Matters of distribution, for example, are not purely about economics—they are informed and shaped by matters of cultural recognition and political representation" (p. 276). Educational reforms, however, too often focus on one form of injustice in ways that limit the possibility for equity. Many multicultural efforts, for example, reflect the politics of recognition and focus solely on representation in the curriculum. Weak or superficial approaches to multicultural education have even been shown to reproduce essentialized ideas regarding marginalized and minoritzed groups, thereby rendering them simultaneously invisible and hypervisible. In *Resisting Asian American Invisibility*, we will examine the impact of misrecognition on Hmong students.

ANTI-ASIAN RACISM

Race and racism are intimately intertwined in the history of the United States, and racism permeates dominant culture, policies, and institutions. As a form of social injustice, racism embodies unequal distribution of material resources, misrecognition, and lack of representation. Race shapes opportunities; it determines the social value assigned to groups and the opportunities to exercise citizenship rights. Race and racism are produced and reproduced in our schools in ways that render students of color invisible and/or hypervisible. Dominant racial discourses frame race, racism, and racial inequality largely in Black-and-White terms. Positioned at the top of the racial hierarchy, Whites are characterized as the norm and Whiteness is equated with American citizenship. Blackness and Black people, on the other hand, are defined as the ultimate racial threat to White people, the White nation and White supremacy. Throughout U.S. history, anti-Black racism has required Black bodies to be feared, hated, contained, and disciplined (Feagin, 2013; Sexton, 2010).

The Black-and-White racial paradigm reflects the realities of a history rooted in White supremacy and the enslavement and economic exploitation of Black people, but it erases the complex reality that racism has multiple expressions. As Omi and Winant (2014) argued in their seminal work *Racial Formation in the United States*, different racial groups are subjected to different racial projects. While different racialized groups (i.e., non-Whites) experience different forms of racism, racialized groups and experiences of racism do not exist in isolation from one another. In her work on the relational nature of race, Natalia Molina (2018) argues that "the lives of racialized groups affect each other across time and space, even when they do not directly cross paths" (p. 101). That is, discourses and even policies regarding one racialized group can influence how other groups of color are understood and treated. Chinese Americans who lived in the Mississippi Delta during the Jim Crow era, for example, were initially categorized as Blacks and only later viewed as being distinct from both Whites and Blacks (Lee, 2017).

Asian Americans occupy an ambiguous position within the dominant Black-and-White racial paradigm; they are at times left out of the picture entirely or are assumed to have overcome racism (thought of as "nearly White"), and at other times they are seen as part of the larger group of "people of color." The idea that Asian Americans are "nearly White," "honorary Whites," or "White-adjacent" reflects the fact that some East and South Asian Americans have achieved educational and economic success as reflected in the model minority stereotype. While some Asian Americans have achieved relative success, this does not mean that Asian Americans do not face racism. Anti-Asian racism has historically been rooted in xenophobic ideas regarding the supposed cultural, moral, economic, political, and physical threat of Asians. At this very moment, the United States and the entire globe are in the midst of the COVID-19 pandemic, and Asian Americans are experiencing an uptick in anti-Asian racism that has been fueled by racist and xenophobic discourses regarding the virus. In response to the increase in anti-Asian racism, a coalition of Asian American–Pacific Islander organizations, AAPI Equity Alliance, launched Stop AAPI Hate (http://www.asianpacificpolicyandplanningcouncil.org/stop-aapi-hate), where Asian Americans can report incidents of discrimination, and within the first month of operation the group received nearly 1,500 reports of coronavirus discrimination from Asian Americans across the United States.

The history of Asian Americans demonstrates that anti-Asian racism has taken the form of exclusionary immigration and naturalization policies and narratives that position Asian Americans as permanent outsiders to the nation. The relative absence of Asian Americans in dominant understandings of race and racism can be partly explained by the fact that Asian Americans have historically constituted a relatively small racial group in the United States because of exclusionary immigration policies. With the passage of the Chinese Exclusion Act of 1882, Chinese immigrants became the first group to be subjected to exclusionary immigration policies. Contrary to narratives that depict the United States as a nation of immigrants, the experiences of Chinese immigrants demonstrate that immigration policies have long been gatekeeping policies that have played a central role in the racial and cultural makeup of the nation (Hing, 2012; Lee, E., 2003). The rhetoric surrounding Chinese exclusion relied on ideas that Chinese immigrants were permanently alien and therefore threatening to the nation (Lee, E. 2003; Ngai, 2004; Takaki, 2008). As historian Mae Ngai explains, "Immigration policy is constitutive of Americans' understanding of national membership and citizenship, drawing lines of inclusion and exclusion that articulate a desired composition—imagined if not necessarily realized—of the nation" (2004, p. 5).

The anti-Chinese sentiment that fueled Chinese exclusion quickly extended to other Asians, including Japanese, Korean, and Indian immigrants (Lee, E., 2003). By the 1920s, Southern and Eastern European immigrants became the subjects of gatekeeping policies. While these immigrants faced discriminatory policies and practices, they were classified as members of the White race and therefore had the right to naturalized citizenship. As historian Erika Lee noted, "Whiteness permitted European immigrants more access to full participation in the larger American polity, economy, and society" (p. 38). Indeed, throughout the history of the United States Whiteness has been key to the terms of inclusion in the nation (Molina, 2010). While White immigrants are absorbed into the nation within a generation and have the option of identifying with their ethnic origins, multiple-generation Asian Americans remain identified as perpetual foreigners whose status is tied to their ancestral homelands.

The image of Asian Americans as perpetual foreigners continues to be a central racializing discourse into the 21st century, reflecting what political scientist Claire Jean Kim refers to as a form of civic ostracism that casts "Asian Americans as immutably foreign and unassimilable with Whites on cultural and/or racial grounds in a way that excludes Asian Americans from civic membership" (Kim, 2000, p. 16). As political scientists Natalie Masuoka and Jane Junn observed, Americans view foreigners and foreignness as being threatening to the nation and "the racial category of Asian was synonymous with 'outsider'" (2013, p. 55). Xenophobic narratives regarding Asian Americans as perpetual foreigners are perpetuated by popular media and even by politicians. Popular cultural representations of Asian American cultures, including jokes about Asian languages and accents, paint Asian Americans as quintessentially un-American (Lee, R. G., 1999).

Research confirms that Asian Americans are discriminated against because of their race or ethnicity, their native language and/or Asian accent (Goto, Gee &

Takeuchi, 2002; Kim et al., 2011). The stereotype that Asian Americans are perpetual foreigners is implicated in anti-Asian harassment of Asian American youth in K–12 schools. Indeed, Asian Americans report higher levels of racial discrimination than other groups of color (Mouttapa et al., 2004). Asian American youth experience racial discrimination including physical (e.g., slapping and pushing) and verbal harassment (e.g., name-calling, mocking accents) by non-Asian peers (Lorenzo et al., 2000).

RESISTING ANTI-ASIAN RACISM: THE POLITICS OF BEING THE MODEL MINORITY

On April 5, 2020, *The New York Times* reported that "Throughout New York and New Jersey, small groups from the Chinese-American community are uniting to fight the pandemic in this country even as they face racist remarks and some physical attacks" (La Gorce, 2020). The article explained the efforts of Chinese American professionals to gather medical supplies for local hospitals even as they face an uptick in racist attacks in the wake of the coronavirus pandemic. Across the United States, Asian and Asian American groups have been engaged in similar efforts in their communities. Andrew Yang, the former Democratic presidential candidate, encouraged Asian Americans to "embrace and show our Americanness" by helping neighbors, donating money and supplies and even wearing red, white and blue (Yang, 2020). The model minority performance of civic engagement encouraged by Andrew Yang is a direct response to anti-Asian racism that casts Asians Americans as perpetual foreigners who are a threat to the nation. Those who espouse this strategy for coping with anti-Asian racism hope that performing a model minority identity will demonstrate that Asians are worthy citizens.

Indeed, Asian Americans have a long history of trying to convince the dominant group that Asians deserve to be included in the nation. In her historical examination of the formation of the model minority stereotype, Ellen Wu (2014) found that Chinese American leaders in the post-WWII era engaged in self-stereotyping in an effort to convince White Americans that Chinese Americans were worthy and deserving American citizens. Their strategy included building on dominant ideas regarding the family and citizenship and emphasizing Chinese American families as socially conservative and strict. As Wu argues, "The conceit of the meritorious Chinatown family constituted a fundamental precondition for the emergence of Chinese Americans as definitively not-black model minorities" (p. 182).

Research on Chinese Americans who lived in the Mississippi Delta during Jim Crow points to similar strategies. The first Chinese immigrants in the Mississippi Delta were viewed by Whites as essentially "Black" and thus barred from White schools, White organizations, White neighborhoods, and White social life (Loewen, 1988). Through a strategy that included entrepreneurship, the development of social capital in the form of ties to powerful Whites, accommodation to dominant White cultural norms, and the performance of a nonthreatening identity, Chinese immigrants in the Mississippi Delta carved out a distinct social position between the Black community and the White community, which included admission to White public schools prior to the Brown decision (Lee, 2017; Loewen, 1988; Quan, 1982).

Although various Chinese and Japanese American communities embraced the performance of deservingness during the first half of the 20th century, the dominant White society did not identify Asian Americans as model minorities until the civil rights era. During this period the mainstream press advanced the image of Asian Americans as hardworking, law-abiding, family-oriented immigrants who had achieved economic and academic success, thus demonstrating that equal opportunities for people of color existed. Not insignificantly, the positioning of Chinese and Japanese Americans as model minorities was predicated on the idea that Black and brown communities were somehow lacking, and therefore responsible for any inequalities they faced. In other words, the idea that Asian Americans are model minorities has always relied on anti-Blackness and has always served as a racial wedge between Asian Americans and other groups of color (Lee, S. J., 2009). Since the civil rights era the idea that Asian Americans are model minorities has become a widely accepted stereotype and continues to be a point of contention within Asian American communities, with some embracing the label and others critiquing it as a tool of racism.

Since the late 20th century, the idea that Asian American students are high-achieving model minorities has dominated educational discourses. The model minority image of Asian Americans has resulted in Asian Americans being grouped with White students in discussions of the racialized achievement and opportunity gap. While many Asian American scholars and activists contest the model minority stereotype as being racist and masking the complex experiences of Asian Americans, other Asian Americans embrace and perform the model minority image. Most recently, for example, Asian American plaintiffs against Harvard University have drawn on the image of Asian Americans as model minorities, and notions of meritocracy, to argue that race-conscious admissions policies disadvantage Asian Americans (Kim, 2018). Both ideas regarding meritocracy and the notion of Asian Americans as model minorities rely on anti-Blackness and ultimately uphold White supremacy (Kim, 2018; Moses et al., 2019; Park & Liu, 2014).

While the model minority stereotype suggests that Asian Americans have overcome racism, educational scholarship suggests that some Asian American communities embrace model minority behavior to resist racism. A growing body of research reveals that Asian immigrant parents' emphasis on education stems from their concerns regarding racism in the broader society, and the assumption that high academic achievement may protect their children (Dhingra, 2020; J. Lee & Zhou, 2015; S. J. Lee, 2009; Louie, 2004; Park, 2020). Furthermore, some Asian immigrant parents have been shown to adopt a narrow focus on STEM fields based on the assumption that these fields will be more objective (Conchas & Pérez, 2003; J. Lee & Zhou, 2015; S. J. Lee, 2009; Louie, 2004). Even the "Tiger Mom" parenting style associated with Asian Americans may be a response to concerns regarding discrimination (J. Lee & Zhou, 2015).

Furthermore, the current rise in anti-Asian racism related to the COVID-19 pandemic illustrates that the prevalence of the model minority stereotype has not erased the image of Asian Americans as perpetual foreigners. Some Asian American scholars have argued that the model minority stereotype and the stereotype of Asian Americans as dangerous perpetual foreigners are two sides of the same coin. Indeed, many of the same characteristics associated with the model minority stereotype—hardworking, family oriented, and quiet—are linked to the perpetual foreigner stereotype as well (Masuoka & Junn, 2013). The idea that Asian Americans are somehow always outside the nation contributes to the relative invisibility of Asian Americans in contemporary conversations about race. In other words, the racialization of Asian Americans as essentially outside the category of "American" has rendered Asian Americans irrelevant in matters of race, racism, and racial inequality.

RESISTING ANTI-ASIAN RACISM: PANETHNICITY AND CROSS-RACIAL COALITIONS

In contrast to the strategy employed by those Asian Americans who engage in self-stereotyping as model minorities, Asian American activists in the 1960s directly challenged racism and other forms of social inequality. While the activism of early Asian American immigrants remained within single ethnic groups (e.g., Chinese Americans, Japanese Americans), Asian American activists at the height of the civil rights era embraced a panethnic identity as Asians and/or Asian Americans. By organizing multiple national-origin groups under a pan-Asian label, Asian American activists focused on common experiences with racial discrimination. This strategic response allowed ethnic groups with relatively small populations to form a bigger voice in the fight against racism (Espiritu, 1992). Asian American activists during this period also built cross-racial coalitions, particularly with African American activists (Maeda, 2005; Prashad, 2002). The scholarship on Asian American political activism suggests that Asian American activists were not just focused on equal rights for Asian Americans but concerned broadly about anti-racism, ending economic exploitation of the working class, and ending global imperialism. Describing the imaginings of Asian American activists, historian Daryl Maeda wrote, "They dreamed ambitiously of global transformations and multiracial, international coalitions even as they acted locally" (p. 4).

Demographic changes in the Asian American population in the late 20th and the 21st centuries have posed challenges to the pan-Asian coalitions forged during the height of the civil rights era. During the 1960s and early 1970s Chinese, Japanese, and Filipinos made up the majority of those classified as Asian American. Today, Asian Americans trace their roots to over 20 countries in East Asia, Southeast Asia, and the Indian subcontinent. Among these are over 1.2 million Southeast Asian refugees who fled the wars in Southeast Asia starting in 1975 and settled in the United States. The diverse histories, languages, cultures, religions, and social class and educational backgrounds of those who are lumped together in the Asian American category make uniting under a common racial category difficult.

While Asian Americans made up a mere 1% of the total U.S. population in 1965, in 2018 Asians were estimated to make up 5.8% of the total U.S. population (https://www.census.gov/quickfacts/fact/table/US/PST045218). Indeed, one quarter of all immigrants who arrived in the U.S. since 1965 trace their origins to Asia, and today Asians make up the fastest-growing racial group in the nation (Lopez, Ruiz & Patten, 2017; Budiman & Ruiz, 2021). More recent Asian immigrants and refugees often view the Asian American category as a strange American invention that is being forced on them, remarking that they "become Asian" when they land in the United States (Lee, 2009).

Southeast Asian Americans have raised particular concerns about the Asian American category, arguing that it masks the complex histories and experiences of their communities. In other words, many Southeast Asian Americans have argued that they experience invisibility within a racial group that is often invisible in the dominant racial framework. The Southeast Asian category is itself a panethnic category that erases linguistic and cultural differences, but Southeast Asians who were displaced as the result of the Vietnam War (e.g., Hmong, Cambodians, Lao, Vietnamese) share an experience as refugees. Pointing to important social class differences among Asian Americans, Yen Le Espiritu (2006), has argued that "if Asian Americans are to build a self-consciously panAsian solidarity, they need to take seriously the heterogeneities among their ranks and overcome the narrow dominance of the professional class and that of the two oldest Asian American groups" (p. 418). Similarly, Loan Dao (2020) notes that through the 1990s the Asian American movement evolved in ways that exposed the social class differences between East Asian Americans and Southeast Asian Americans in which Southeast Asian "refugees embodied the client in need of assistance, in need of saving, and in need of voice" (p. 13).

Asian Americans express a variety of attitudes toward cross-racial solidarity. Since the 1960s, some Asian Americans have maintained a commitment to cross-racial coalitions in their resistance to racism, but this commitment has not been consistent across time or among all Asian American groups. More politically conservative Asian Americans have historically remained relatively silent on anti-Black racism and racism against other non-Asian groups. Asian Americans involved in the lawsuit against Harvard's race-conscious admissions policies, for example, have generally been silent about racism against non-Asians, which has served to support White supremacy and anti-Blackness. As we write, Asian American communities are divided in their response to the current uprisings against police brutality and anti-Blackness in the wake of the murders of George Floyd, Breonna Taylor, and Ahmaud Arbery, among countless others. Various Asian American organizations have demonstrated both recognition of the relative privilege experienced by Asians Americans and the importance of fighting against anti-Black racism within Asian American communities and in the larger society. Still other Asian Americans, however, continue to view Asian American interests as being largely separate from those of the Black community. The Hmong American community, for example, was divided over the murder of George Floyd because one of the officers involved in the murder is a Hmong American man. As we will show, Lakeview's Hmong American communities are also divided in their interpretations of racism and their strategies for fighting the invisibility and hypervisibility experienced by Hmong people.

COMMUNITY-BASED EDUCATION AS RESILIENCE AND RESISTANCE

In the face of forced assimilation and institutional racism, minoritized communities, including Asian American immigrant and refugee groups, have long relied on co-ethnic/co-racial community-based educational spaces (CBES) to supplement traditional schools (Baldridge, 2019; Reyes, 2007; Wong, 2010; Zhou & Kim, 2006). Scholarship on CBES reveals that these spaces play a central role in supporting resistance to the hegemonic forces of traditional education for youth of color (Baldridge et al., 2017). CBES can foster connections to heritage languages and cultures, encourage healthy ethnic/racial identities, support academic achievement, and offer opportunities for youth to develop critical citizenship, including the skills to challenge the inequalities facing their communities through community action (Baldridge, 2014; Kirshner, 2007; Kwon, 2013).

Immigrant and refugee parents in the United States have historically been concerned with maintaining their distinct heritage languages. While some critics of multiculturalism have raised fears that the current generation of immigrants is rejecting English, generations of immigrants since the earliest settlers have sought to preserve their ethnolinguistic practices, often relying on co-ethnic community-based language schools (Fishman, 2014). For example, since the late 19th century, Chinese immigrants have established Chinese language schools to help the second-generation preserve language and cultural background (Zhou & Kim, 2006). After World War II and through the 1960s the number of Chinese language schools declined, but with the influx of post-1965 Chinese immigrants there has been a reemergence of Chinese language schools and other youth-centered community-based spaces (Zhou & Li, 2003). Scholarship suggests that immigrant groups have had limited success in achieving the goal of maintaining heritage languages through participation in language schools, but co-ethnic language schools have helped to support a connection to ethnic cultures (Olneck, 2009).

Recent scholarship on contemporary Asian immigrants suggests that parents turn to language schools to support ethnic-racial socialization and the broader educational needs of their children (Park, 2020; Zhou & Li, 2003). Growing numbers of middle- to upper-middle-class East and South Asian Americans rely on supplemental education, both nonprofit co-ethnic community-based education and for-profit institutions, to support their children's academic growth (Dhingra, 2020; Park, 2020; Zhou & Kim, 2006). There is a dearth of scholarship on heritage language schools for Hmong and other Southeast Asian American communities, but research suggests that Hmong and other Southeast Asian communities are concerned about maintaining their heritage languages. In their descriptive study of co-ethnic Asian afterschool programs and language schools, Paik et al. (2017) discovered that Cambodian,

Hmong, and Lao communities across the country have established nonprofit after-school and language programs. Some programs offered academic enrichment and almost all included some emphasis on culture.

In addition to preserving ethnic language and culture, and fostering academic achievement, CBES can also support youth activism and inclusive civic engagement among minoritized youth (Dyrness & Sepulveda, 2020; Flanagan & Christens, 2011; Ginwright, 2007, 2010; Ginwright & Cammarota, 2007; Kirshner, 2007; Kwon, 2013). CBES that focus on race can successfully disrupt deficit discourses regarding youth of color (Baldridge, 2014; Kwon, 2013). The success of these programs depends on meaningful and trusted relationships between adults and youth, and the inclusion of a larger sociopolitical analysis (Baldridge et al., 2017; Ginwright & Cammarota, 2007; Gonzales, 2015). Some CBES for Southeast Asian American youth use culturally relevant arts programming to encourage social critique (Ngo, 2017b; Reyes, 2007). For example, Ngo's (2017b) study of a Hmong American community-based arts program revealed the way one CBES used theatre to explore youths' culture and to foster critical consciousness. One recent study of a Southeast Asian community-based educational space found that the program empowered youth to challenge symbolic violence in schools and in the broader society by providing opportunities for youth to make sense of the legacies of colonization, war and political violence, displacement, poverty, and racism on their families and communities (Pheng, in progress). In *Resisting Asian American Invisibility,* we aim to build on the scholarship on CBES by exploring what Hmong adults and youth in Lakeview want from community-based education.

ROAD MAP FOR THE BOOK

In Chapter 2 we introduce the racial and cultural context of Lakeview and the three research sites that are central to our multi-sited ethnography. We also discuss our team approach to ethnography, including a discussion of our respective positionalities and political commitments as researchers. Chapter 3, "Invisibility and Hypervisibility at UHS" (with Linda M. Pheng), focuses on the academic and social invisibility experienced by Hmong American youth at University Heights High. We examine school policies and practices, such as English learner programs, that impact Hmong students.

Chapter 4, "Middle-Class Hmong Leadership and the Push for Inclusion" (with Mai Neng Vang), focuses on how middle-class Hmong professionals make sense of the problem of invisibility and their strategies for challenging invisibility. We examine their efforts to gain recognition for the Hmong community through their work with the school district and other dominant institutions. This group of Hmong professionals is particularly concerned with the inclusion of Hmong history and culture in the curriculum and with the representation of Hmong staff in the schools. They view education as the route to social mobility and political inclusion for the next generation of Hmong Americans.

Chapter 5, "Solidarity Holds Our Unity Together (SHOUT)" (with Choua Xiong), focuses on SHOUT, a politically progressive community-based educational space that focuses on resisting and challenging the invisibility faced by low-income Southeast Asian and Black communities. While middle-class Hmong professionals are primarily concerned with issues facing the Hmong community, the members of SHOUT are invested in cross-racial alliances between low-income Southeast Asian American communities and the low-income Black community. Furthermore, SHOUT is committed to fighting anti-Blackness as the heart of racism. Their educational programming centers on critical pedagogy and active resistance to dominant institutions.

In Chapter 6, "Disrupting Invisibility," we reflect on what the stories in our study reveal about the dangers and harm of invisibility, and the possibilities for disrupting invisibility. We conclude by exploring the possibilities of culturally sustaining pedagogy for Hmong and other Southeast Asian American communities. We argue that a culturally sustaining pedagogy has the potential to address some of the concerns raised by both the middle-class Hmong professionals and the politically progressive Hmong activists.

CHAPTER 2

Hmong Americans in Lakeview

Like the Roman god Janus, Lakeview has two faces with contrasting personalities. Some residents, particularly White middle-class ones, view the city as a liberal oasis that offers a high quality of life with its extensive system of parks, numerous farmers' markets, growing downtown, and cultural diversity. In contrast, many residents of color see a city long marred by racism and racial disparities that are masked by the city's liberal façade. Residents of Lakeview also express markedly divergent views of the public schools, with some proclaiming that the schools are diverse and academically rigorous and others arguing that the schools reproduce existing racialized inequalities. The two visions of the city and the city's schools are so strikingly different that it would be easy to think that people are describing two different places. Indeed, Lakeview's neighborhoods are segregated by race and class in ways that contribute to the disparate visions of the city.

Lakeview's self-image as an inclusive and politically progressive city is linked to the broader culture of niceness upon which the image of "Midwest nice" is based. Although being "nice" may appear to be an unassailable virtue, an emerging body of scholarship illustrates the role of the culture of niceness in the perpetuation of inequality (Castagno, 2014, 2019; Ladson-Billings, 1998). Educational anthropologist Angelina Castagno (2019) asserts that the culture of niceness protects the status quo by requiring "us to reframe potentially disruptive or uncomfortable things in ways that are more soothing, pleasant, and comfortable" (p. x). Niceness as a political concept is like tolerance as a concept insomuch as both encourage "that we should all simply behave in ways that demonstrate acceptance of others" (Castagno, 2019, p. xv). Like tolerance, niceness leaves structural inequalities and the status quo untouched.

Despite the existence of persistent racial inequalities, Lakeview enjoys a national reputation as a liberal oasis in a state that has grown increasingly polarized. As political scientist Kathy Cramer (2016) argues, the political divide in Wisconsin reflects an important rural versus urban divide that exists in much of the country. In fact, it is common to hear self-described Lakeview progressives, mostly White people, point to Lakeview's exceptionalism as a liberal mecca. Those who espouse the exceptionalism of Lakeview assume that Lakeview residents are more politically enlightened and inclusive than other Wisconsinites. Lakeview residents express their progressive politics and support for diversity through their voting patterns and participation in social justice–oriented protests and through their displaying of yard signs supporting Black Lives Matter and other progressive causes. As with American exceptionalism, however, Lakeview exceptionalism leads to a kind of double standard where Lakeview residents are highly critical of the racism that they assume more rural residents possess but remain largely unaware of their own racism and privilege. Although many rural residents in Wisconsin assume that communities of color are getting all the resources in urban areas, the story of Lakeview challenges this assumption. Like many of the White rural residents of Wisconsin in Cramer's study (2016), communities of color in Lakeview argue that policy makers have long ignored their concerns.

In Lakeview, progressive political perspectives mix with a culture of Niceness to produce a city fraught with contradictions. Lakeview attempts to be socially progressive and yet has struggled to adequately address racial inequalities. It is a growing city that has become more racially and economically diverse in the last 20 years. In 2017 the population of Lakeview was approximately 250,000 with the following racial breakdown: White 74%, Asian 9%, Hispanic 6%, Black 6%, American Indian .4%. Although the White population is still by far the largest group, its population is older than that of other races. The county in which Lakeview is situated has also seen an expansion in its population and a similar growth in racial diversity, with a significant increase in the Latinx and Asian American populations in the last 20 years. Wisconsin has the third largest Hmong population in the United States; Lakeview has had a significant Hmong community since the 1980s. The largest Asian American groups in Lakeview today are the Hmong, Chinese, Korean, and South Asian. The East Asian American and South Asian American populations have largely been drawn to the area's tech industry and local universities.

In the nearly 20 years since Stacey's fieldwork for *Up Against Whiteness*, concerns regarding the racialized opportunity gaps, particularly the Black and White achievement gap, have become central to the public discourse in Lakeview. Concerns regarding the disparities in education and other arenas were well known among residents of color and predate the reforms following 2001's No Child Left Behind legislation. In 2020 one local Black leader wrote an op-ed in which he outlined the over 50-year struggle to address educational disparities between the Black and White communities in Lakeview. NCLB pushed the school district to confront the Black–White achievement gap more aggressively, and a 2013 report published by a local nonprofit organization drew further attention to the racial disparities in education, employment, health, and criminal justice faced by the African American community in Lakeview and the county. The local report revealed that 42% of the African American high school students in the county did not graduate on time, compared to 12.7% of White students in the 2012–2013 school year. African American students, in other words, were 3.3 times more likely to miss this key benchmark than their White peers. While the report did not examine other communities of color, the authors acknowledged that other groups of color experience inequalities in the county, and they have since examined issues facing Native Americans and Latinos. Grouped in the pan-Asian category, the experiences of Hmong and other Southeast Asians remain largely invisible.

The school district is more diverse than the city of Lakeview, and while most residential neighborhoods in Lakeview are segregated by race and social class, the schools are racially, economically, and linguistically diverse. During our research the racial makeup of the Lakeview School District was 18% Black/African American; 9% Asian; 20% Hispanic; 44% White; 9% mixed race; less than 1% Pacific Islander; less than 1% Native American. In addition to its racial diversity, the district serves over 75 language groups, and 48% of the students are designated low-income. During our fieldwork just over 25% of students in Lakeview were designated English learners (ELs), with Spanish being the most common home language for ELs and Hmong being the second most common. The school district serves approximately 27,000 students across nearly 50 schools; while it serves an increasingly diverse student population, the teaching staff is over 85% White.

As in other racially and economically diverse districts, the Lakeview School District struggles to address both the concerns of the communities of color and the interests of the vocal and powerful White middle-class population in the school district (Lewis & Diamond, 2015; Turner, 2020). In 2010, for example, a group of predominately middle-class White parents in Lakeview raised concerns regarding what they argued were the inadequacies in gifted education in the district and at University Heights High School (UHS) specifically. In an effort to address racialized achievement gaps, UHS had implemented a policy of inclusion that led to detracking classes and the practice of embedded honors or allowing select students to do honors work in mixed group classes. Many observers interpreted the concerns raised by the advocates for gifted education as an attack on detracking efforts and on equity efforts more broadly. As we will discuss later in this chapter, UHS is one of our research sites and the subject of Chapter 3.

The Lakeview School District has attempted to address these disparate interests by broadening the concept of inclusion to incorporate all students. This interpretation of inclusion has led to the implementation of policies and programs for different groups of students, including programming for gifted students and for students in the "academic middle." Not insignificantly, most students identified as gifted in Lakeview are White and middle class and the majority of those identified for programming targeting the "academic middle" are students of color and/or first generation to college. Thus, the district's implementation of inclusivity operates much the way that niceness operates in that it may inadvertently reproduce the structures of inequality (Turner, 2020).

In Lakeview, as in districts across the nation, efforts to address the racialized achievement gap center on the collection of data, particularly test scores, graduation rates, and attendance. This intense focus on testing, data, and accountability can be traced to the 2002 passage of No Child Left Behind (NCLB), the neoliberal policy that continues to influence education today. *Neoliberalism* is a theory of political economy that centers the value of individual entrepreneurial freedom, supported by private property rights, free trade, and free markets (Harvey, 2007). NCLB reflected neoliberal assumptions that the most important purpose of education is preparing economically productive workers and that schools should embrace market logics. Within neoliberal educational discourses, testing data is assumed to be an objective measure of individual merit and of school quality (Apple, 2004; Turner, 2020). Addressing differences in test scores is seen as a way to promote racial equality so that students from all racial backgrounds can participate in the economy (Au, 2010, 2016; Hursh, 2007; Turner, 2020). As Hursh (2007) explains, "neoliberal discourse focuses on standardized testing as a means of providing both a 'quality indicator' to the consumer and 'objective assessments' of student learning withing educational markets" (p. 500). Within this political context, racial equity is understood in terms of the individual student and raising individual test scores and thereby narrowing the racialized achievement gap is seen as an antiracist goal because it allows individuals to compete. It should be noted that decades of neoliberal educational policies have done little to address racialized inequities in education and may even have magnified Black and Brown students as academically incompetent. As Wayne Au (2016) argues, "low-income students of color (as well as their teachers and their schools) are rendered visible as failures through high stakes, standardized testing" (p. 52).

If racial groups do not experience an achievement gap, then it is assumed that they are doing well and do not suffer from racial barriers. Like most districts across the nation, Lakeview groups together Asian Americans from various ethnic groups into one category. Their data suggests that Asian Americans overall are doing well in school. As we will discuss in Chapter 4, a group of middle-class Hmong leaders worked for years to get the Lakeview School District to disaggregate the data on Hmong students because they believed that the aggregate data on Asian American students masked the academic issues facing Hmong students. The first disaggregated data on Hmong students in Lakeview revealed that Hmong students were academically behind their White peers, and the majority were still categorized as English learners. During our fieldwork there were 835 Hmong students in the district, down about 3% from 2011–2012, when data on Hmong was first collected. The fact that Hmong students are still regularly categorized as ELs shocked and troubled middle-class Hmong advocates because nearly all Hmong American students are U.S.-born, and many are even the children of U.S.-born Hmong parents. When we were approved to conduct research in the Lakeview school district, our district liaison was an individual responsible for educational services for English learners, which suggested to us that the school district continued to view Hmong students as being the responsibility of the EL staff. Tellingly, there has been increasing attention to the gap between ELs and their English-proficient peers in Lakeview and throughout the state of Wisconsin (Wisconsin Policy Forum, 2019).

TEAM APPROACH TO MULTI-SITED ETHNOGRAPHY

Stacey launched the current study in the summer of 2015 with a team of Southeast Asian American graduate students that included Choua Xiong, a Hmong American PhD candidate who is trilingual in Hmong, Thai, and English; Linda M. Pheng, a second-generation Khmer American PhD candidate, bilingual in Khmer and English; and Mai Neng Vang, a Hmong American doctoral student bilingual in Hmong and English. When our research team first started discussing the project in the winter of 2015, our original goal was to explore what had and had not changed for Hmong youth in Lakeview schools over the 17 years since Stacey collected the data for *Up Against Whiteness*. We were interested in whether and how current educational policies and conversations regarding diversity, equity, and race had changed the educational context for Hmong youth at UHS. Over several months of conversation our project evolved to include a focus on both formal and community-based education, and to include the perspectives of local Hmong leaders and parents as well as youth. The data presented in this book reflect ethnographic fieldwork conducted between the summer of 2015 and December 2017.

Ethnographic research has generally been conducted by lone researchers, but team ethnography is becoming increasingly more common as researchers recognize the benefits of multiple perspectives (Creese et al., 2008). All members of our research team were actively involved in data collection and analysis. In the tradition of in-depth ethnographic fieldwork, our research focused on various types of observations, which ranged from relatively passive observations to full participation (DeWalt & DeWalt, 2010). We gathered data through semistructured interviews with Hmong students at UHS, teachers and staff at UHS, Hmong parents and Hmong community leaders, staff, and youth workers at the two community-based sites, and youth who participated in programming at the two community-based educational spaces. Most of the data was collected individually, but we also made it a point to collect some data in pairs or as a whole team. We held regular team meetings to discuss data collection, emerging themes, and ongoing analysis. We engaged in an iterative approach to data analysis, moving back and forth between data and analysis, reviewing relevant literature, and engaging in "memo-making" that explored links between multiple levels of data (Birks, Chapman & Francis, 2008). Our analysis involved inductive and deductive approaches to our data as we engaged in observations, conducted interviews, and wrote fieldnotes and memos (Emerson, Fretz & Shaw, 2011). We triangulated data from interviews, observations, and other sources (e.g., social media, newspapers), and looked for confirming and disconfirming evidence throughout the process of analysis.

Our approach to ethnography was informed by scholars who encourage researchers to make connections and theoretical claims beyond the single case (Bartlett & Vavrus, 2017; Burawoy, 1998; Weis & Fine, 2012). Like other critical researchers, we were focused on uncovering power and inequality, particularly with respect to issues of race, immigrant and refugee background, social class, and linguistic background. As critical scholars, we intentionally looked for linkages across time and space, eschewing the notion of a bounded or isolated case (Bartlett & Vavrus, 2017; Weis & Fine, 2012). Following Weis and Fine (2012), we sought to "render visible the relations between groups to structures of power, to social policies, to history, and to large sociopolitical formations" (p. 173). We also applied the insights of Burawoy's extended case method of ethnography "in order to extract the general from the unique, to move from the 'micro' to the 'macro,' and to connect the present to the past in anticipation of the future, all by building on existing theory" (1998, p. 5).

Our research team conducted ethnographic fieldwork at University Heights High School, and with two groups of Hmong American community leaders in their

respective community-based educational spaces. Additionally, we conducted observations at public events in Lakeview, and we examined education policies regarding English learners and other relevant materials (e.g., local newspapers, social
media). University Heights High is a comprehensive 4-year public high school and
the focus of Chapter 3. We agreed that University Heights High should be one of
our high school sites and were fortunate to gain access. We were also interested
in conducting research at Western High School, because of its reputation for having
the most Hmong high school students in Lakeview, but we were not successful in
gaining access. Gaining research access to University Heights High involved negotiating a formal bureaucratic process; the process of identifying and gaining access
to community-based educational spaces for Hmong youth was more fluid and
informal. We relied heavily on Choua and Mai Neng's social networks to identify
Hmong American leaders involved in educational advocacy and community-based
educational spaces for Hmong youth. Through our social networks we identified
several middle-class professional Hmong Americans who were involved with an
organization we call Hmong Education Advocates (HEA). Chapter 4 focuses on
middle-class professional Hmong leaders, HEA, and the summer camp sponsored
by members of HEA. Chapter 5 focuses on the second community-based organization; we call it SHOUT, which stands for Solidarity Holds Our Unity Together.
A grassroots, community-based, nonprofit organization serving some of the most
economically and socially marginalized members of the Black and Southeast Asian
American communities, SHOUT is known nationally within politically progressive
circles for their work fighting gender and racial violence.

   While we are naming Wisconsin as the state in which our research was conducted,
we are using pseudonyms for the city and for all individuals and organizations to
protect the confidentiality of our participants. All quotes from participants are tran-
scribed verbatim. According to the 2010 U.S. Census, Wisconsin has the third largest
Hmong population (49,240) in the United States. Unlike in California (91,224) and
Minnesota (66,181), Hmong communities in Wisconsin are spread throughout the
state and are not concentrated in one single area. The Hmong American community
makes up .86% of Wisconsin's population (49,240/5,686,986) (Pfeifer et al., 2012).
Forty percent of the Hmong population works in the manufacturing industry compared to 18% of the state's population. While the Hmong American community's
poverty rate has decreased over time, they remain one of the poorest ethnic groups in
Wisconsin and the United States. Furthermore, Hmong American communities have
one of the largest youth populations in comparison to the general population and the
Asian American population (44% under the age of 18) (Pfeifer et al., 2012).

   Finally, while we recognize that there is an ongoing debate among Hmong
people in the United States regarding the terms used to describe the community (e.g.,
Hmong, Hmong American, Miao/Meo or HMoob), we will be using Hmong and
Hmong American to refer to our participants since these are the terms most com-
monly used by 1.5 generation and 2nd generation Hmong people living in the United
States. We recognize that there are two main subgroups within the Hmong American
communities: Hmoob Dawb (White Hmong) and Moob Lees (Blue Mong) (Lee &
Tapp, 2010). While we do not want to minimize the complexity of the differences

among Hmong families and communities, for the purpose of readability we will be using the spelling "Hmong"; this is not intended to exclude Blue Mong.

RESEARCHER POLITICS, ETHICS, AND POSITIONALITY

It is now commonly understood among ethnographers and qualitative researchers in general that research is always political and never neutral. The acts of data collection, data analysis, and representation are rooted in relations of power. Researchers make decisions about what questions to ask, which groups to study, which stories to tell, and how to tell these stories, and our decisions have consequences for our participants. As many critical researchers have argued, too much social science research has perpetuated harm, damage, and violence (Ladson-Billings, 2012; Lee, 2015; Tuck & Yang, 2014). Our research is guided by the principles of humanizing research to center "the building of relationships of care and dignity and dialogic consciousness raising for both researchers and participants" (Paris & Winn, 2013, p. xvi). Our research team worked to develop meaningful reciprocity with our participants. For example, our research team provided academic resources, and delivered several workshops to train SHOUT organizers about school data and race and racialization. We worked with Mr. Thao on a proposal for funding to support an initiative for Hmong students. Although this proposal was not successful in gaining funding, we connected HEA summer camp coordinators with university students interested in tutoring Hmong youth. Our commitment to humanizing research extends to issues of representation; we have attempted to capture our participants' stories and put them into a larger context.

Political and ethical concerns regarding research are deeply connected to issues of researcher identity, and we end this chapter with our positionality statements. Our positionality influences the types of questions we ask, the things we observe, the themes we find important, the analysis we make, and the way we represent our participants and their lived realities. Because of this, any analysis and any representation are "incomplete, partial, selective" (Riessman, 2008, p. 50). The lives and histories of our participants as well as the political, social, and economic contexts in which they live are much more complex than our words can capture, but we are obligated to try to represent their stories with dignity and nuance. Although positionality statements can never capture an individual's full and complex identity, we are providing extended positionality statements to highlight the aspects of our identities that are most relevant to our work as researchers working with the Hmong American community in Lakeview.

Stacey J. Lee: I am a middle-class, middle-aged, 3rd generation Chinese American cisgender woman, lesbian, and university professor. I grew up and went to elementary school and junior, and senior high in a predominately White middle–upper middle-class suburb of California and went on to attend private institutions of higher education. My identities and experiences are quite different from the Hmong American youth and adults in our study, and this knowledge influenced my research decisions.

I grew up English dominant, and my mother, who was a high school teacher, monitored my grammar like a hawk. I grew to understand that her attention to my grammar came from her belief that "speaking proper English" would protect me from racism. While I have always been most comfortable speaking English and can only read and write in English, I spoke Chinese and a blend of Chinese and English with my paternal grandparents with whom I lived during the summers. Despite being a dominant English speaker, like most Asian Americans I faced racialized assumptions that I was not fluent in English. Comments such as "Your English is really good" still ring in my ears. During our fieldwork when I heard Hmong youth speaking Hmonglish, I was reminded of the Chinglish that I used as a child with my grandmother. Like many Hmong elders, my paternal grandmother had virtually no formal education, but she had a vast wealth of knowledge from her childhood in a small village in China and her experiences as a Chinese immigrant. I draw on her knowledge and resilience every day. Thus, there were moments when I realized that despite the significant differences between me and our participants there were small but important points of resonance that shaped my understanding of our participants.

I'd had the privilege of learning from and writing about Hmong American students from 1996 to 2005. I decided to take a pause from focusing my scholarship on Hmong and other Southeast Asian American communities around 2008. Although I was always mindful of the dangers of doing research that might unintentionally contribute to essentializing Hmong communities, I recognized that as a cultural and linguistic outsider there were limits to what I could learn (Lee, 2015). Furthermore, I knew that there were growing numbers of Hmong and other Southeast Asian educational researchers in the pipeline, and I wanted to step back to make room for their voices. In the spring of 2015, I was awarded a Vilas Mid-Career Investigator Award by the University of Wisconsin–Madison and wanted to use some of the funds to support my graduate students. When I told Linda, Choua, and Mai Neng about the award and my search for a new project they suggested that we do a collaborative project to follow up on *Up Against Whiteness*. As we described earlier in this chapter, the research evolved to include parents, adults, and community-based educational spaces.

As a research team, we reflected on our respective positionalities in making decisions about how to divide the research responsibilities. Thus, Choua and Mai Neng took primary responsibility for the two Hmong community-based organizations because of their cultural and linguistic knowledge, and Linda took primary responsibility for fieldwork at UHS. I spent time observing in all three sites to make sense of the similarities and differences across sites. I also conducted interviews with participants in all three sites. Not insignificantly, the middle-class professionals associated with HEA appeared to be more comfortable with me and my presence than the adults at SHOUT. I found that youth were more wary of me during this time at UHS than they had been in my previous fieldwork at UHS. Thus, at UHS Linda did all the interviews with the students. My identity as an education professor facilitated interactions with faculty and staff at UHS.

I have learned a tremendous amount through my experiences conducting team-based ethnographic fieldwork in Lakeview. The opportunity to think through data and analysis with a team allowed us to consider different perspectives. In the end, this work confirms to me that there isn't a single ideal positionality, and that all researchers can bring something unique and important to the field as long as they remain curious, respectful, and humble.

Linda Marie Pheng: I am a Khmer American cisgender queer woman pursuing a doctoral degree in Educational Policy Studies at the University of Wisconsin–Madison. While I am not Hmong, my Khmer refugee family has experienced genocide, war, and displacement in Cambodia. Khmer communities across the United States, like the Hmong, Lao, and Vietnamese, also continue to grapple with intergenerational trauma while navigating the racialized aftermath of an unsuccessful resettlement. In addition, like the youth in our study, experiences of race, poverty, and marginalization are woven into my educational experiences.

I was also enrolled in ESL in elementary school despite being American born, and tested out in 2nd grade. As a young person, I was embarrassed by my family's poverty, which stung most acutely at school. A 6th-grade P.E. teacher once made an example of me for being inappropriately dressed by pointing out that I wasn't wearing good athletic sneakers for Field Day. I had one pair of shoes that academic year—slightly too big white canvas slip-ons an older cousin handed down to me. My closest friends and I would bunch together in the lunch line at the register, covering for one another to hide that we received free breakfast and lunch and never missed a meal. Such experiences informed how I navigated fieldwork for this study, especially at UHS.

At UHS, I paid close attention to what youth wore and what they ate for lunch, the water bottles they carried, and whom they seemed to be hanging out with. These seemingly trivial details helped build a case file of sorts that might hint at the socioeconomic background of a young person. While race is central to the marginalization of the students in this study, class, or rather poverty, creates a daily struggle for many Southeast Asian American families. Furthermore, understandings of and responses to poverty have implications for how we adopt (e.g., Sheng Yeng) or challenge (e.g., Kendall) dominant ideologies such as the model minority stereotype. I tried my best not to ask questions that would potentially trigger negative reactions in participants. Youth can seem surprisingly forthcoming to adults, but sometimes that bravado or nonchalance masks shame and embarrassment. That said, I was caught off guard by young people's directness more than once at UHS, especially when they casually misidentified my age and ethnicity.

I was in my mid-30s when we began the phase of research at UHS. On cold fieldwork days, I could feel every ache in my joints and muscles getting up each morning to catch the bus to get to UHS. I felt old and tired, but apparently, I looked young to UHS staff, teachers, and students. When I arrived at the school between periods, the front desk secretary would ask me if I needed a late pass. She did this a few times until she remembered my face and researcher identity. Meandering through the hallway on the way to Ms. Lee's class, if I forgot to put on the visitor sticker, boys walking in the halls or sitting outside of their classrooms would sometimes ask me for my grade and name, and if they could help me get to class.

I gently replied with "No, thanks" and stated that I was a university researcher studying Southeast Asian American students at the school. To be fair, I also chose to wear hoodies and jeans instead of blazers and dress pants (my teaching attire) to not stand out at school. My youthful face and casual attire helped me to fit into the school environment as I looked of similar age to the largest population at UHS.

The Asian Club students never mistook me for a high school student. The student leaders were notified in advance that a UW graduate student was visiting their club, so the expectation of my presence mitigated some of the initial awkwardness I felt entering the space. The Asian Club was made up of primarily Hmong students during the fieldwork, so at the very first meeting I felt shy at potentially intruding into what seemed to be (and would later prove to be) a Hmong space. Thankfully, the club president facilitated a "two truths and a lie" icebreaker that helped new members get to know one another. At my turn, I became embarrassed when many Hmong students, and the lone Khmer student in the room, thought I was misleading them about being Khmer (see Chapter 3). As a lighter-skinned Khmer person, I have been the recipient of such disbelief about my ethnic and cultural identity all my life. The discomfort that I feel when others doubt my Khmer heritage is similar to the discomfort that I feel when people ask me, "Where are you from?" I was relieved when the students quickly moved on to the next person and did not further interrogate my lineage as others have done in the past. In addition to observing the preponderant ethnicity, I noticed that there were more girls than boys in the club. This distribution, and my own identity as a cisgender woman, contributed to why there are more interviews with girls than with boys.

It has not escaped me that my ethnic misidentification by the Asian Club members is an experience they name as also happening to them at the school. As people of color in the United States, and specifically as Southeast Asian Americans, we have all contended with misidentification and misrecognition along nexuses of race, ethnicity, language, and class. Sometimes, we do something similar to one another, as we have unconsciously learned the racialized and classed narratives embedded in Southeast Asian American identities. The findings of the book not only speak to these experiences and the harm that arises for Southeast Asian Americans, but also highlight the work being done in community-based educational spaces for recognition of and resistance against the structures that render invisible our identities, cultures, and struggles. I am grateful for the opportunity to participate in this study because it has allowed me to both connect with the spaces that I needed as a young person and contribute to the type of scholarship that I once thought was impossible as a new graduate student.

Mai Neng Vang: I identify as a cis-hetero Hmong American woman from a working-class refugee family. I was born in a Thai refugee camp and came to the United States a month before turning 4 years of age. My family was resettled in a predominantly White town in northwestern Wisconsin, where I lived until moving away for graduate school at 22 years old. I am a first-generation college student and the first in my extended family to go to graduate school. In college, as part of a scholarship my first year, I joined a cultural psychology research team to do research on Hmong parenting. It was also in college that I learned the language to talk about the racialized reality that I was (am) living. I became resentful of research as I began to perceive the colonial relationship that research often reproduces between the academy and my community. Since my junior year of college, I have been critically reflecting on what it means for me to be a Hmong researcher within my own community.

As I am a Hmong-identifying person, the adults from the Hmoob Meskas Summer Camp (HMSC) space seemed to consider me an "insider." I noticed that there were times when they would tell me about their families or an experience related to being Hmong and then they would trail off and say, "You know how it is." This signifies to me that they assume that I really do know "how it is" because they consider me a cultural insider. Additionally, because I look young and am petite in stature, I was also able to establish rapport with students fairly easily. One student proclaimed that when she first saw me, she thought I was "one of [them]," a student like herself.

This research is personal for me. It's personal not just because I was working with a community that I identify with ethnically; it was also not just because I developed close relationships with the people I was working with. This research is also personal for me because I can see my 10-year-old self in the students I worked with at the HMSC. Because all of them are second- or third-generation Americans, I cannot claim to fully know what it feels like to be them and I cannot claim that I fully understand their experiences. However, I could relate to a lot of the stories that my students shared with me—I could empathize with a lot of their frustrations, their pains, their joys, because I have gone through similar experiences as a Hmong child growing up in a predominantly White town. I also shared with a few of the HMSC students my own struggles with internalized racism and experiences navigating discriminatory institutions. I wrote the following poem during a "writer's block" when I was writing my thesis as a reminder to myself of why my work, my scholarship, the telling of my participants' stories, is important, even if it is hard (and even re-traumatizing):

I am still learning to love
those parts of myself
that I rejected twenty-five years ago
for though you cannot see
the scars that 14 years
of public schooling have left,
I am reminded every day
that I fight so hard
so that one day:

no HMoob child will say to herself
that she won't speak HMoob at school
so her classmates will befriend her

so no HMoob child will believe that
her culture and her people
are unintelligent and undesirable

so no HMoob child will be embarrassed
to pack for lunch
the food her mom cooks at home

so no HMoob child will feel the burden
of having to explain who the HMoob are
and where we come from

so no HMoob child will have to wonder
where she goes to visit the "homeland"
her parents talk so fondly of

so no HMoob child will have to question
whether she's "HMoob enough"
or how she can be "more Americanized" to fit in

so that all HMoob children
will feel valued in their skin
and see that they too are worthy of love.

—internalized inferiority

Taking pride in who I am as a first-generation Hmong American took a long time in coming. I was embarrassed to be part of the Hmong culture because the messages that I had received from the media, some of my teachers, and even some Hmong adults were that Hmong people are not intelligent; Hmong youth are deviant; Hmong culture is "traditional" and not "modern" like American culture; Hmong culture is "backwards" and not "progressive" like U.S. society. For 8 years of my public schooling (4th through 12th grade), I refused to speak Hmong during school hours (I spoke Hmong only when at home or translating for my family). Through the hostile stares of my non-Hmong peers and requests from teachers toward myself and other Hmong students to speak in English, I had been made to feel that my native language was not welcomed in school spaces. My elementary school Hmong peers and I would equate testing out of ESL with having a higher intelligence. I tested out of ESL in 3rd grade and was no longer pulled out of classrooms for ESL sessions, but I yearned for the community and sense of belonging that the ESL space provided for my peers and me. The summer before my 5th-grade year, my family moved to a different school within the same district and I was retested for ESL placement. I remember being frustrated at this retesting since I had already tested out. This constant testing contributed to my thinking that in order to be academically and economically successful in this country, one must be able to speak, read, and write English proficiently.

As a researcher, I strive to nuance our understandings of what it means to be a Hmong person in this country. Tuck (2009) asks researchers to refrain from adding to "damage-centered research," which is research that frames communities as "defeated and broken" (p. 412). Tuck argues that this type of research works to pathologize communities, wherein the community is defined solely by the oppression that they face. She suggests that rather than focus on how communities are damaged, research should attempt to encompass "desire" in order to push back against the dominant frameworks that situate communities of color as deficient. For me, it is important to highlight the agency that minoritized communities have exercised and continue to engage in—even while being surrounded by restrictive structures.

Gao Moua and Mr. Thao were two of the first local Hmong community members that I met when I came to graduate school; we were all introduced by a mutual acquaintance. In negotiating access into the HMSC space, Gao Moua and I discussed what the HMSC needed so that I could give back to the program while collecting data. Gao Moua was enthusiastic about my research and indicated that any analysis and data that I was able to provide them in order to garner more support for the program would be great. She also felt that my presence as a graduate student in the HMSC space would be positive role modeling for the young participants to aspire to. Gao Moua explained that she tries to recruit local college students as volunteers in the program for this very reason. Through my fieldwork, I participated as a volunteer and worked directly with HMSC teachers, students, and nonacademic staff. I was asked to provide feedback about the curriculum, programming activities, and other areas for improvement. I continued to support the program in the years following data collection through donating to the yearly fundraising gala, attending their events, and teaching lessons during the school year when the program piloted their monthly programming.

Through fieldwork and simultaneous analysis, I came to realize that as I learned about spaces of empowerment and healing for the participants in our research project, I was also trying to heal from my own racial trauma. Because of this and because I care deeply about the people I worked with through the research, there were moments in the analysis and write-up of the data that I found it difficult to decide how to contend with areas of tension in the work. I remember going through the transcripts of interviews and becoming emotional all over again with participants as they shared their lives. I remember wondering how or if I should write about someone's pain or harms they have caused. How do I as a researcher bearing witness to pain, joy, love, healing, and sorrow do justice to my communities in protecting us but also calling out our hurt so justice can be served?

Choua Xiong: There are several aspects of my positionality that shaped the research design, data collection, and data analysis. I am a Hmong American refugee daughter who grew up in a suburban, predominately White neighborhood in Wisconsin. I was the first in my family to obtain any postsecondary degree, and the oldest child to my young parents. I became a mother during the fieldwork period of this ethnography. All of these social identities and experiences influenced the ways I built relationships and interacted with the participants at SHOUT.

SHOUT works with individuals who identify as girls, women, LGBTQ, elders, and Southeast Asian and Black people from impoverished communities. My own experiences growing up in a low-income, patriarchal, Hmong, and refugee family positioned me with the cultural knowledge to contextualize and navigate the dynamics at SHOUT. As a student activist, I also understand and share SHOUT's commitment to organizing work. Being young, married and a mother gave me many opportunities to relate to the demographics of the staff, executive team, and community members at SHOUT. Over the 18 months that I conducted research with SHOUT, I was lucky to witness the struggles and successful moments that SHOUT experienced during their journey to build community and youth activism.

I recognized the privilege I hold as a highly educated Hmong person at SHOUT, and I acknowledge that many of the young people and youth workers do not have the same relationship to formal schooling as I. Thus, I made intentional decisions to use my academic knowledge to help students identify and build their own skills such as writing, public presentation, and time management. There were many moments where I felt I did not "belong" at SHOUT because my day-to-day life is different from that of SHOUT members—my family had a roof over our heads, I was not constantly hungry, I did not struggle to stay focused in school as a child, I had the navigational skills to go see a doctor even if they were really racist, I could talk to authority figures like police officers because I had the linguistic and communication skills needed. In these moments, I was reminded that being in graduate school gave me the confidence to challenge racist systems in ways that these young people at SHOUT could not.

Prior to becoming a "researcher" at SHOUT, I knew the co-executive director, Pa Zao, through both formal and organizing spaces. When I became a graduate student, I reached out to learn more about SHOUT with the intention of participating in their programs. This relationship and connection were central to our research team's access to SHOUT as an ethnographic site. Although I had primary responsibility for research with SHOUT, it was the combined synergy of all three graduate students and Pa Zao that led to our mutually productive relationship. The relationship between the three graduate students and SHOUT disrupted the violence too often committed by traditional researchers. Linda and I wrote more specifically about how these types of reciprocal relationships enable social justice research that is coproduced by the community (Lee et al., 2020). Throughout our formal period of research we fostered reciprocity. For example, I piloted Hmong language programs for youth and elders at SHOUT.

The research team's access to and relationship with SHOUT has continued beyond our time as researchers because all of us are committed to promoting long-term and equitable relationships. My role as a SHOUT community member requires me to ask for feedback and have continual conversations with the organization. It is important to me that this relationship remain ongoing and that my work with SHOUT is at the capacity that is useful for the organization. I currently participate in SHOUT's social and political activities such as teach-ins, phone banking, creating educational resources, demonstrations, and testimonies.

CHAPTER 3

Invisibility and Hypervisibility at UHS

Stacey J. Lee and Linda M. Pheng

With an apologetic shrug, the principal explained that she didn't know how many Southeast Asian American students attended the school but assumed they were a relatively small group compared to the growing number of Latino students. Then she suggested that I speak to the ESL staff, which was like a flashback to 15 years ago. While Hmong students were hyper-visible years ago, they are invisible today, but I'm still being sent to the ESL team to find out about Hmong students.

Stacey's fieldnotes, Sept. 22, 2016

As with the city of Lakeview and the Lakeview School District, perspectives on University Heights High range from those who hold it up as a pillar of academic excellence and cultural diversity to those who critique it for its failure to adequately serve minoritized youth. Not insignificantly, opinions regarding UHS generally diverge along race and class lines with Black, Latinx, and Southeast Asian American communities expressing frustration regarding the persistent racialized inequalities at the school. Most White, middle-class residents laud UHS for its academic excellence and diversity but acknowledge the existence of racial inequalities.

There is evidence to support both perspectives regarding UHS, a fact that all members of our research team noted. On the one hand, University Heights High is regularly among the high schools with the most National Merit Semifinalists in the state. Furthermore, walking through the halls, a first-time visitor is likely to notice both the diversity of the student population and the school's efforts to foster an inclusive school culture. We began our fieldwork during the lead-up to the 2016 presidential election, and while direct discussion of the candidates was rare, there were stickers and handmade signs indicating support for LGBTQ students, Muslim students, immigrant students, and Black Lives Matter posted on classroom doors throughout the school. Following the 2016 election, scores of UHS students participated in a walkout to protest the election of Trump. Posters for various activities and clubs ranging from forensics to K-pop to Machine Learning and Data Science lined the hallways, suggesting that there were spaces for all students. There were also several racial and/or ethnic affinity clubs, including ones for Black, Latinx, Native American, and Asian American students. In many ways, UHS appears to be an idyllic large high school with something to offer every student. On the other hand, the school is overcrowded and academically and socially segregated by race and linguistic background. The following fieldnote illustrates the overcrowded conditions and racial segregation at UHS.

> I arrived at lunchtime and the halls are packed with students eating everywhere—in the halls, in stairways, classrooms and outside on the lawn. Some students were sitting alone and studying or staring at phones, but the vast majority were in groups of 2 to 20. Some students ate food purchased from the cafeteria, but others ate salads, sandwiches, wraps or snacks from Trader Joe's, Whole Foods, other local stores or the food trucks. As usual, most students were in same race groups with the biggest exception being the East (?) Asian American youth sprinkled into several predominately White friendship groups. In fact, it seems like most of the students in the main corridors were White.
>
> Stacey's fieldnotes, March 9, 2017

Black and other students of color are behind White students in all student achievement areas; most of the National Merit Semi-finalists, for example, are White or East Asian American students. With over 2,100 students in grades 9–12, University Heights High is also technically overcrowded, and it is easy for an individual student to get lost in the crush. As if to express their social and academic marginalization at UHS, Hmong and other Southeast Asian American students were often found gathering near the school exits or in dark and isolated school corridors.

We conducted research at University Heights High School from September 2016 through May 2017. During our research the University Heights High student population was approximately 53% White, 19% Hispanic, 12% Black, 10% Asian, and 6% mixed race, with over 30% eligible for free or reduced lunch. As a large comprehensive high school, UHS offers traditional academic courses, career and tech education, and classes in fine and performing arts. Reflecting the growing middle-class Hmong American population in Lakeview, there were two teachers at University Heights High who identified as Hmong, and a Hmong bilingual resource specialist. Hmong and other Southeast Asian American (SEA) students represent a small portion of the student population at UHS, and in informal conversations with educators we found that Hmong and other Southeast Asian American students were generally lumped together with other Asian ethnic groups and referred to as "Asians." While Hmong students were viewed as a distinct group with a specific history and culture when Stacey collected data for Up Against Whiteness early in the 2000s, the unique needs and experiences of Hmong and other SEA students were hidden by the "Asian" label in 2016–2017. As the field note that opens this chapter suggests, Hmong students are often overlooked, and when they are acknowledged are assumed to be the responsibility of the ESL department.

Linda took primary responsibility for the research at University Heights High. Initially we had some difficulty identifying Hmong and other Southeast Asian students for our study since few members of the staff could help us identify Southeast Asian American populations and many confused Hmong students with the more recently-arrived Nepalese and Tibetan student populations. Our fieldwork at University Heights High included regular observations of academic spaces, including regular academic classes, ESL classes, and AVID classes. We also observed students during extracurricular activities and in social spaces, including the Asian Students' Association, other clubs with Southeast Asian American students, and during lunch. We interviewed self-identified Hmong and other Southeast Asian American students, and teachers and staff who worked with this population. Finally, we analyzed publicly available documents from the school, district, and state in order to provide context for the school.

We estimate that there were approximately 60–65 Hmong students at University Heights High during our research. Additionally, there were smaller numbers of Lao, Khmer/Cambodian, and Vietnamese students. In interviews, Hmong and other Southeast Asian American students reported feeling socially isolated and academically adrift. Several Southeast Asian American students at University Heights High reported that they believed that the Western High across town was a more welcoming space for Hmong and other Southeast Asian American students. Although we were not able to gain permission to conduct fieldwork at Western High School, district data reveal that Western has the largest Hmong student population in the district. We also learned that Western offered a class in Hmong language that many of our participants viewed as concrete evidence that Western was responding to the concerns of the Hmong students.

THE ACADEMIC WORLD OF HMONG AMERICAN STUDENTS AT UHS

Among Lakeview's predominately White educated citizens UHS has always enjoyed a reputation for its academic excellence. Each year nearly half of the 12th grade class takes at least one AP exam, and UHS students go on to colleges and universities throughout the country. While UHS has long had an image as an academically rigorous school, the focus on college-going has increased dramatically since Stacey conducted fieldwork for *Up Against Whiteness*. Neoliberal educational discourses and policies, particularly the idea that all students should aspire to post-secondary education, have permeated the school. Students' schedules are packed with academic classes and a variety of extracurricular activities meant to prepare them for college or work. UHS's college-going culture is layered on top of concerns regarding the persistent racialized achievement gap that is reflected in course-taking, relationships with teachers, grades, test scores, and awards.

Despite the fact that nearly half of the student population are students of color, White students took center stage in most of the classes we observed. The only exceptions to the White-dominated classroom cultures were ESL and AVID classes. As in Stacey's previous research at UHS (Lee, 2005), White students were more likely than students of color to speak during class discussions, ask questions about assignments, and engage in casual and easy banter with their teachers. Many of our Hmong student participants complained that White students dominated classroom discussions. The ease with which White students interacted with the predominately

White teaching staff reflected their shared White and middle-class linguistic styles (Bourdieu, 1991; Eckert, 1989; Heath, 1983; Lareau, 2011). At times White students' race and class privilege took the form of racial microaggressions toward students of color. We observed, for example, White students correcting the language usage of students of color more than once. Most of our Hmong student participants reported that White students dominated classroom discourse, and many said they had witnessed White students engaging in microaggressions in classes. Gia La, the president of the Asian Club, reported that White students were often disrespectful toward non-White students in class. She provided an example from her Law & Ethics class where she was the only Asian student among a "bunch of White kids only." She said that during the White students' presentations she made it a point to listen and "respect them," but during her presentation they were "just doing their own thing, on their phones, snapchatting." A general culture of disrespect combined with White privilege left Hmong students feeling marginalized in their classes.

Most UHS teachers we spoke with were unsure whether they had any Hmong or other Southeast Asian students in their classes, and several teachers confused Hmong students with Nepalese students. Hmong and other Southeast Asian students rarely spoke in their classes unless directly called on by the teacher, and they generally did not seek their teachers out for assistance. When we asked students why they didn't interact more with their teachers most simply shrugged and said they didn't feel comfortable. Mr. Lor, a college administrator and active member of the Hmong community, offered an interpretation of Hmong students' reluctance to ask for help. Mr. Lor said that he had noticed that many Hmong students appeared to be hesitant to ask their teachers for help because they didn't want to "seem like they need help." He went on to explain that Hmong youth might be sensitive to criticisms regarding Hmong people needing "handouts" and therefore are trying to appear self-sufficient. Our observations confirmed Mr. Lor's hunch that Hmong students were hesitant to ask for help. Sadly, however, the fact that most Hmong students were quiet in their classes contributed to their invisibility.

There were a few teachers, however, with good rapport with students of color, including Hmong students, and their classes had more balanced student participation. Gia La explained that she was generally quiet in her classes because they were dominated by White students but felt comfortable talking in Global Studies class because the teacher was "super energetic . . . and treated all students the same." Ms. Archer, a history teacher, was identified as an exemplary teacher by several students, including our Hmong participants. A middle-aged White woman, Ms. Archer regularly engaged students in discussions about race and social class, and provided opportunities for all students, including students of color, to participate. Susannah, a Hmong girl, described Ms. Archer as "awesome" and explained that she liked the class because she could ask questions that weren't completely on topic and Ms. Archer and her student teacher would always answer the questions. One day, for example, Susannah asked about Angel Island and the student teacher gave an impromptu talk on Chinese immigrants at Angel Island. As the fieldnote below illustrates, Ms. Archer took opportunities to correct students' assumptions in ways that encouraged understanding across difference.

Students were in small groups discussing housing reform during the Progressive Era and the conversation turned to Section 8 housing. The White students in Susannah's group made problematic assumptions about Section 8 housing being "unsafe" and being located in "bad" neighborhoods, and two Black students responded by stating that Section 8 housing is "just for poor people and people who need help." Hearing the conversation, Ms. Archer reiterated the points made by the two Black students and gave more background to the program.

Linda's fieldnotes, March 16, 2017

Ms. Archer's attitude was always very matter of fact and calm, which allowed students to make mistakes without being humiliated. In other words, Ms. Archer positioned all students as learners and teachers. As these examples reveal, Hmong students felt most comfortable in classes where teachers recognized all students as learners and were also willing to challenge White students' racist and classist assumptions.

Although most adults at UHS did not know much about Hmong or other Southeast Asian American students, several teachers made comments that suggested they saw differences among their Asian American students. At times the term "Asian" was used as an all-encompassing panethnic category, but at other times it appeared to be code for Hmong, other Southeast Asians, Nepalese, and Tibetan students. The 60–65 Hmong students made up approximately 30% of the total Asian American student population at UHS. The fact that Hmong students were the only Asian ethnic group that the district collected disaggregated data on made it impossible to know the ethnic breakdown of the Asian American student population at UHS, but the demographics of Lakeview reveal that Chinese and Koreans are among the larger Asian groups. Remarking on the differences among Asian American students, a few teachers asserted that many of the "other" Asian American students at University Heights High were adoptees from China or Korea. East Asian American students were generally not in ESL or AVID classes, tended to socialize with White middle-class students, and appeared to live up to the standards of the high-achieving model minority (Lee, 2009). These teachers suggested that these supposedly adopted students were more socially integrated into the fabric of the school because they were growing up in White families. Ms. Lee, one of the Hmong teachers, laughed and said that she'd heard that rumor about Asian American adoptees. Shaking her head, Ms. Lee explained that she thought that only some Asian American students were adoptees and that the others were the children of middle-class East Asian American professionals. Although we did not systematically track how many East Asian American students were adoptees, we did encounter East Asian Americans who were adoptees and other East Asian Americans who lived with their birth parents. The narrative about East Asian American adoptees, however, shaped perceptions about who Asian American students were and how family background shaped social and academic integration.

Within a couple of visits to UHS we learned that teachers and students viewed ESL and AVID as the two spaces responsible for serving the Southeast Asian American student population. AVID is also understood to be responsible for all groups of color at the school, and the ESL department is seen as being responsible for Southeast Asian American and Latinx students.

TRAPPED IN ESL

An Asian male teacher walks into the class—I think he's a teacher, so now there are 3 staff members in the classroom. This teacher glanced at me, but looks more interested in Kendall; actually, he only talks to Kendall and looks to be explaining math concepts to her only . . . in English? In Hmong? OH! He's the Hmong BRS [bilingual resource specialist]. That's kind of odd. I did ask Kendall later who he was and she said, "One of two Mr. Lees," and she doesn't know why he comes to observe her and look at her binder once in a while.

                                                              Linda's fieldnotes, Nov. 16, 2016

Consistent with the district-level data on Hmong students, most of our Hmong American participants were designated English language learners and approximately half were still identified as needing language services in high school. All the Hmong students we met at UHS were U.S.-born and had been identified for ELL services when they entered Lakeview schools, which for many was in kindergarten. There were important differences in the schooling identities and experiences between those Hmong students who were still identified as needing services and those who had exited ESL. Hmong American students who were still labeled ELLs and receiving services were generally confused and embarrassed about still being in ESL, suggesting that the EL label was stigmatized. Hmong students who received ESL services were less confident academically and more socially marginalized than their peers who no longer were in ESL.

The head of the ESL program, Ms. Henson, arrived for the interview with Stacey with a printout of the ELLs who listed Hmong as their heritage language, commenting that she knew that Stacey would want the official data. In keeping with policies implemented in response to No Child Left Behind, Lakeview identifies English language learners and tracks their progress toward English language proficiency through annual standardized exams. According to the Lakeview School District website, English language learners are defined as students who have had "significant exposure to a language other than or in addition to English." Wisconsin requires school districts to identify English language learners upon enrollment in the district using a home language survey, and students identified as potential English language learners are given an English-language proficiency assessment shortly upon enrollment. While Lakeview educators use the terms "English language learner" and "English learner," critical language scholars argue that these terms focus on students' perceived limitations in much the way that the term "limited English proficient" does at the federal level. Instead of focusing on perceived deficits, these scholars argue for the term "emergent bilingual," which reflects an asset-based perspective and recognizes the fluidity of language (García, 2009b; García & Kleifgen, 2010).

Wisconsin is among the 40 states, territories, and federal agencies that belong to the WIDA Consortium, which provides standards, assessments, research and professional development related to the "academic language development and academic achievement for children and youth who are culturally and linguistically diverse" (WIDA Mission and History, https://wida.wisc.edu/about/mission -history). Based on the results of the initial screening tool, students whose scores reflect that they have limited English-language proficiency are referred for services. In this context, "limited English proficiency" is defined as having language skills that may contribute to "difficulty in performing ordinary classwork in English." Parents/guardians may refuse ELL services for their children, but all students who are identified as ELLs must be assessed for English language proficiency on a yearly basis regardless of whether they receive services.

Holding the printout, Ms. Henson told Stacey that the school-level data showed that there were 56 Hmong students labeled English learners at the school and that twenty-six of these students had achieved the needed score on the proficiency test to be exited from the ESL program. Native Hmong speakers make up the second-largest group of ELs in the school and in the district. Pointing her pen at the printout, Ms. Henson explained, "26 are 6s. Oh yeah, 9 of them are 5s, 11 are 4s, 3 are 3s, 4 are 2s and it looks like 3 of them are 1s." The numbers referred to the students' scores on the WIDA ACCESS for ELLs, which assesses the following English skills: speaking, listening, reading and writing. Students are given a score/level based on their performance with Level 1 defined as "entering" and Level 6 defined as "reaching." At level 6 students are considered fully proficient and then monitored for two academic years before being reclassified. These students, however, continued to carry the EL designation next to their names in classroom rosters for two or more years.

Throughout the conversation with Stacey, Ms. Henson referenced students' ACCESS scores and spoke about the importance of using "data" and "evidence" to make decisions about ELs. She explained that students received services through a range of formats depending on their ACCESS level. Level 1–3 students were generally placed in sheltered classes taught by ESL-certified teachers, and intermediate level students were generally in mainstream classes and received sporadic services through bilingual resource specialists (BRS) who visited mainstream classes at the request of the mainstream teacher. Wisconsin's bilingual statute requires school districts to provide bilingual services in schools that have at least ten students who speak the same non-English language in grades K–3 and serve at least 20 students who speak the same non-English language in grades 4–12 (115.97.2-4). UHS had one Hmong BRS during our fieldwork.

The approximately 300 English learners at UHS were served by 10 ESL-certified teachers and several bilingual resource specialists. Ms. Henson noted, however, that the complexities of scheduling and testing made it difficult to adequately serve all the students, and students identified as intermediate or above received only sporadic services. Within the Lakeview School District there has been growing concern regarding the district's struggle to provide adequate services to English learners, with a 2015 school district report revealing that approximately 25% of students at ELL levels 1–5 were not receiving ELL services to support any of their core academic courses. Ms. Henson explained that most of the students in the intermediate group, including Hmong speakers, were long-term English language learners (LTELLs), and that the district had recently become focused on whether and how long-term ELLs in the district were being served. The state of Wisconsin defines LTELLs as those who have not achieved English proficiency (e.g., 1–5 on the ACCESS assessment) after 6 to 8 years, depending on whether they entered Wisconsin schools in kindergarten or later. According to 2015 Lakeview School District statistics, approximately 35% of ELL students at the secondary level fall into the category of long-term ELLs. In the following excerpt from the interview with Stacey, Ms. Henson explains that an analysis of district data revealed that many long-term ELs were not getting appropriate language support, which contributed to their difficulties exiting the program.

> We've gone through a district facilitated redesign. After looking at data and noticing how many of our students were actually not getting deliberate language instruction or contact with an ESL teacher and some of the long-term ELLs or upper-level ELLs that were just kind of floating out there and struggling for themselves we really had to look at how can we provide services for them, because they are legally obligated to receive those. So, without disrupting or concentrating them all into shelter courses, because we wanted to give them rigorous curriculum. We wanted them to have the opportunities to advance with the rest of their mainstream peers.

As Ms. Henson indicates, the decision to use bilingual resource specialists to support mainstream teachers was a deliberate attempt to integrate long-term ELLs into mainstream classes and to have mainstream teachers take more responsibility for ELLs.

Long-Term English Language Learners and Academic English

Long-term English language learners have gained attention during the era of testing and accountability, with some scholars arguing that these students face unique educational challenges that have been overlooked by schools (Menken et al., 2012; Olson, 2014). Although long-term English learners are understood to be "orally bilingual for social purposes," they are identified as having low levels of academic English that contribute to their underachievement (Menken et al., 2012, p. 121). Much of the scholarship characterizes long-term English learners as lacking proficiency in both English and in their native language, marking them as doubly deficient or "semi-lingual" (Cummins, 1979). Advocates for long-term English learners argue that the academic struggles faced by this group are the direct result of inconsistent and inadequate services. Indeed, this is the perspective that Ms. Henson advanced in her description of the problems facing long-term English learners in Lakeview. In response to evidence of inadequate services, Lakeview's response has been to focus more attention on providing support for LTELLs to develop academic English.

Academic English, broadly defined as "the language used in school to help students acquire and use knowledge," is described as being distinct from social language (DiCerbo et al., 2014, p. 448). The concept of Academic English has been fundamental to current language policies and practices targeting English learners, particularly understandings of LTELLs. As Shohamy and Menken (2015) observe, testing policies privilege language for academic purposes, view academic language as being distinct from language for social purposes, and are instruments of power that reproduce inequality. WIDA, for example, distinguishes between communication and language use for social versus instructional purposes, and the ACCESS exam is designed to assess academic language proficiency. Some scholars have raised concerns regarding the difficulty of the WIDA ACCESS exams, particularly the unreasonably difficult exit criteria that create the LTELL class of students (Sherwood, 2018). At UHS and throughout the Lakeview School District there was a shared understanding that LTELLs are those who struggle to master academic English.

The concept of "academic English," however, has been criticized for promoting a dichotomous view of language use and for being based in deficit views of the home languages of emergent bilinguals (DiCerbo et al., 2014). The concept of academic English rests upon the dominant language ideology, which reflects the monolingual White norm (Lippi-Green, 2012). As linguistic anthropologist Stanton Wortham (2008) points out, language ideologies reflect the fact that social status and language use are intertwined in ways that link language to "associations between "educated" and "uneducated," "sophisticated" and "unsophisticated," "official" and "vernacular" language use and types of students" (p. 37). Nelson Flores (2020) argues that "academic language is a raciolinguistic ideology that frames racialized students as linguistically deficient and in need of remediation" (p. 22).

Thus, even as school districts across the country, including Lakeview, focus on long-term English learners and the development of academic English, critical scholars are highlighting the racist and deficit assumptions upon which these concepts are based. In their critical analysis of the impact of the LTELL label on students, Flores et al. (2015) assert:

> We view the LTELL label as one that has done more harm than good. It has pathologized students through normalizing a racist system that privileges speakers of one variety of a language and discounts students' full linguistic repertoire and its place in schools. The label has become "the new semilingual," further disadvantaging students who fall within it, while failing to challenge the epistemic racism of idealized monolingualism that has made the label possible. (p. 130)

From this perspective, the LTELL category and the fixation on academic English reflect and reproduce inequalities along race and linguistic lines. In fact, research suggests that high-stakes testing policies have played a central role in legitimizing the discourse on language and academic partiality and the subsequent growth of the LTELL category (Flores et al., 2015; Koyama & Menken 2013; Shohamy & Menken, 2015).

Hmong LTELLs, Hmonglish, and Outsider Status

Kendall was identified as an intermediate level EL based on her WIDA ACCESS scores and thus received occasional support in the form of assistance from the Hmong

BRS when assistance was requested by a teacher. Like other Hmong students categorized as long-term English learners, Kendall expressed confusion regarding her status as an English learner and about when and why the BRS appeared in her classes. In fact, most of our student participants expressed confusion and shame about being labeled ELLs, which contributed to feelings of marginalization in the school. As the field note at the beginning of this section demonstrates, the Hmong BRS would typically appear unannounced in class and focus on the Hmong ELLs while the rest of the class continued. This attention was almost always unwanted and simply served to highlight the student's linguistic differences in a negative light, thereby reinforcing emergent bilinguals' outsider status at UHS. Kendall's description of the Hmong BRS as the "other Mr. Lee" suggests that she knew that he was Hmong, but we learned that she didn't feel like he was someone she trusted or could count on for support.

Mr. Lee, like many of the ESL staff, was concerned with helping students master academic English as measured by standardized tests. He focused on students' ACCESS scores and could readily cite a student's scores and the WIDA areas of competence but knew little about the students as individuals and didn't appear to recognize their strengths. In fairness, the contexts of testing and accountability promoted a narrow focus on testing and Mr. Lee seemed to understand his job as helping students to pass the test. When Stacey asked Mr. Lee about the testing, he posited that many students didn't take the tests seriously. He explained that he told students, "You are second language, and you have to show that you can do it," and he went on to explain that he tried to impress upon students that if they didn't pass the test they would have to take it again the following year. As his words suggest, he recognizes that Hmong English learners are assumed to be deficient, and he wants students to strive to overcome this deficit positioning. That said, he said little to challenge the deficit perspective regarding LTELLs and appeared to accept the idea that LTELLs were deficient in both English and Hmong.

The fact that so many Hmong American students still qualify for ELL services in high school is perplexing and troubling to many in the Hmong community. At school district events parents and community leaders all questioned why Hmong youth remain trapped in ESL when they speak English; district leaders generally responded by saying the community needed to be patient as the district improved services for ELs. Hmong communities across the nation have expressed frustration regarding the high numbers of Hmong American students classified as English learners (Xiong, 2012). Xiong's (2012) quantitative analysis reveals that the majority of Hmong American students who are placed into ELL programs are second-generation students who have been born in the United States, and like other Hmong American scholars he considers this an urgent issue for educational policy.

Mr. Lee understood that many members of the Lakeview Hmong community were confused about the fact that so many Hmong students were still categorized as ELLs, and he said that he tried to explain to parents that while most Hmong students were U.S.-born and spoke English, they were "struggling with academic English." When Stacey pressed him to say more, he simply stated that speaking and writing in academic English prove to be challenging for many Hmong students. The reality is that many students struggle with writing, including native

English speakers who are "fluent" in English, but the discourse around "academic English" implicitly suggests that it is a problem associated specially with being English learners. Thus, as critical language scholars argue, the idea of "academic English" promotes a deficit perspective of emergent bilinguals (Flores, 2020). In fact, both Hmong students who still received ELL services and those who had exited the program referred to LTELLs as students who aren't "good enough with English," thereby suggesting that they have internalized deficit perspectives.

Like the majority of Hmong students at UHS, Kendall is multilingual and communicates in English, Hmonglish and Hmong. With her Hmong peers, Kendall most commonly speaks Hmonglish, a form of "code-meshing" that includes English, Hmong, and other linguistic repertoires (Canagarajah, 2011). Code-meshing, defined as interweaving various linguistic repertoires, is distinct from code-switching, which is the separating of languages based on context (Young et al., 2014). Although we couldn't identify a common or shared definition of Hmonglish among the youth or among Hmong adults, our observations suggest that Hmonglish involves the use of Hmong words and phrases along with the use of various forms of English, including standard English and African American Vernacular English. We observed Hmong American youth speaking Hmonglish at lunch, during Asian Club meetings and in out-of-school spaces. As Kendall explained in an interview, she feels marginalized and uncomfortable "in rooms when you have to speak only English." The use of Hmonglish reflects the fact that "Hmong American immigrant youth are navigating multiple cultural repertoires and creating 'Hmonglish' identities that draw on multiple discourses of being in the world" (Ngo, 2015, p. 1). In her research on Southeast Asian American youths, Reyes (2005) found that many of the Southeast Asian youth who lived in low-income neighborhoods spoke a "hybrid variety that frequently incorporated features of AAVE as well as features of Mainstream American English (MAE) and of Vietnamese, Khmer (Cambodian), Lao or other home languages of the teens" (p. 515). Similarly, the Hmonglish spoken by our participants incorporated features of mainstream or standard English, Hmong, and African American vernacular (AAVE), which reflected the various cultures encountered in their daily lives.

From the standpoint of current educational policies regarding emergent bilinguals, Hmonglish represents a flawed form of both English and Hmong. This deficit perspective regarding Hmonglish stems from a language ideology that reflects monolingual, White, upper-middle-class, educated perspectives (Cushing, 2020; Lippi-Green, 2012). The assumptions that languages are uniform, distinct and should remain separate (monoglossic language ideology) leads to the view that code-meshing or the mixing of linguistic forms is problematic (Flores & Beardsmore, 2015; García, 2011; García & Solorza, 2020). From this dominant perspective, code-switching may have useful educational applications, but code-meshing is simply seen as incorrect use of language(s). The belief that speakers should maintain rigid boundaries between languages has led to a vision of bilingualism as double monolingualism (García, 2011). Countering the deficit and monolingual perspectives in dominant educational policies and practices, critical language scholars celebrate the fluid and creative language practices reflected in code-meshing (Flores, 2019; García, 2009a). Similarly, in their call for the recognition of code-meshing in classrooms, Young et al.

(2014) assert that code-switching amounts to "linguistic segregation" that encourages internalized racism among Black students who speak AAVE.

The scholarship on raciolinguistics, which points to the co-naturalization of race and language whereby the "linguistic practices of racialized populations are systematically stigmatized," can also help make sense of the deficit perspectives regarding both Hmong and Hmonglish (Rosa & Flores, 2017, p. 623). Pointing to the linguistic components of Asian American racialization, Reyes (2016) argues that the perpetual foreigner stereotype of Asian Americans leads people to assume that Asians will only speak a foreign language and/or be nonnative English speakers with Asian accents. These assumptions support the belief that Asian Americans are all English learners. While the perpetual foreigner stereotype positions Asian Americans as linguistic outsiders, the model minority stereotype promotes the idea that Asian Americans are smart and high achieving. Together the two stereotypes lead to the assumption that Asian Americans are intelligent but better suited for math and science related disciplines than fields that require superior language skills.

In contrast to Asian Americans, Black people are too often stereotyped as unintelligent and Black speakers are viewed as being inarticulate. Commenting on the racialized assumptions about Black people, Alim and Smitherman (2012) assert that White Americans "interpret Black linguistic forms as signs of Black intellectual inferiority" (p. 24). Our research demonstrates that race, class, refugee status, and language intersect in the process of Hmong youths' racialization. When Hmong Americans first arrived in the United States as refugees, they were cast as traditional, backward, and preliterate. The ongoing struggles with poverty among many Hmong youths and their use of Hmonglish, which draws on AAVE have led to their ideological blackening (DePouw, 2012; Lee, 2005; Ong, 1999, 2003). As such, we argue that Hmong youths suffer from deficit perspectives regarding their language(s) in ways that marginalize them in school settings.

Although we heard Hmong youth speaking Hmonglish in informal spaces in and out of school, we did not observe code-meshing among Hmong students in their classes. In fact, most Hmong students we observed in their classes rarely spoke unless directly called upon by their teachers. Hmong students' relative silence in classroom settings appears to reflect the students' recognition that the dominant culture holds deficit ideas regarding Hmong, Hmonglish, and any nondominant form of English. All of our participants recalled non-Hmong children using fake "Asian" sounds to taunt them or their Hmong peers in elementary school. In high school, messages about their language(s) were communicated through EL policies and practices and through the actions of their non-Hmong peers. The fact that so many Hmong American youth continue to be eligible for English language learner services in middle and high school sends a powerful message to students that their languages are lacking.

On several occasions we witnessed White middle-class students policing the language of students of color who used nonstandard forms of English in class. The White students we observed appeared to view their corrections as forms of help, reflecting a performance of Whiteness associated with white saviorism (Matias, 2013). Teachers attempted to control the policing of languages by redirecting conversations, but these redirections did little to challenge the idea that White students were the experts on appropriate language use and that speakers of nonstandard English were deficient. In one instance an English teacher took the opportunity to explain to the class that there were different forms of English and that all forms were welcome in class. While this teacher's intervention was an important challenge to White privilege, overall, White middle-class students marked UHS as their space. It is not surprising that all of our Hmong participants suggested that they were less comfortable in classes with White students.

Finally, it is important to point out that our fieldwork suggests that attitudes about Hmonglish vary within the larger Hmong community, with many Hmong elders and middle-class professionals viewing Hmonglish as evidence of both language loss and deficiency in English. Previous research has found that code-meshing among Hmong youth can lead to criticism from both Hmong elders and White peers and adults (Canagarajah, 2011). Although most Hmong American youth at UHS were observed speaking Hmonglish with their co-ethnic peers, there were Hmong students who never used Hmonglish in our presence. Sheng Yeng, a high-achieving student, for example, spoke standard English at school and Hmong at home. Born in the United States, she reported that she had been in ESL until she tested out in 6th grade. The daughter of a college-educated mother, Sheng Yeng aspired to a career in the health professions. Significantly, Sheng Yeng explained that she tried to live up to the stereotype that Asians are smart and expressed critical opinions about many of her Hmong peers for not working hard enough in school and being "ghetto," which included the way they spoke and acted. As noted earlier, language is a performance of identity and for Sheng Yeng the avoidance of Hmonglish appeared to be linked to her performance of a high-achieving Asian (Reyes, 2016).

COLLEGE READINESS PROGRAMS

I'm in Ms. Lee's AVID class and students are piling in more quickly. She directs me to sit in a chair close to her desk. I don't want to sit there but I know where other students sit and I know kids can be territorial with their chairs so I sit there. Oddly, I don't see any White kids; well, it's AVID. The students, most of them look at me and are curious about me. I spot two Asian kids. Today, Ms. Lee's agenda is to give back a Cornell note-taking assignment. It seems like many students have screwed up the assignment and she's telling them just that.

Linda's fieldnotes, Nov. 10, 2016

Several programs have emerged in Lakeview and across the state of Wisconsin aimed at addressing the significant and persistent racialized achievement gap. In keeping with the heightened emphasis on postsecondary education in the 21st century, many of these programs focus on college preparation. We identified and interviewed Hmong American and other Southeast Asian American students in two precollege programs—Uplift (UP) and AVID. UP is a precollege enrichment program run through a local university. We didn't observe any Uplift activities because they occurred outside of UHS and we didn't have IRB approval to conduct research in Uplift spaces, but we did interview Hmong American youth who participated in Uplift. AVID, described as a college readiness program for the "academic middle," is a national nonprofit adopted by a network of over 7,500 schools across the UnitedStates. The Lakeview School District first adopted AVID in one high school in 2007 to "address persistent achievement and opportunity gaps." AVID targets students "who are capable of completing rigorous curriculum but may need additional support, mentoring and/or information to meet the requirements for enrollment in post-secondary education" (https://www.avid.org/). The typical AVID student is the first generation to go to college and many are students of color and/or from low-income backgrounds. While the official discourse frames AVID as a program for promising students, we found that AVID students at UHS had more ambivalent attitudes about being in AVID. Many students, for example, viewed being in AVID as confirmation that people think they need extra help that White students don't need.

As Linda's fieldnote suggests, AVID was understood to be a space for students of color at UHS. At other high schools in the district White working-class students regularly participated in AVID, but most of the White students at UHS came from middle- to upper-middle-class backgrounds and were therefore outside of the targeted population. The UHS AVID program did not collect disaggregated data on Asian American students, but we estimate based on family name and/or language background that there were approximately 16 Hmong students and a few other Southeast Asian American students spread across the four AVID elective courses at UHS. Notably, some of the Hmong and other Southeast Asian American students in AVID were still classified as English learners and receiving services.

AVID is designed to address equity by providing students access to rigorous academic content and the social capital to navigate schooling. By ensuring that low-income students, students of color, and those from first generation to college have access to knowledge that will lead to academic success and higher education, AVID reflects the social justice tenet of *redistribution* which focuses on redistributing resources (Fraser et al., 2003). In other, words, AVID provides important academic resources (e.g., advising, academic classes etc.) to students who have historically been excluded from the knowledge necessary to gain access to higher education. The scholarship on AVID suggests that the program has a positive impact on college attendance (Bernhardt, 2013; Mathews, 2015; Smith et al., 2014; Watt et al., 2011). A local Lakeview report on AVID found that students in AVID had better attendance and improved grades. Our observations of the AVID classes confirm that AVID teachers focus on preparing students for college, reflecting the redistributive purpose of AVID. The four AVID teachers at UHS followed the AVID curriculum that focused on study skills (note-taking, organization, and time management), homework assistance, and college guidance. We found that AVID teachers spent a great deal of time encouraging the development of pro-school identities and behaviors, emphasizing the importance of being on time and taking the time and care to submit high quality work. Reflecting the tenets of a college-going culture, teachers repeatedly spoke about students' future lives as college students where they would be expected to work independently.

In addition to teaching students study skills and pro-school attitudes and giving them guidance about postsecondary education, AVID teachers took time to develop a sense of belonging and community. In Mr. Hamilton's (a White man in his 30s) class, for example, students were asked to give presentations about themselves and their families as a way to develop public speaking skills and to get to know each other. During these presentations students shared both stories of struggle (e.g., racial profiling, poverty, housing insecurity) and stories of resilience and hope (e.g., educational aspirations) while their classmates listened quietly and attentively. Although students across racial and ethnic groups were generally friendly with each other, our observations revealed that AVID students chose to sit in same-race groups. In fact, students joked about the racial segregation in AVID and explained that AVID class was a space where they got to be with their "own people" in a welcoming environment.

Ms. Lee was one of the few Asian American teachers at UHS and she often drew on her own experiences with cultural and racial stereotypes to connect to students of color. One day, for example, she talked about her experiences being referred to as "the little Oriental girl," which led a Black student to respond by saying that was like calling a Black student a "chocolate drop," which led the students to erupt in laughter. During another AVID class, Ms. Lee used an example about the assumptions that people have about Hmong people to make a point about stereotypes. Upon hearing Ms. Lee mention Hmong people, the one Hmong student in the class who was generally quiet, perked up and shared an example from her family.

Both Ms. Lee and Ms. Born (a White woman in her 30s) regularly incorporated discussions of interpersonal racism and structural racism into their curricula. During one unit they had students read and discuss a range of issues related to race, including the achievement gap, housing inequality, racial stereotypes and the social construction of race. The following field note is a typical example of the kinds of conversations AVID students engaged in during the AVID elective class.

> They have been talking about race and the achievement gap in class, and about "positive" and negative stereotypes about racial groups they've heard. Ms. Born reminded them that some of them laughed at some benign stereotypes while some of them responded with distaste, and she asks them, "Can we change stereotypes?" At which point a Vietnamese student asks: "How are stereotypes spread?" And this spurs an active and lively discussion.
>
> Linda's fieldnotes, March 29, 2017

As this field note illustrates, Ms. Born encouraged students to think critically and ask questions about the race, including their assumptions about other racial groups. While the class had a lively atmosphere, which Ms. Born encouraged, she also pressed the AVID values of organization and preparation.

Although AVID teachers worked to challenge racial stereotypes, there were moments when the students reproduced hegemonic narratives about race. The model minority stereotype commonly circulated among students of all races. For example, during a small group discussion of the achievement gap in Ms. Lee's AVID class, a girl (non-Asian) stated, "Everyone performs less than White students!" And a boy (non-Asian) yelled out "Not Asians!" Ms. Lee didn't hear the comments and the students in the small group just laughed. Although non-Asian students knew that not all Asians were high achieving, they assumed the Asian American students who weren't high achieving model minorities were the exceptions to the norm.

A central theme in AVID classes was the importance of personal responsibility, which Ms. Born would often remind them of by saying "Good scholars are well prepared scholars." Ms. Lee emphasized the idea that personal responsibility was particularly important given the racism in the larger society. For example, after having students watch Adichie's "The Danger of a Single Story," in which Adichie warns her audience about the dangers of hearing only a single story about a person, group or country. After the students watched the Ted Talk, Ms. Lee connected the idea of stereotypes to their behavior and the unintentional messages they may be sending to teachers. After expressing her disappointment at the quality of work she had just graded, Ms. Lee asked students what messages they might be sending when they turned in low quality work, which prompted students to respond: "Low quality work says you're lazy and don't care" and "[Low quality work] shows we don't care about our education." Lessons about personal responsibility extended to lectures about the importance of treating each other with respect.

> In addition to personal responsibility, Ms. Lee is also stressing that she wants to change the culture of the class. They have a habit of talking negatively to one another (dissing). She says, "You have people telling you, even teachers, that you don't belong because of your skin color, language, background, why say those kind of things to each other?" She wants the class to change how they talk and interact with each other.
>
> Linda's fieldnotes, Nov. 30, 2016

As the field note illustrates, Ms. Lee regularly encouraged students to defy low expectations rooted in racism. AVID students did not simply passively accept everything Ms. Lee said in class and some actively questioned and resisted her lectures regarding personal responsibility. During one of Linda's observation, for example, Ms. Lee was giving one of her standard talks about punctuality when one of the more talkative Southeast Asian American (not Hmong) students spoke up and said that recent science suggested that school started too early for teens. During these debates, Ms. Lee would typically shake her head or laugh. Despite these minor disagreements, her AVID students and the students of color from her other classes regularly congregated in her room to eat, study and talk.

By holding students to high academic standards, addressing topics and issues that connect to students' identities, nurturing engaged citizenship and providing opportunities for critical discussion, Ms. Lee, Ms. Born and Mr. Hamilton were all engaging the core tenets of culturally relevant pedagogy (Ladson-Billings, 1995). AVID classes were generally lively and interactive, and students of color appeared to be more invested in the conversations in AVID classes than they were in other academic classes. Hmong and other SEA students were typically quiet in AVID classes, but they reported feeling more comfortable in AVID than other classes, which appears to be connected to the fact that teachers in AVID acknowledged race and racism. Kendall, for example, generally looked miserable and withdrawn in her classes but was always relaxed and prepared in her AVID class.

BEYOND ACADEMICS: HMONG AMERICAN STUDENTS' SOCIAL WORLDS

Actually, the Asian Club kids are quite peripheral to the school. . . . The marginality of the Hmong kids is also clear in the case of Kendall and the Hmong B-boys who occupy the corners of the school in the "special education" corridor.

Linda's fieldnotes, May 25, 2017

White students' behavior in the hallways and on school grounds reflected their sense of ease and belonging. During lunch and passing periods White students were generally found laughing, playing music, singing, lounging on the floors, tossing water bottles at each other and generally goofing around. In contrast, most students of color occupied the physical margins of the school—basement, cafeteria, and near the exits.

While there were certainly some mixed-race friendship groups, these were the exceptions rather than the norm. Our observations revealed that Asian American students, particularly East Asian American students, appeared to be the most likely to socialize with students outside of their racial group, specifically with White students. Most Hmong and other Southeast Asian American students were likely to be found hanging out with their co-ethnic peers or alone. As noted at the beginning of the chapter, UHS boasts a range of extracurricular activities and clubs, and most of these were also largely segregated by race and/or ethnicity. When we asked students to describe UHS, most mentioned both the racial diversity and the racial segregation. Gia La, the president of the Asian Club, simply stated "I don't think UHS is really a school where people are welcoming."

While White students' behavior at UHS communicated a sense of belonging in the school, Hmong American and other students of color complained about the daily racial microaggressions they faced in the school. As discussed previously, some microaggressions were expressed as deficit assumptions about students of color, as in the examples of White students correcting the English used by students of color. At other times microaggressions involved name-calling and mockery that reflected specific racialized narratives. Some incidents happened in classrooms when teachers were busy and others in the hallways and during lunch. The following field note reports an example of a racial microaggression that drew on and reproduced the idea that Asians are perpetual foreigners.

The kids are doing a gallery walk assignment to prepare them for a final exam position paper. The students are working in small groups and at one point I hear a Latino boy ask an Asian girl how to say "Hi" in her language. She replied with "Ni hao" and he then responded with, "No, ching chong." The Asian girl doesn't respond and continues to work, but then a Black girl who witnessed the exchange, rolled her eyes and in a sarcastic tone said, "Now, we are all just educated little children here, aren't we?" She is the only one to defend the Asian girl. After the Black girl spoke up, the Asian girl turned to the boys (Latino boy who made the comment and and some White boys) in the group and said, "I'm not gonna accept being fucking Chinese. I'm Tibetan. You guys do so many disrespectful things that I don't say anything." And one of the White boys said, "Like, breathe"—suggesting that she was overreacting.

Linda's fieldnotes, March 30, 2017

The response of both the Asian/Tibetan girl and the Black girl suggests that racialized microaggressions were fairly common at UHS. As is often the case with microaggressions, the boy's comment was said as a joke and drew on commonly known stereotypes (Sue et al., 2016; Wang et al., 2011). The fact that the Tibetan girl is most upset about being mistaken for Chinese suggests that this incident stung because it rendered the history and experiences of her ethnic group invisible. Many Hmong students also complained about being mistaken for being Chinese, a mis-ethnicization that rendered their ethnic group invisible. Parker, a Hmong youth who reported struggling academically and socially throughout most of his schooling, complained that everyone (non-Asians) think all Asians are Chinese, which meant he "always ha[s] to explain who I am to people."

While some students were able to seemingly shrug off racialized microaggressions, others admitted that these events were traumatic. Susannah remembered that on her second day at UHS a Black student asked her "What the hell are you?" After she told him she wasn't Chinese, the student said, "Go back to your country." Racialized microaggressions such as this are particularly troubling to Hmong people as they do not have a nation-state and are stateless (Xiong, 2021). Susannah said this incident made her feel like she "wanted to crawl into a hole and die." Both of these examples reflect the persistent stereotype that Asian Americans are perpetual foreigners whose seemingly strange cultures and languages put them outside the nation (Lee & Hong 2020; Ng et al. 2016). Although the examples of microaggressions involved students of color expressing anti-Asian racism, in their interviews our Hmong American participants reserved the most significant criticism for White students, whom they viewed as entitled, insensitive, and exclusive.

Like the adults at UHS, students of all races generally used the term Asian to describe all Asian American students, and many non-Asian students seemed to assume that all Asians were Chinese. Although non-Asian students seemed to have little knowledge about the ethnic differences among Asian Americans, they appeared to notice differences in achievement among Asians with some living up to the image of high achievement and others who were not doing as well. Hmong and other Southeast Asian American students recognized ethnic differences among

Asian Americans, but they also referred to two groups of Asian Americans at the school. On the one hand they identified students who belong to Asian Club, sit at the Asian table, stick to themselves and might be in ESL or AVID. Most of these students were understood to be Hmong. On the other hand, there were the high achieving Asian Americans, mostly Chinese students who socialized with other Chinese students and with White students. A few Hmong students pointed to differences between Southeast Asians and Chinese students (often code for all East Asians), arguing that Chinese students were more privileged.

Asian Club

The Asian Club is officially described as a club for Asian students "or anyone interested in Asian cultures, working together or just wanting to have fun." Despite the panethnic name of the club and efforts to broaden the membership to include Asian American students from various ethnic groups as well as non-Asians, most club members identified as Hmong and a few others identified as Vietnamese or Khmer. The large number of Hmong students in the Asian Club led many members to jokingly refer to it as the "Hmong Club." The president of the Asian Club reported that there were 35 official members of the club, but attendance at meetings typically ranged between 7 to 18 students with a relatively equal breakdown of boys and girls, and students across all four grades. Ms. Her was the faculty advisor for the club and meetings were held in her classroom, but club meetings were generally student-led and often included icebreaking games and discussions about club activities and fundraising to support the activities. Many club meetings were spent with students just socializing and eating lunch. We learned for example, that many Hmong girls liked to listen to K-pop and talk about episodes of their favorite K-dramas (Korean dramas) during Asian Club. Speaking in English, Hmong, and Hmonglish, Hmong girls gushed over how pretty Korean actresses were and how good-looking male K-pop stars were. Their conversations suggested that they were drawn to K-pop and K-drama because of a desire to see "cool" Asians in popular culture. Our fieldwork suggests that the Asian Club had two unofficial goals: providing a welcoming social space for Hmong and other Asian American students and enhancing the visibility of Asian American students at UHS. As we will argue, the Asian Club was much more successful in achieving the first goal of creating a social space for Hmong students than they were in achieving their larger political goal of visibility.

The UHS Asian Club was affiliated with the districtwide United Asian Club that brought together students from the different high schools in Lakeview. Like UHS's Asian Club, the United Asian Club was a predominately Hmong American space that was overseen by middle-class Hmong American professionals, including Mr. Lor, who worked in higher education administration. The United Asian Club met once or twice a month and meetings centered on planning events that brought together Hmong youth across the city for social events, sporting events, cultural events (e.g., Hmong New Year's assembly) and events that focused on postsecondary education (e.g., college fairs, college scholarship).

The Asian Club's reputation as a Hmong space was boosted by its membership, the relationship with the Hmong-led United Asian Club, and the club's activities. For example, in collaboration with the United Asian Club, UHS's Asian Club put on an assembly for the Hmong New Year that featured girls dressed in Hmong clothing and doing traditional Hmong dances, Hmong boys breakdancing, and a play that recounted the Hmong origins story. The assembly included students from high schools throughout Lakeview, and students spoke in both English and Hmong to the audience. Although open to the entire UHS community, there were few UHS students in the audience. In addition to district-level staff, there were elementary-aged students and a few Hmong parents in the audience.

Although the students in UHS's Asian Club were almost all Hmong, many students did not previously know each other and had joined the group because they'd heard that the club was a place to meet other Hmong students. During an Asian Club meeting in October of 2016, for example, club members played "Two truths and a lie," and invited Linda to join the game. When Linda remarked that it seemed like they must all know each other because they were all guessing correctly, the president of Asian Club responded, "Oh no, we don't know each other, actually," and another girl jumped in to add, "I just know about him [boy in corner, diagonal of me] because that's my brother." In the field note below Linda takes her turn at two truths and a lie:

> The girl's comment about knowing her brother drew laughs from the group. Then I'm asked to take my turn on the spot. So, I say: "1. I'm Khmer-Chinese, 2. My favorite color is pink, and 3. I'm scared of the dark." They all start guessing at the same time. One girl says, "Your fave color can't be pink because your hair is blue." Another says, "But her jacket is pink." A boy across the room says, "There is no way you're Khmer." So, it's a toss-up between #1 (mostly boys) and #2 mostly girls—I tell them it's #2—my fave color is green. So, they go around and other people take their turn. One boy with the cropped hair shared "I hate school" as his second statement—NO ONE guessed that to be a lie!
>
> Linda's fieldnotes, October 13, 2016

As this fieldnote suggests, students in the Asian Club engaged in good-natured teasing that encouraged a sense of belonging among members, thereby achieving one of the central goals of the club.

As their response to Linda's ethnicity demonstrates, students in the Asian Club recognized and paid attention to ethnic differences among Asian Americans, and even held stereotypes about other Asian Americans. Here, the Asian Club students were remarking on Linda not "looking Khmer" because her skin was too light for a Khmer person. The student who asserted that there was "no way" Linda was Khmer was the only Khmer student in Asian Club. In fact, Linda noted that during her fieldwork various Hmong, Khmer, and Vietnamese students remarked on how light-skinned she was for a Khmer person. The focus on skin color is not simply a neutral observation but one that reflects *colorism* within Asian American communities. Colorism is defined as the status hierarchies within the same ethnic or racial group based on skin color whereby lighter-skinned people are favored (Chanbonpin, 2015; Hunter, 2007; Rondilla & Spickard, 2007).

In Asian American communities, colorism is the product of a complex set of social and historical interactions with gender, immigrant, generational, and class dimensions (Chanbonpin, 2015). Aesthetic preferences in Asian countries, specifically the privileging of light skin, were shaped by classism and attention to status differences. Because less privileged people often labored outdoors, and higher status people tended to work indoors, skin color came to reflect status and worth. Throughout Asia, East Asians, who are generally lighter-skinned, are seen as superior to Filipinos and Southeast Asians, who are depicted as being darker-skinned (Dixon & Telles, 2017; Rondilla, 2009). While the process of racialization in the United States lumps together immigrants and refugees from throughout East Asia, Southeast Asia, and the Indian subcontinent, Asian Americans have transferred colorism to the U.S., where colorism operates within and across racial groups (Bonilla-Silva & Dietrich, 2009).

Some Asian Club members expressed a desire to have a more diverse group of Asian American members, even though they spoke about differences among Asian ethnic groups. They feared that the Asian Club was invisible at the school and thought that drawing non-Hmong members and thus increasing numbers would lead to greater visibility and recognition. In other words, their desire for greater diversity was driven by concerns about the invisibility of the Asian Club at the school, and not by a desire to foster cross-ethnic conversations. Asian Club members consistently referred to the small size of the club and suggested that the relative social power held by both Black students and Latinx students had to do with the fact that both groups had relatively large clubs at UHS. During Linda's first observation of the Asian Club, for example, she remarked that the group looked big, which was met by a loud, "NOoooooooooo. It's not big. That's Western. They're the big group." As noted earlier, Western has a reputation for being the most racially diverse high school in Lakeview with the largest Hmong population, and there was a bit of a crosstown rivalry between Western's Asian Club and UHS's Asian Club.

A petite, fashion-conscious, and friendly 12th-grader, Gia La was the newly elected president of the Asian Club. Gia La had transferred to UHS in the 11th grade and in her relatively short time at UHS was already popular among her Hmong peers and liked by her teachers. As she explains in the following interview segment, Gia La was eager to transform the Asian Club into a more visible group before she graduated and went to college.

> I wanted to step up and be president was because I feel like not just, not just the Hmong culture, but Asian people in general . . . I feel like they're like invisible in high school. Like, you know, there's Black student union, that's a big club. And then there's the, I don't know what that club is called, but it's like all the Hispanic people. They have a really big club too. And, I was like, you know, how come, the only time Asian people are known is when there's egg roll sales. And, it's kind of bothered me. It's like, okay, we only exist when we have egg roll sales. Like, we should do more. Like we should get more involved. I think it's just important to me because, you know,

we're students here too and you know, we're a club just like every other club. We
don't get the support that like other clubs do, but it's also on us, like, we have to
reach out to the school for them to notice us and to reach out to us too.

As her quote suggests, Gia La hoped that the Asian Club could increase the visibility and recognition of Asian American students, and she assumed that increasing
the size of the club would increase Asian visibility at the school. It's important to
point out that she was concerned and frustrated that non-Asians only saw Asians
during egg roll sales. In fact, club members recognized that making and selling egg
rolls was their best way to raise money, but some feared that the sales might inadvertently perpetuate the image of Asians as dehumanized producers of exotic food.
  Gia La was particularly interested in expanding the membership of the Asian
Club to include non-Hmong members but noted that she had been able to convince
only a couple of Khmer and Vietnamese students to join. In the following interview
segment, Gia La reflected on her efforts to get Chinese students to join Asian Club.

Yeah. It's always mainly Hmong students. And I mean, I have tried. I had a study
hall last semester. I had a few Chinese students in my class. I told them about it, but
they just weren't interested. I don't know why. Like it's just, I don't know what it
is, but just, when I ask other ethnicities, they're just not interested. Then when I ask
random Hmong people, they're like, "Oh yeah, okay." But then they come, like, I
don't know what it is. I don't know if it's just because I'm Hmong, so the Hmong
people feel more comfortable, or I don't know. Maybe I have to be Chinese to make
the Chinese students feel like they should come. Like, I asked them all the same questions. I tell them all like the same way. But then, only the Hmong students show up
and all the other Asian students, they don't; I really don't know. *[Note: she sounded
a little frustrated during this segment]*

In the spring semester Gia La successfully recruited a few East Asian American boys
that she knew from her classes to participate in the Asian Club for a district-wide
United Asian Club sports tournament. These boys came to one Asian Club meeting to discuss the tournament and then participated in the tournament.

Some big East Asian looking kids are here for the Asian Club meeting . . . I
can tell they are different because they are not eating the free lunch from the
cafeteria like the Asian Club kids. These East Asian kids are eating home-
packed lunch (very large salads, like a Trader Joe's shopping list) and carrying expensive water bottles/Zojirushi. Oh, these boys are here because they
are signing up to play sports at the tournament (haha), which UHS Asian
Club kids will also participate in.

Linda's fieldnotes April 20, 2017

Although the East Asian American boys participated in the event, they didn't interact much with the Hmong students during the meeting or event, and they didn't
participate in any Asian Club events after this one event. As Linda's fieldnotes

reflect, there were fairly obvious social class differences between most of the East Asian American students at UHS and most of the Hmong and Southeast Asian American students. Hmong students, most of whom were from working-class or low-income backgrounds, referred to the middle-class Chinese and other East Asian American students as being "rich." Indeed, Southeast Asian American and East Asian American students had different social class and cultural backgrounds, different immigration histories, and relatively different experiences in the school, and these differences made a panethnic identification difficult (Espiritu, 1992). While the majority of Hmong and other Southeast Asian American students came from low-income families, most of the East Asian American students were from middle-class families. The class distinctions could be seen in what they ate for lunch (e.g., boxed milk and other food from the cafeteria versus snacks from Whole Foods or Trader Joe's), how they dressed, and where they lived. Hmong and other Southeast Asian students all commuted by bus or car into the predominately White, upper-middle-class neighborhood where University Heights is located. In contrast, the East and South Asian American students could be seen driving to school or walking a short distance to their homes. Parker, for example, asserted that Chinese and other East Asian students "have more privilege than us; Southeast Asians have more struggles" referring to differences in class background and immigration history.

Hmong and other Southeast Asian American students were well aware of the stereotype that Asian Americans were supposed to be good students. Furthermore, they recognized that many of the East Asian American students appeared to live up to the model minority stereotype and feared that Hmong students did not. Although all of our Hmong participants expressed concern that people didn't know about Hmong people or culture, they also feared that students had negative or deficit perspectives about Hmong people. As mentioned earlier in this chapter, Sheng Yeng remarked on the fact that she was one of the few Hmong students who lived up to the stereotype of Asians being high-achieving model minorities. Her concerns regarding the image of Hmong students at UHS led her to avoid socializing with the Hmong students who all sat together at the "Asian" table in the cafeteria; she was initially afraid that she would be "following some racial, stereotypical footsteps" if she joined the Asian Club. Building on the deficit perspective of Hmong students, Sheng Yeng explained "I don't see Hmong kids or Hmong people in general as like the very involved type of people." When Linda asked her to clarify, Sheng Yeng responded by saying that Hmong students weren't involved enough in school. Although Sheng Yeng used the panethnic term "Asian," she appeared to divide Asians into two groups—those who are high achieving and those who are not (e.g., Hmong). This was similar to the way non-Asian students and faculty divided Asian American students.

Previous research suggests that Hmong Americans have been stereotyped as low-achieving or failed model minorities, and Gia La and Sheng Yeng worried that East Asian American students were reluctant to join the Asian Club because they didn't want to associate with Hmong students (Lee, 2005). Gia La and Sheng Yeng wanted to raise the social status of Hmong people at the school and increase the general visibility of Asian American students. Gia La believed that a more ethnically diverse

Asian Club would accomplish both goals. Both Gia La and Sheng Yeng assumed that their non-Hmong peers didn't know they were Hmong because they didn't fit the dominant image of the marginalized Hmong student. Sheng Yeng, in particular, was afraid of being stereotyped as a "typical" Hmong student and wanted to demonstrate that Hmong students can do well in school. Both girls appeared to recognize that the pan-Asian identity offered them some protection from deficit perspectives, but, understandably, they also wanted people to know they were Hmong. Similarly, research on Cambodian students revealed that Cambodian students were stereotyped as being low-achieving, and higher-achieving Cambodian students responded by embracing a panethnic Asian identity, which they assumed would protect their image (Chhuon & Hudley, 2010). As Chhuon and Hudley explain, "Cambodian students also chose to embrace panethnicity in school because they perceived it as a path to a positive academic identity. For example, an Asian American label meant that teachers and students would view them as high achievers, rather than academic strugglers" (p. 350). Trapped by racialized stereotypes of Asian Americans as model minorities and Hmong Americans as failed model minorities, Gia La and Sheng Yeng alternated between emphasizing a panethnic Asian identity and a Hmong identity.

While Gia La and Sheng Yeng wanted the Asian Club to be a space that raised the status of Hmong students and heightened the visibility of Asian American students in general, most of the other Hmong students in the Asian Club were primarily invested in creating a space where they felt they could belong. Ultimately, the relatively small size of the Asian Club and the challenges they faced in diversifying club membership prevented the club from gaining greater visibility. Although Gia La wasn't able to fully realize her goals of increasing the membership of Asian Club and increasing the visibility of Hmong and other Asian American students at UHS, the club did provide a space for Hmong and other Southeast Asian students to connect with other Hmong and Southeast Asian students and create a place of belonging.

CONCLUSION

UHS is like a giant factory in which kids are produced in different parts of the school for different opportunities. Kids like Kendall are put through the conveyor belt and end up in the "mediocre" pile because of too little care and attention, which is ironic since she is both an ESL and AVID student and she's supposed to be receiving more support than a regular student. . . . Actually, most kids of color are in the mediocre pile while White kids seem to be in the "premium products" section. They get more attention from teachers because they know to speak up more.

Linda's fieldnotes, May 25, 2017

In the 1990s a local paper noted that Hmong students were the most marginalized group at UHS (Lee, 2005). In *Up Against Whiteness*, Stacey argued that 1.5- and second-generation Hmong youth were judged by the dominant standards of Whiteness—idealized White middle-class norms—and found to be deficient. At the time, the Hmong community had been in the United States for approximately 25 years and while they were no longer newcomers, their history as refugees had not been entirely forgotten. The dominant group, including educators, knew that the Hmong community struggled with poverty and that Hmong youth struggled in school, but they didn't fully appreciate the barriers created by refugee policies and educational policies and practices. Rather, the problems experienced by the Hmong community were seen as being tied to the Hmong culture and/or to the youths' adaption to "urban" culture. As such, the academic struggles and high rates of poverty within Hmong communities rendered them a failed model minority. Unable to fit into the model minority image, Hmong American youth at University Heights High and in other educational institutions in the United States were subjected to an ideological blackening—a form of hypervisibility or misrecognition. The ideological blackening reflected an implicit anti-Blackness and allowed dominant institutions to escape responsibility for reflecting on their role in marginalizing Hmong American students.

While there have been significant changes at the school and within the Hmong student population over the years, we found that Hmong and other SEAA students were still among the most marginalized and invisible at UHS. All the Hmong students we spoke to expressed concern about the invisibility of Hmong people at UHS and in Lakeview. At the turn of the 21st century Hmong students occupied a position as relative newcomers at UHS, but approximately 10 years after the last significant group of Hmong refugees were resettled in the United States in 2005 many teachers and most students knew little about Hmong people, culture, or history. The large student population at UHS made it easy for students to get lost in the crowd, but we argue that this is more than a story about small numbers. While our Hmong participants used the term "invisibility" and we agree that there were ways in which Hmong youth were literally unseen, our data suggests that there were moments where Hmong students were hypervisible at UHS. We argue that the term *misrecognition* is a more accurate reflection of Hmong students' struggles with invisibility and hypervisibility at UHS. Our fieldwork reveals that Hmong students are rendered invisible and/or misrecognized by the culture of Whiteness at UHS, by the overwhelming Asian American category, and by neoliberal educational policies. Misrecognition was linked to a low status and a lack of belonging at the school, which contributed to Hmong students' concerns regarding Hmong people being stigmatized (Fraser et al., 2003; Fraser, 2009).

While all Hmong youth complain about the invisibility of Hmong people at the school and in the city, some students are more successful at navigating the dominant space of UHS than others. The most academically and socially successful Hmong students at UHS identified as cisgendered girls like Gia La and Sheng Yeng. Although none of the students spoke explicitly about the role of gender or gender identity in their experiences at school or in the Lakeview community, we found that Hmong girls were more active in Asian Club, and more likely to have positive things to say about their teachers, which is consistent with previous research that has found Hmong girls doing better in school than boys (Lee, 2005; Lo, 2017). The most marginalized Hmong students at UHS were long-term English learners who experienced multiple forms of vulnerability, including poverty.

Unlike many low-income immigrants and refugees who attend poorly resourced and segregated schools that are assumed to account for their academic struggles, our Hmong participants attended a reasonably well-resourced school with a significant number of White students and a reputation for academic excellence. A growing body of scholarship has found that racial inequalities also exist in well-resourced schools like UHS, and scholars point to the system of beliefs, values, norms, practices, and performances that constitute Whiteness in the persistence of inequalities in these schools (Dhingra, 2020; Lee, 2005; Lewis and Diamond, 2015). Dhingra (2020), for example, argues that "teachers, predominately white, reinforce a 'hidden curriculum'—that is, informal norms for what constitutes proper behavior, dress, attitudes, and discipline in schools" (p. 44). Colorblindness and color-evasiveness or what Zeus Leonardo describes as "the unwillingness to name the contours of racism" are central to this hidden curriculum of Whiteness (Leonardo, 2002, p. 32).

Whiteness allows White people to be seen as individuals but doesn't afford the same individuality to racially minoritized groups. Teachers at UHS recognized White students as individuals with different interests and talents as evidenced by their participation in various clubs or activities, but identified Hmong students only with ESL or the Asian Club. Although most teachers at UHS were complicit in perpetuating a culture of Whiteness at the school, Hmong students' most critical comments were directed at White students, not teachers. Hmong students and other students of color recognized that some of their White teachers were working to be more inclusive, but they complained that White students were racist and privileged. At UHS, White middle-class students were the biggest beneficiaries of Whiteness, and their entitlement was demonstrated in their everyday actions in the hallways and in classrooms. We were particularly struck by the way White students dominated classroom discussions and corrected the English used by classmates of color. Even when White teachers pushed back and told White students about different forms of English, White students appeared to be certain in their understanding that standard English was the only correct form of English. We argue that their assumptions about the singular correctness of standard English reflect the assumptions of colorblindness central to Whiteness. Importantly, Whiteness and color-evasiveness were also reflected in the supposedly objective educational policies that labeled many Hmong students long-term English learners.

The panethnic "Asian American" category worked to render Hmong students both invisible and hypervisible. As many scholars have argued, one of the unintentional problems with the panethnic "Asian" category is that it glosses over cultural and historical differences among Asian Americans. At UHS, Hmong students complained that their non-Asian peers didn't know anything about Hmong people and that many non-Asian students assumed that all Asians were Chinese. Aggregate data on Asian American students also worked to mask or hide differences among Asian Americans at UHS. Hmong students who remain trapped in ESL were hypervisible because they were seen as being less academically successful than other Asians. In fact, Hmong students' relationship with and attitude toward ESL services have shifted significantly since Stacey's earlier fieldwork at UHS. In *Up Against Whiteness*, 1.5-generation Hmong students identified the ESL program as offering a safe space of belonging. In this earlier work, ESL teachers were among the most ardent advocates for Hmong students and many 1.5-generation Hmong students spoke fondly of their ESL teachers and the opportunities and support offered by the program. In contrast, the Hmong American youth in our current study are all U.S.-born and -educated and do not understand why they remain categorized as ELs, a label they experience as stigmatizing.

The emphasis on academic English embedded in current educational policies and practices reflects deficit-based approaches to emergent bilinguals. Hmong students who are unable to demonstrate a mastery of academic English are labeled long-term English learners, marking them outside the norm of ELs. Unfortunately, our data demonstrate that Hmong youth have all internalized an understanding that the EL category is the equivalent of being marked as academically incompetent. Like placement in lower-track classes, the EL designation negatively affects academic self-esteem (Tyson, 2011). Hmong students who remained trapped in ESL were confused and embarrassed by their designation and by the services provided. The two Hmong students who were most connected to the school and doing well academically had tested out of ESL, but they recognized that many of their Hmong peers remained trapped in ESL. Research has demonstrated that ELs are often tracked out of academically rigorous courses because of the assumption that students must master academic English before gaining access to challenging academic content, with long-term ELs suffering the most (Callahan, 2005; Callahan et al., 2010). Relatedly, recent research shows that teachers hold lower expectations for students labeled EL (Umansky & Dumont, 2021). Like other neoliberal educational polices that are purportedly colorblind and aim to address racial inequities, policies surrounding English learners in Lakeview reproduce race, class, and linguistic inequities (Turner, 2020).

The AVID program represents one of the biggest institutional changes at UHS. Some scholars have correctly argued that AVID provides access to the academic hierarchy but doesn't challenge the hierarchy or academic structure (Lewis & Diamond, 2015; Ochoa, 2013). While we agree with these criticisms about AVID, we found that AVID teachers at UHS used AVID to create culturally relevant spaces where racially minoritized students were provided with opportunities to interrogate race and racism while learning academic skills. Most Hmong students at UHS, however, did not participate in AVID. One of two Hmong American teachers at UHS taught in the AVID program but many Hmong students only knew her through the Asian Club, which was the only space of belonging open to all Hmong students. The Asian Club's struggles to expand membership highlighted the limits of Asian American panethnicity at UHS and contributed to a sense that the Hmong identity was stigmatized at UHS.

In short, University Heights High is a case study of how the misrecognition of Hmong Americans plays out in Lakeview schools. While the four comprehensive high schools in Lakeview have unique cultures and histories, all have relatively small populations of Hmong American students and all struggle with racial inequities. In the next two chapters we will focus on how Hmong American adults and youths in Lakeview make sense of and resist the misrecognition and invisibility of Hmong students.

Middle-Class Hmong Leadership and the Push for Inclusion

Stacey J. Lee and Mai Neng Vang

> It's also the . . . one of the most important ones in the sense that getting an education helps open many doors and get you out of poverty into—be more affluent, as well, as just whether you want to run for office or open up a business, having an education really helps that person—individual, and so education kind of became one of the corner pieces of some of the racial justice things I work on.
>
> Mr. Thao, Hmong community leader

In the approximately 15 years between the time Stacey collected the data for *Up Against Whiteness* and the time we embarked on this study there has been a significant growth in the number of college-educated, middle-class professional Hmong Americans living and working in Lakeview and the surrounding community (Pfeifer et al., 2012; Smolarek et al., 2019). Most of these women and men work in K–12 education, higher education, city and state government, or for nonprofit organizations. As individuals who have successfully used formal education to achieve material security, they see education as the surest way for the Hmong community to move out of poverty and become equal members of society. Mr. Thao's quote at the beginning of this chapter illustrates this faith in the power of formal education, and an understanding that there is a connection between economic standing and civil liberties (Xiong, 2021). Middle-class professionals expressed concern that too many Hmong American youth were struggling in school, which they argued made them vulnerable to being trapped in generational poverty and associated problems.

Some of the middle-class professionals are members of the 1.5 generation who came to this country as refugees when they were children, entered schools as English learners, and were among the early group of Hmong Americans to earn college degrees. Other middle-class professionals are second-generation Hmong Americans born, raised and entirely educated in the United States. Importantly, members of both cohorts have children in local schools and had personal experiences as former ESL students. Like the Hmong American high school students who identified as "traditional" in Stacey's earlier study, the middle-class professionals have a positive attitude toward school, and embrace biculturalism and bilingualism (Lee, 2005). While they are willing to make certain cultural accommodations to the dominant society in order to achieve social mobility and financial security, they remain deeply concerned with cultural preservation.

Middle-class professionals came to educational advocacy as part of a broader political awakening and concern for the barriers facing the Hmong community in Lakeview, in the state of Wisconsin, and in the nation. Mr. Thao, recognized by many of the middle-class professionals as one of the central educational advocates for Hmong students, is illustrative of this group. Mr. Thao came to the United States as a refugee when he was a child and his family was resettled in a predominately White community where he was one of the few Hmong students in the local schools. He holds a graduate degree in a STEM field but became involved in community work and educational advocacy when he realized that the Hmong community did not have a voice in the dominant society.

Mr. Thao emphasized that there are "traditional" Hmong leaders in the community who provide important services for the community, but he explained that these leaders struggle to navigate the public education system because they are not English proficient and do not possess the requisite knowledge about how the U.S. educational system functions. The category of traditional community leaders is shifting and complex, but historically these leaders have been exclusively cisgender, married, middle-aged Hmong men, and leadership positions were usually passed down to married sons. Recently, however, these leadership positions have shifted to also include some Hmong women. The majority of these traditional leaders are working-class and lower-middle-class married couples with little to no college education. Although most can speak conversational English, they feel most comfortable speaking Hmong and are uncertain about how to engage in educational advocacy beyond pushing their own children to do well in school. The group of traditional leaders also includes men and women who were part of the 2004–2005 refugee wave. These 2004–2005 refugee leaders have little to no formal education and limited English fluency. Traditional leaders are responsible for moderating clan disputes and organizing community events such as the Hmong New Year celebration. Like other immigrant and refugee parents, traditional leaders want their children to succeed in school, but they face significant sociocultural obstacles that make it difficult for them to navigate the education system and to advocate for Hmong youth (Delgado-Gaitan, 2004; Valdes, 1997). A large body of scholarship shows that parents with limited formal education and those from working class backgrounds, like those of immigrant background, face barriers to parental involvement (Desimone, 1999; Lareau, 2000; Turney & Kao, 2009). Because their educational aspirations for Hmong youth are similar to those held by their middle-class co-ethnics, traditional leaders have ceded authority for educational advocacy to the middle-class professionals.

Mr. Thao explained that upon moving to Lakeview there were a few incidents revealing anti-Hmong sentiment in Wisconsin that made him recognize the need for Hmong leaders to advocate for the community in dominant society. In particular, he cited a 2007 incident involving a university law professor who made disparaging remarks about Hmong culture, particularly gender relations, that many members of the Hmong American community found offensive and misinformed. Mr. Thao explains his political awakening in the following quote:

> I started realizing that there wasn't a voice for the Hmong community, whether it's here in Lakeview or Wisconsin in general. And so that's what kind of prompt me to start being more vocal about, "You know, we should have the same rights and should we . . . we should have equal rights as well," when we talked to elected officials as well as just community leaders in Lakeview and just about equity, right? I mean the Hmong community, it's one of those communities that gets left out in the fringes because they feel that they are, you know, the hardship of communicating and language barrier and cultural barrier, they kind of just get left out there and so . . . that's kind of how this role came about for myself.

Mr. Thao's community advocacy evolved to include educational issues because he believes that formal education is central to the success of the next generation of Hmong Americans.

Gao Moua, another middle-class professional community leader, explained that she had been involved in advocating for the Hmong community for a number of years and became specifically interested in educational issues when her own children started school.

> You know, it's, it's really, when you're a little bit distant from the school system, you think that everything is okay. But then as the parents, when you have the kids in the school system, your firsthand experience really wake you up and say, "Holy cow, this is still happening."

Gao Moua spoke specifically about her concerns with ESL, the absence of culturally relevant curriculum, cultural stereotyping, and the low expectations faced by Hmong students. Early in her children's education she had attempted to participate in the Parent Teacher Organization (PTO) at her child's school but found that she couldn't make her voice heard "because it's all White parent . . . all White folks wants to do things their way. They don't make room for you." Gao Moua explained that watching her children struggle with racial stereotypes and identity issues led her to push the PTO to address multiculturalism, but her efforts were met with indifference.

> You know, I'm trying to tell them about we need to do events for it, teach the kids their identity issues, you know, so even White kids, they need to know where they come from, too right? And they need to know that other people are from other parts of the world. But then they also need to know that some of their friends are born right here in the same hospital and they shouldn't assume that because they look different then they're from somewhere else.

Significantly, Gao Moua argued that cultural pluralism is good for all children, including White kids. As she talked about her experiences with what she referred to as the "politics" of the PTO, Gao Moua shook her head with frustration, and suggested that White parents did not appreciate the importance of multicultural issues for "understanding that this country is made up of different people from the world." Gao Moua's experiences are consistent with research that shows that PTOs in racially diverse schools are often dominated by White parents and that participation in PTOs is linked to greater visibility and power than other forms of parent engagement (Cucchiara, 2008; Posey-Maddox, 2013). As Posey-Maddox has observed, "Parent-teacher organizations can serve as a useful window through which to examine issues of exclusivity, power, and access in public school settings" (2013, p. 236).

Gao Moua and other middle-class Hmong advocates understood that parent involvement with formal school structures, as represented by parent–teacher organizations, provides parents with important access to institutional power and control over their children's education; they were concerned about the barriers to involvement faced by Hmong parents (Delgado-Gaitan, 2004; Lareau, 2000; Turney & Kao, 2009). Reflecting on the difficulty she has had with the Lakeview School District, Gao Moua suggested that she felt it was her duty to advocate not only for her children but for the Hmong community.

> And so we, so we enter a school in that route and we continue to be the advocate because there's so much gaps in them that, you know, what amazed me is like if parents like me, who really know how to navigate systems, still experience this, can you imagine the parents who don't speak any English and who don't take part in the community to really speak up? What do they feel like? Right?

Like other Asian immigrants and refugees, Gao Moua points out that some Hmong parents experience language barriers to their participation in schools. Indeed, language barriers appear to contribute to the fact that Asian immigrant parents commonly report feeling unwelcome at children's schools (Turney & Kao, 2009). As her quote suggests, Gao Moua was well aware that she had relative privilege compared to many Hmong parents but still encountered problems in dealing with the schools.

HMONG EDUCATION ADVOCATES (HEA)

Middle-class professional advocates regularly asserted that because the Hmong community is largely invisible, their concerns go unrecognized and unaddressed. Furthermore, they reasoned that the Hmong community was less visible than other communities of color in Lakeview because they were a small group, had fewer resources, and had historically been too quiet. Mr. Thao believed that the lack of recognition relative to other groups of color reflected and contributed to status differences between the groups. He explained, "While the Urban League and United

Latinos provide services to their respective communities, the Hmong community has no such direct service organization. With limited or no funding support from the larger Lakeview community for programs designed to address Hmong assimilation and self-sufficiency, the Hmong community feels isolated and students and parents are disconnected from the schools."

Recognizing the need for a stronger Hmong voice in the Lakeview School District, a group of middle-class Hmong professionals in Lakeview and surrounding communities, including Mr. Thao, organized an educational advocacy group called Hmong Education Advocates (HEA) to make the needs and voices of the Hmong community known to the school district. These leaders positioned themselves as the bridge between school district leaders and the Lakeview Hmong American community. HEA was founded in 2011 but did not become fully active until 2012. The organization began with 15 members, with three of them being part of the executive board. Chou, one of the original members of HEA, explained that they created the organization to "advocate the school district to make an effort to provide services to the Hmong community."

While middle-class advocates in HEA occasionally used terms such as Asian and Southeast Asian, their educational advocacy was specific to the Hmong community. In fact, they argue that the Asian category renders Hmong people and their concerns invisible. For example, when asked whether he believed that Hmong people face discrimination in society, Mr. Thao adamantly asserted, "I think we do! Because they think we're Asian! They don't know what Hmong is." Mr. Thao is rejecting the panethnic "Asian" categorization and claiming a distinct ethnic identity as Hmong. In short, HEA wants schools to recognize the distinct history, culture, achievements, and suffering of the Hmong people. In calling for the recognition of the distinctive nature of Hmong culture and history, middle-class leaders are espousing a politics of difference that reflects the concerns of multiculturalists (Kymlicka, 1995).

HEA's vision, as stated on their Facebook page and account as well as on each of their meeting agenda and meeting minutes, is to "advance the Hmong community through maximizing their educational experiences and opportunities." Moreover, they list four missions: (1) To enhance student success by supporting their educational needs; (2) To provide educators and professionals with the tools and resources to help students succeed; (3) To educate and support parents in their students' academic success; (4) To collaborate with existing organizations and programs to foster student success. During the first couple of years, HEA held monthly meetings and also met quarterly with the superintendent of the Lakeview School District starting in May 2013. HEA's meetings with the superintendent were part of their intentional efforts to develop social capital with institutional leaders. Interestingly, their willingness to participate in our study appeared to be motivated in part by a desire to strengthen connections with the University of Wisconsin. HEA and other middle-class advocates asserted that success in K–12 education was key to going on to college and to being ready for gainful employment after high school.

HEA had an email subscription list of over 70 members, but during our observations in 2016 only about five or six members regularly attended the monthly meetings, including three members of the executive board. HEA meetings were formally run with attendance sheets and printed agendas, and typical agenda items included communications with university student organizations, communications with local school districts, and strategies for how to connect with mainstream leaders in Lakeview. Although attendance at monthly meetings was relatively low, they communicated often via email to their listserv, forwarding job announcements (usually for Hmong-specific services) and information regarding the Hmong summer enrichment program and the Hmong Professionals Network (both run by Gao Moua).

Members of HEA suggested that without greater advocacy on their part the school district would not prioritize the needs of Hmong students. Chou, for example, suggested that the school district only responded when communities made themselves heard.

> First, it's not a priority and secondly, budget cut, right? Uh, so if parents, the community is not vocal about it, then it's—I mean, no news is good news, right? If they don't need then the Latinx and the Blacks vocalize daily that their kids can't learn, they are falling behind, and then they will focus more on Black kids and Latinx kids.

As the last sentence in Chou's quotation suggests, HEA members believe that the Black and Latinx communities in Lakeview get more attention than the Hmong community. While HEA members acknowledge that the Hmong community is smaller than the Black and Latinx communities, they suggest that the attention that these other communities receive is due to the vocal advocacy of those communities. They were aware of what other communities of color were doing in terms of educational advocacy and occasionally modeled their actions after other groups. HEA, for example, was modeled after a Latino group. Still, they did not appear to embrace an identity as people of color or to engage in cross-racial coalition efforts on a regular basis.

Mr. Thao, Chou, and other HEA members regularly referenced the fact that the Black–White achievement gap in the greater Lakeview area had gotten attention after the publication of a local report in 2013. Although they were sympathetic about the barriers faced by the Black community, they expressed concern that Hmong and other Southeast Asian communities remained largely invisible in local discourses regarding educational inequities. For Mr. Thao, invisibility was both an expression of inequality and a central contributing factor to the ongoing inequality faced by Hmong Americans. HEA focused on advocating for disaggregated data on Hmong students and fighting for culturally relevant pedagogy, bilingual education, and the hiring of Hmong staff in the district.

DISAGGREGATING HMONG DATA

Mr. Thao began his fight to have the Lakeview School District disaggregate the data on Hmong American students before the formation of HEA. The focus on data has been central to neoliberal educational reforms, and Mr. Thao understood that in order to get the district to recognize the needs of Hmong students he needed to get the district to gather the data (Au, 2010, 2016; Hursh, 2007; Koyama, 2011; Lipman, 2013). Like most school districts across the nation, Lakeview disaggregates data by racial categories but did not disaggregate data on Asian American students by ethnic group. Pointing to the limits of the panethnic Asian American category, Mr. Thao argued that aggregate data rendered invisible the academic concerns of Hmong American students. Furthermore, he believed that aggregate data on Asian American students supported the idea that Asian Americans were all high achieving model minorities. Mr. Thao explains his several-year struggle to get the Lakeview District to disaggregate the data on Hmong students, which he ultimately achieved in 2013 when a new superintendent was appointed to the Lakeview District:

> So, for a long time, they would just take the Hmong data and just lump it in with the Asian data and so that really skewed things. And that really was saying the Asian students were doing pretty well in [Lakeview]. And so three superintendents later, I finally got the school board members supportive of my idea and this new superintendent says, "Yea, we could do that for you." And so, 3 years ago was the first when the Hmoob data was pulled out of the Asian American data. And so, what that showed was in that first year, about 92 percent of Hmong students weren't proficient in reading. And 78, I think, percent weren't proficient in doing math.

Since 2013, Mr. Thao has collaborated with the district to disaggregate the data on Hmong students based on students' last names (which he notes is not a perfect system but helps to provide an idea of Hmong American students in the district). The disaggregated data from the 2015–2016 academic year reveal that the vast majority of Hmong American students in the district are identified as English learners (88%), and three-quarters (76%) are eligible for free or reduced lunch. The data also demonstrates that while Hmong American students have relatively high graduation rates (80%), high attendance rates (94.8%) and low behavior incidents (8%), they score below district averages in math and reading proficiency in grades 3–8.

Armed with this data, HEA has argued that the disaggregated data demonstrates that a large number of Hmong youth are trapped in ESL and graduating from high school with limited academic skills, which will make them vulnerable to being trapped in low-wage jobs. By calling for disaggregated data, Mr. Thao and HEA were engaging in a strategy advanced by many critics of the model minority stereotype who argue that the stereotype contributes to the institutional neglect suffered by Asian Americans (Lee & Kumashiro, 2005); Museus & Chang, 2009; Museus & Kiang, 2009; Teranishi, 2010). Many Asian American education scholars and advocates have advocated for disaggregated data on Asian Americans, arguing that aggregate data erases the diverse and complex experiences of Asian Americans by obscuring differences related to ethnicity, social class, language, generation, history, gender, sexual orientation, religion, disability, immigration status. The Southeast Asia Resource Action Center (SEARAC), one of the leading Southeast Asian American civil rights organizations in the US, has advocated for disaggregated data for years. SEARAC (2020) argues that aggregate data masks the issues faced by various Southeast Asian ethnic groups and that disaggregated data is critical to illustrating the challenges and identifying the solutions to the inequities facing Southeast Asian American communities. Some school districts are beginning to respond to the calls for disaggregated data, including the Los Angeles Unified School District, the nation's second largest school district, which announced in 2019 that they would begin disaggregating data on Asian Americans in an effort to improve the educational services for specific communities.

As educational researcher Oiyan Poon and her colleagues have argued, however, the focus on ethnically disaggregated data on Southeast Asian American students may inadvertently contribute to the reproduction of deficit thinking about Southeast Asian communities and to the reification of the model minority stereotype (Poon et al., 2015; Poon et al., 2017). She argues that when scholars highlight the academic struggles faced by Southeast Asian Americans, the strategy "essentializes AAPI ethnic groups based on educational achievement, bifurcating AAPIs into presumed low-achieving ethnic groups (e.g., Southeast Asian Americans, Filipino Americans, NHPIs) and high-achieving ethnic groups (e.g., East Asian Americans, South Asian Americans). Such simplistic assumptions overlook dynamism and fluidity of diverse lived experiences" (pp. 21–22).

In fact, while the middle-class professional leaders are concerned with invisibility, they are also concerned with the kind of visibility or hypervisibility that the Hmong community has endured. Specifically, they expressed concerns with the "negative" stereotypes facing the Hmong community, including the reliance on public assistance among Hmong American families, youth gangs, early marriage among girls, Hmong boys dropping out of school and the idea that Hmong men are inherently violent. These ideas have been advanced in some of the academic scholarship, in the media, and in popular culture. The University of Wisconsin law professor who was embroiled in controversy with the Hmong community in 2007, for example, drew on these stereotypes in describing Hmong gender norms. Clint Eastwood's 2009 film *Gran Torino* also called on stereotypes about Hmong males as gang members and mixed these with essentialized images of Asian Kung Fu masters, which led one Hmong American reviewer to describe the experience of watching the film as "a feeling of disjunction, of malrecognition" (Jalao, 2010). The stereotypes of Hmong men as gang members and warriors have been linked to the ideological blackening of Hmong American youth in dominant discourses (DePouw, 2012; Lee, 2005). Importantly, ideological blackening relies on and reifies the inherent anti-Blackness in dominant society and reinforces White dominance. Without challenging anti-Blackness, middle-class advocates appeared to be eager to distance themselves from ideological blackening.

The dilemma for middle-class professional community leaders was how to fight invisibility without contributing to deficit narratives of the Hmong American community. Their strategy involved simultaneously highlighting the ways the Hmong community is "model" and arguing that schools have rendered Hmong experiences, culture, and history invisible in ways that damage Hmong youth. Drawing on model minority discourses, which position Asian Americans as hard-working, family-oriented, and law-abiding, these Hmong leaders pointed to the low incidence of behavior issues among their youth as evidence that Hmong families teach their children to be respectful and to value education.

In the following quote, Gao Moua, a middle-class professional who cofounded a summer program for Hmong American children and youth, draws on model minority discourses in explaining the invisibility of Hmong American students:

> And so it's like our kids have to be a little bit more visible. Our kids are on a double-edged sword because we teach our kids to be respectful, don't challenge teachers, don't ask too many questions, right? And then when they go school, they don't do that part [act out]. So, they seem, when they go to school or class, and not absent— they're here, so that's good enough. They're behaving, so they don't get the substance of the material that they are learning. So, with that, we continue to get high graduate rates, and that puts another edge to us, but again, we are not preparing our kids for the higher education because they don't have the deep-down substance for higher education.

While Gao Moua clearly recognizes that many Hmong American students have not achieved the academic success associated with the model minority, she emphasizes that Hmong families encourage the behavioral and cultural characteristics that are associated with the model minority stereotype. While she doesn't explicitly name any other racial or ethnic groups, she seems to be suggesting that other groups are disrespectful and regularly challenge teachers' authority. Gao Moua appeared to be frustrated that Hmong children are rendered invisible because they don't have behavioral problems. Like many scholars, Gao Moua is suggesting that the educational needs of Hmong youth go unseen and unaddressed because they don't cause problems (Lee, 2005; Ngo & Lee, 2007; Um, 2003).

Reflecting the broader discourses of neoliberalism, middle-class Hmong American leaders invoked the language of economic self-sufficiency and self-reliance as central goals for the Hmong community, and they believed that formal education was crucial to achieving these goals. Gao Moua, for example, emphasized the goal for the Hmong community was to be "productive citizens" and she expressed concern regarding the high rates of Hmong Americans who were on public assistance. In the following interview segment, Gao Moua explains her understanding of what it would mean for Hmong people to be productive citizens in the United States.

SL: You used the phrase *productive citizens*. Can you say a little bit more about what you mean by that?

Gao Moua: That is referring to what I said earlier about our parents' sacrifices as to have better opportunity and I'm sure you probably heard this, parents always wanted to make sure that you don't beg other people for food, you don't tell another people to pay the bill. They're always preaching, making sure that you become productive, that you support yourself and you be able to give back to the community and economic self-sufficient, um, family. Everything that as a human being, you need to be functional so you don't rely on other people to support you. And I think that's even more critical now that we are here and our parents are seeing homeless people. It's such a rich country. Like, how do people become homeless? And now they're starting to realize, "Oh, because the social structure is not supporting the families, but that's why these family are fragmented and they're doing that."

As her quote illustrates, Gao Moua argues that the idea that economic self-sufficiency is central to productive citizenship is shared by Hmong elders. She suggests that concerns regarding self-sufficiency have become more pronounced in the United States where economic opportunities and poverty coexist, claiming "It's even more critical for parents to want kids to be productive knowing that the risk is higher here than, you know, in Laos or in Asia because it would be a shame to feel that 'Oh, my kids is not doing well, and my kids is a liability to society.'" Significantly, federal policy regarding Southeast Asian refugees prioritized economic self-sufficiency (Caplan, 1985; Haines, 1982; Jew, 2014). This focus on economic self-sufficiency reflects neoliberal ideas regarding the relationship between gainful employment, good citizenship, and belonging (Ong, 2003). In keeping with neoliberal ideologies, Gao Moua views poverty as an individual failure rather than the result of systemic race and class inequality. She also calls upon traditional and essentialized ideas of the proud Hmong family that teaches the values of self-respect and self-sufficiency. Interestingly, she suggests that it is the dominant American culture than threatens the sanctity of the Hmong family, making Hmong youth vulnerable to the dangers of economic dependency.

While Gao Moua is concerned about how many Hmong families rely on public assistance, she makes an exception for the elderly and those with disabilities.

If it is naturally that you born that way, then that's fine. But you know, if you say we're capable, you should be able to help yourself. So that's where we're looking at the productive is really living to that legacy, expectation from the grandparents who brought us here and saying, "Okay, to maintain my image and my expectation, these are what we need to do."

In other words, Gao Moua divides those on public assistance into two categories—the deserving poor and the undeserving poor. Those she labels deserving of public assistance include the elderly and those with disabilities who can't be faulted for suffering from poverty. Gao Moua argues that the young and able-bodied, on the other hand, should work, "be functional" and not "rely on other people to support you." From this perspective, the undeserving poor are an embarrassment to their Hmong elders and the larger Hmong community. Similarly, Mr. Thao drew on ideas of deservingness in his efforts to advocate for elderly Hmong people during welfare reform in the late 20th century.

How do we get the advocacy that's needed for these parents, who, you know, through no fault of their own, who can't work because of the language barrier and culture barrier, the fact that they are, you know, older, but yet they're getting their benefits cut, for no reason other than the fact that they fought for the U.S. and came here, was challenging for many families.

As this quote suggests, Mr. Thao was painfully aware of the racialized stereotypes surrounding welfare dependence in the Hmong community and he worried about contributing to deficit perspectives of his ethnic group. Thus, he emphasized that Hmong elders need public assistance "through no fault of their own," suggesting that they are deserving of support while others may not be as deserving. Like other Hmong advocates, Mr. Thao also invoked the image of the "good refugee" who fought alongside the United States, in his characterizations of Hmong elders (Vang, 2021; Xiong, 2016, 2022).

Mr. Thao, Gao Moua, and other middle-class advocates drew a bright line between the elderly and disabled, who were viewed as deserving of public assistance, and younger and able-bodied Hmong people who should work for a living. Their understanding of poverty is similar to what Michael Katz referred to as the idea of "poverty as problem of persons," which views poverty as being rooted in moral, cultural and/or biological problems (Katz, 2013). As Gao Moua suggests, for the elderly and the disabled, poverty is connected to a biological problem that can't be helped. Poverty among young able-bodied Hmong people is attributed to the failings of the dominant American culture and the failures of the American educational system. Thus, middle-class advocates view the fight for educational equity to be key to the fight for economic self-sufficiency and citizenship.

CONCERNS REGARDING ESL

Pointing to data that revealed that the vast majority of Hmong students in Lakeview were labeled English learners and tracked into ESL services, middle-class advocates argued that Lakeview schools were failing the Hmong community. Middle-class and traditional leaders had come to understand that the "English learner" designation was a label that followed their youth through school, limited academic opportunities, and contributed to deficit ideas about Hmong youth. These leaders were particularly concerned that students trapped in ESL were locked out of higher track classes that prepared students for higher education, a concern that is supported by research (Callahan et. al., 2009). Furthermore, they expressed concern about the process for identifying students as English learners, including the home language survey that they believed targeted their children for testing and ESL services.

In addition to criticizing official policies, a few leaders also spoke about the ethnic and racial profiling they had experienced or witnessed. Gao Moua, for example, recalled her experience registering her eldest son for school and the pressure she faced to enroll him in services for English learners.

But when my son entered school and we went to the parent orientation, the principal of that school directed me to the Hmong parents' group and say, "Oh, Hmong parents go over here." And the other group is on the other side. So I said to her, "Oh, I could speak English. I like to go to the mainstream." And she said, "Oh no, we have Hmong for Hmong parents," you know, and so she was insisting that I go to that one. And so that was the first thing that didn't rub me right. And so, I share my experience with my husband, and you know, my husband, he would speak up. So, he went to the board, school board meeting and share the experience.

Gao Moua was concerned that if she were put in the Hmong parent group that her son would be placed in ESL. She explained that she had heard from other Hmong parents that Lakeview educators often assume that Hmong children cannot speak English and need to be in ESL. While Gao Moua and her husband took their concerns to the school board, many Hmong parents do not feel comfortable questioning the schools. Gao Moua went on to explain that she and her husband appreciate the need for ESL services for newcomers but are critical of policies that place fully bilingual children like her son in ESL.

And we, we really believe about support for the ESL student where, you know, ESL programs should be there to help kids who just arrived and have the need for support. But for kids like ours, who are born here in the United States, we don't think that they should be in ESL. Right? So, we talk about that part and whatever happened in the administration office, we quickly were known as the parents who are anti-ESL. So, we didn't get a very warm welcome into the school system because we were, you know, making a distinguish between the rights to go to mainstream parents' group and the right not to put our kids in ESL and so forth.

As the end of this quote suggests, Gao Moua believes that their educational advocacy led them to being labeled as problematic parents. When our research team met with school district staff to discuss Hmong parents' concerns regarding English learner policies, we were told that parents had to trust the district and give them time to work out the issues. In fact, earlier research on Hmong parent engagement suggested that parents did trust that teachers and schools knew best how to teach their children, but parents like Gao Moua are no longer sure that trust is warranted (Thao, 2003).

While Gao Moua and other middle-class leaders have faced barriers in their advocacy, they did make some important inroads. In an effort to educate Lakeview school district staff about the concerns of Hmong parents, middle-class advocates worked with the school district to organize focus groups where Hmong community members shared their experiences in the schools. Gao Moua recalled one focus group in which a parent reported that when she met with her son's 6th-grade teacher to discuss his struggles in math, the teacher's response was, "I thought your son didn't speak English." This teacher's response is problematic for numerous reasons, including the fact that she hadn't taken the time to find out whether he spoke English, and the automatic assumption that his struggles in math were related to language.

The assumption that Hmong students, including second- and third-generation students, do not speak English reflects the persistent stereotype that Asian Americans are perpetual foreigners. The scholarship on raciolinguistics points to the co-naturalization of race and language whereby the "linguistic practices of racialized populations are systematically stigmatized regardless of the extent to which these practices might seem to correspond to standardized norms" (Rosa & Flores, 2017, p. 623). In other words, raciolinguistics demonstrates the way race and language intersect in the reproduction of inequality experienced by students of color who speak languages other than English. Dominant assumptions regarding the presumed deficiency of bilingual Latinxs' English and Spanish, for example, trap students in linguistic remediation (Flores, 2016). Similarly, the assumed inferiority of the Hmong language shapes policies and practices toward native Hmong speakers. As noted in the chapter on University Heights High School, current policies surrounding English learners advance a largely monolingual orientation and deficit perspective regarding heritage languages spoken by students of color (Flowers, 2019).

Middle-class advocates understand that students who are tracked into and then trapped in ESL are not getting access to the academic content necessary for college. Research on tracking and high school English learners demonstrates that the misguided belief that English fluency is a prerequisite for academic success has led to English learners being excluded from higher level content-area academics (Callahan, 2005; Kanno & Harklau, 2012). Middle-class professionals and the few traditional leaders we spoke to have grown increasingly suspicious of the district's language policies, particularly ESL policies, which they view as a barrier to social mobility. Some parents reported that they were even hesitant to report that Hmong was spoken in the home because they did not want their children to be placed in ESL.

During an informational session hosted by HEA in 2017 for parents of English Learners in the Lakeview school district, Mai Neng observed that Hmong parents voiced concerns that they had over their children's placement in ESL services (Vang fieldnotes, April 7, 2017). Among the concerns were questions about the accuracy of (yearly) placement tests. One young Hmong dad shared that when he saw the test, the questions were difficult to answer even for him as someone who has an education. Parents also spoke about their own negative experiences being labeled as EL affecting their views of ESL services and contributing to their hesitancy in accepting services for their own children. An older Hmong man who works as a bilingual resource specialist in the district commented that in his years of working with parents in the district, he noticed that parents want ESL services, but fear that teachers treat students who are labeled as EL differently. This provoked some conversation around the stigma attached to being labeled EL and receiving ESL services. The conversations between HEA members, Hmong parents, district staff, and university professors during this event highlighted the questions, concerns, and suspicions that the community had regarding how schools and the district serve EL students, and specifically Hmong EL students.

Although middle-class and traditional parents and leaders were concerned about their children being trapped in ESL, they were also afraid that their children were losing the Hmong language. Indeed, they were frustrated that their children were considered English learners when most of the youth were actually more comfortable speaking English than Hmong. These leaders argued that without Hmong language skills the younger generation would not know who they are or be able to communicate with their elders. Their fears regarding language loss are well-founded, as research suggests that language loss is common in immigrant communities, with second- and third-generation Americans succumbing to the broader forces of linguistic assimilation (Alba 2004; Portes & Rumbaut 2001). In Xiong & Xiong's (2011) analysis of nationally representative data, for example, they found that the odds of speaking only English among second-generation Hmong Americans were nearly three times that of the first generation. Furthermore, Xiong and Xiong (2011) warn that, "Given the centrality of oral tradition in Hmong social life, the loss of native language skills could spell challenges for Hmong society in more ways than just individual miscommunication" (p. 14). In particular, they point to the importance of the Hmong language for connecting to "collective ideas and memories" that can't be communicated in English. Thus, middle-class and traditional leaders want the schools to help their youth become fully bilingual and biliterate in order to function in both the dominant society and within the Hmong community.

Within the Lakewood school district, there are three types of language services: traditional English as a second language (ESL) services, developmental bilingual education (DBE), and dual language immersion (DLI) programs. While ESL and DBE services are only accessible to those labeled as English learners (EL), DLI programs in the district are open-access for all students. Bilingual education scholars and LatCrit scholars have long-warned about the "gentrification" of DLI programs, concerned with whose interest gets privileged in such programming as the interests of White middle-class parents converge with those of Spanish-speaking parents (Morales & Maravilla, 2019; Valdes, 1997; Valdez et al., 2016).

The Lakeview School District sponsored a listening session for Hmong community members to provide information about different language programs for ELs, including a proposal for a new Hmong DBE program. During this community session, several concerns regarding the Hmong DBE program were brought up by participants (several of whom were HEA members who had strategized the week before about talking points to highlight). Here is a snippet from Mai Neng's field-notes from that meeting:

School District staff told community members that in both DBE and DLI programs, core curriculum is taught in both languages, but differ mainly in who was part of the classroom: DBE classes consist of only EL native speakers while DLI classes consist of both native speakers and non-native speakers. One of the concerns was about the integration/segregation and socialization of DBE students with "mainstream" students if students are spending the majority of their day in a classroom with other EL students. Other concerns included the logistics of implementing a Hmong DBE program, the first of its kind in the district (i.e., student recruitment, resource allocation, research in preplanning stages, who will get hired to teach, creating a curriculum that is about "bilingualism, biliteracy, and biculturalism," etc.). Mr. Thao spoke up in the meeting to question the equity of the number and types of language programs available across the district. He pondered why in the proposed plan there was only one Hmong DBE program and five Spanish DLI programs when there currently existed ten Spanish DLI programs and two Spanish DBE programs in the district.

Mai Neng's fieldnotes, Oct. 6, 2015

As this fieldnote demonstrates, Mr. Thao and other HEA members had some reservations about the district's DBE program for Hmong speakers. In previous HEA meetings, Mr. Thao and HEA members had discussed wanting to advocate for a Hmong DLI program but realized there may not be enough buy-in from non-Hmong parents to convince district staff. Thus, the HEA members agreed that they would support the proposal to create a Hmong DBE program but would hold the district accountable for addressing the concerns that they had regarding such a program.

CALLS FOR CULTURALLY RELEVANT PEDAGOGY AND HMONG STAFF

Reflecting the politics of recognition, HEA leadership asserted that the educational challenges facing Hmong students were due to the invisibility of Hmong perspectives and voices in schools. Specifically, they attributed the academic struggles of Hmong students to a lack of culturally and linguistically relevant pedagogy and the relative absence of Hmong teachers, administrators, and staff in the district. According to those who espouse the politics of recognition, the lack of recognition has a negative impact on the way marginalized communities view themselves. Taylor (2021) explains that identity is strongly influenced by the way other people view us, and that an individual or group of people suffer when society fails to see them in a positive light.

Middle-class and traditional leaders want Hmong youth to learn about the achievements, sacrifices, struggles, and resilience of the Hmong people, and to feel a connection to and appreciation for their native culture. Here, Hmong leaders were engaging in the politics of cultural difference that emphasized a coherent and largely unchanging version of Hmong culture that reflected the strategic essentialism performed by other Hmong leaders (Ngo, 2013). Furthermore, HEA leaders argued that the invisibility of Hmong perspectives in educational dialogues in the city perpetuated inequalities, and they expected state institutions to rectify the problem of misrecognition. In short, they viewed the fight for recognition as being about issues of the self-worth of their community, the social status of their community, and economic opportunities for the younger generation.

Middle-class Hmong leaders and traditional leaders critiqued the schools for their Eurocentric and subtractive approach to Hmong and other minoritized communities and argued that schools should help Hmong students maintain a connection to their cultural and linguistic backgrounds and give them an understanding of their histories. Lee, a middle-class parent, described the assimilative forces that exist within American society.

> I think your ethnic journey and your ethnic identity is very crucial to you being a, a person of substance, a person of character. And without it, I think you would be losing something very crucial to who you are. And I think that's something that's opposite of what American culture can offer you. Because in American culture, a lot of the times, the idea of assimilation or the idea of this melting pot theory where every people, group, should come and assimilate to become one. When you do that, you fail to see the, a lot of the nuances that comes along with culture and the richness of that. And you fail to see perspective as well.

Lee, like other middle-class leaders and parents, argued that assimilation strips individuals of important aspects of their identities. Traditional Hmong leaders such as Mr. Yang also expressed concerns regarding the Eurocentric curriculum in the schools.

> If there were classes to teach [about Hmong language and culture], it would be ideal and better for our kids. Because there are none in school, our kids don't know how to speak Hmong anymore.

Their concerns were consistent with the large body of research that highlights the fact that mainstream schooling, including assimilationist policies, curricula, and pedagogies, are designed to strip youth of their linguistic, cultural heritage and identities (Lee, 2005; Ngo, 2017a; Valenzuela, 1999).

HEA, other middle-class leaders, and many of the traditional leaders advocated replacing the assimilationist curriculum that dominates schools with culturally relevant pedagogy for Hmong youth. They are fighting for the representation and integration of Hmong culture and history in the curriculum. As with other relatively small ethnic groups who have experienced forced assimilation and exclusion from the Eurocentric curriculum, Hmong communities across the country struggle to find appropriate and accurate teaching resources. A Hmong teacher involved with HEA protested the lack of culturally responsive materials for Hmong youth, stating that teachers "don't have a lot of, like, even simple picture books for the kids to do research on." She explained how excited she was when one of her Hmong colleagues, another member of HEA, gave her a poster encouraging youth to read with a picture of General Vang Pao:

> It should be in my classroom, but it's at home for my siblings. But I'm like, "Oh my gosh! This is the kind of posters that my teachers should have had!" You know, 'cuz there was a lot of us. I think we had more Hmong kids than White kids.

As her quote illustrates, Sheng's desire for culturally appropriate material for her students stems from her own experiences as a student who longed to see her culture represented in the curriculum.

In conversations with the school district, Mr. Thao consistently advocated for culturally relevant pedagogy for Hmong students, and he explained that he first heard other ethnic groups talking about cultural relevance and then googled it and read more about Dr. Ladson-Billings's work. Middle-class leaders argue that the absence of culturally relevant pedagogy and the presence of assimilationist policies and practices have played a central role in the academic struggles faced by Hmong youth. Mr. Thao argued that low test scores among Hmong students were due to the lack of a culturally relevant curriculum for Hmong students in Lakeview schools. Like many who embrace the discourse of culturally relevant pedagogy, Mr. Thao focuses on cultural competence but does not pick up the focus on more critical aspects of culturally relevant pedagogy, which seek to encourage critical dispositions that challenge structural inequality. Indeed, for middle-class Hmong leaders, the central goals of culturally relevant pedagogy are improved academic achievement and a connection to their culture and history.

In addition to calling for culturally relevant pedagogy, HEA and other middle-class advocates called for greater Hmong representation in school district staffing. Sheng explained that each time the Hmong leaders met with the superintendent they asked:

> "Why aren't you hiring Hmong people?" Or, "Why aren't you, like, having position that require bilingual? And then like, specify that you want a Hmong person?" Because when you look, they *do* have a lot of posting for like Spanish, and we're like, "But, Hmong? We also need that too because we are the third biggest population."

Sheng went on to argue that it didn't make sense that there was only one Hmong person in the school district administration when Hmong speakers represent the third largest language group in the city. For Sheng and other middle-class leaders, representation in school district staffing was crucial for having an equal voice and for providing Hmong students with role models.

The twin goals of greater representation of Hmong staff and greater inclusion of Hmong culture and history in the curriculum have been central to the educational advocacy of Hmong communities in the Twin Cities of Minnesota, in Fresno, California, and in various communities in Wisconsin (Ngo, 2017a). In Wisconsin there are ongoing statewide efforts to pass legislation that would require schools to teach Hmong history and culture. Since the early 2000s, bills requiring the inclusion of Hmong history in Wisconsin schools have been introduced but have been unsuccessful. In response to the increase in anti-Asian racism since 2020, a group of bipartisan lawmakers have introduced legislation that would require school boards to offer curriculum on Hmong Americans and Asian Pacific Islander Desi Americans, but these bills have not passed either (Falk, 2022). Like many Hmong American leaders across the United States, the middle-class advocates in our study support legislation that would require teaching about Hmong history, culture, and contributions. They argue that their history as U.S. allies in Laos gives them a legitimate claim to the resources necessary to preserve their culture and remember their histories.

In short, HEA leaders asserted that the silence regarding Hmong perspectives in the curriculum and the paucity of Hmong educators in the schools contributed to Hmong youths' identity confusion, internalized racism, intergenerational tensions, and ultimately to the achievement gap. Middle-class leaders' rhetorical strategy involved emphasizing the distinctive aspects of Hmong culture, which set them apart from other groups.

COMMUNITY-BASED EDUCATION: THE HMONG MESKAS SUMMER CAMP

While middle-class professionals engaged in strategic advocacy in the school district, they also worked to create culturally relevant programming for their youth in out-of-school spaces. Mr. Thao explained that several parents, professionals, and college students came together in 2013 to discuss ways to close the "achievement gap" of Hmong students in their community. Mr. Thao shared that:

> Hmong parents were saying, "Hey, we're seeing our kids struggle. And we're also seeing that there's not a lot of resources from the school district to support our kids. And thirdly, we recognize that the Hmoob language is being lost too. So, what can we do to do all three, right? Make sure that the—to preserve the language and culture, to make sure we support our kids so that they do well in school, so they do graduate, and, and how do we share our concern with the larger community."

As a result of these conversations, the Hmong Meskas Summer Camp was created to provide a safe and supportive learning environment for Hmong students. Parents felt that teaching children about their language, culture, and history can lead to higher self-esteem, pride, and confidence, which can then lead to improved academic performance (especially on standardized tests). Founders of this program believed that in fostering pride and confidence among students, the program could support students to become productive citizens who could go on to college and contribute to the larger society.

The Hmong Meskas Summer Camp (HMSC) is a 6-week community-based summer program that Mr. Thao and Gao Moua started in 2013. According to the staff and volunteer manual, the mission of the camp is to "develop productive citizens and leaders" by teaching elementary and middle school-aged students about their Hmong cultural heritage and in turn "enhancing academic skills." The students in the summer camp include children of middle-class Hmong families and from working-class and lower-middle-class traditional Hmong families.

During the summer of 2015 when Mai Neng conducted fieldwork at the camp, programming ran every weekday from 8:00 a.m. to 4:00 p.m. There were 34 students who ranged in age from 5 to 14 years enrolled in the program. The Hmong staff included three teachers, two program coordinators, and one cook (a mother of one of the students). One of the teachers held a part-time position that was funded by the Lakeview School District. Mr. Thao and Gao Moua, the two cofounders of the program, were in the space on a voluntary basis, part-time. In addition to the paid staff, there were a total of 11 volunteers, including Mai Neng. Seven of these volunteers were parents. The other volunteers were college students or recent college graduates.

There was an enrollment fee associated with students' participation, which was $75 a week, for a total of $450 for the whole summer. Of the 34 students, however, only seven students paid full price for their participation. Other students were granted a half or full scholarship based on income level, and if a family enrolled multiple children there was a discounted price for the family. Additionally, parents could also offset some (or all) of the costs by volunteering with the program. Gao Moua explained the goals of the HMSC program to Mai Neng:

> It's really three fold going on at the same time, and that is the *Hmong* pride. I think, *thaum lawv paub txog Hmoob cov txuj ci, lawv paub hais tias Hmoob tseem ceeb* when they know about Hmong arts and talents, they understand that Hmong is important . . . and *lawv thiaj li paub zoo siab hais tias,* "Oh, you know, *Hmong's* not bad" so *kom lawv tsis txhob txaj txaj muag ua Hmoob* they are no longer ashamed and embarrassed to be Hmong . . . and the other fold is developing a sense of community *rau cov me nyuam Hmoob. Rau qhov* it's really hard for *peb cov me nyuam Hmoob* our Hmong kids to be in a safe space where they can be themself. And so one of the goal at the program is really giving them that safe space to be *Hmong,* to laugh at each other, to cry with each other, to be *Hmong* and to be able to . . . just be ourself. And so that safe space is really what we're creating for them so *kom lawv tuaj es lawv sib sib ncawg, lawv tsis xav sib ncaim,* they can build relationships with one another, they don't want to part with one another you know . . . and then the third fold is to really to boost *lawv qhov* their academic . . ."[1]

Through Gao Moua's explanation of the program's goals, it is clear that the HMSC hopes to do three things: (1) foster a sense of pride in being Hmong, (2) provide

---

1. *Translation:* "It's really threefold going on at the same time, and that is the Hmong pride. I think, when they know about Hmong arts and talents, they understand that Hmong is important . . . and they realize, 'Oh, you know, Hmong's not bad,' so they are no longer ashamed and embarrassed to be Hmong. And the other fold is developing a sense of community for our Hmong kids. Because it's really hard for Hmong kids to be in a safe space where they can be themself. And so one of the goal at the program is really giving them that safe space to be Hmong, to laugh at each other, to cry with each other, to be Hmong and to be able to . . . just be ourself. And so that safe space is really what we're creating for them so they can build relationships with one another, they don't want to part with one another, you know . . . and then the third fold is to really to boost their academic."

a safe space to learn and be Hmong, and (3) promote academic success as a result of the first two goals.

The program has three academic levels: Zaub Qhwv (beginner), Zaub Ntsuab (intermediate), and Zaub Paj (advanced). When Mai Neng asked Houa, one of the coordinators and a teacher in the program, how they divided students up into the levels, he explained, "The students were primarily split up by age, and they were then split up again by academic success." He elaborated on what he meant by "academic success," clarifying that he was referring to how students performed on the pretest that they took at orientation. This test was meant to help staff gauge students' Hmong literacy levels. Houa stated that if a student tested as well as Level 3 students, then regardless of their age they would get placed into the higher-level class.

The curriculum was set up so that each week, the lesson plans were focused on a different theme. The first week, students learned about kinship. Week two was focused on Hmong history. The third week was on Hmong customs. In the fourth week, students learned about Hmong cultural arts and crafts. Then, week five, students learned about different religious beliefs within the Hmong community. And finally, the last week was devoted to a review of everything students had learned over the summer. It was also a week where staff purposely did not make lesson plans so that they could structure time for students to work on their performances and final projects for the HMSC banquet.

The staff said that they wanted to work with the students in the HMSC program because they want to help students foster a sense of cultural pride—something that they felt they grew up not having. For example, Sai, another one of the teachers, explained that he really believed in the HMSC program because of his own experiences with internalized racism:

> I felt like when I grew up—throughout school, my childhood, I didn't really, like, acknowledge being Hmong. You know, they made us, like, sing Hmong songs or stuff like that, but it's like, it wasn't a really important part of me until it hit me in college. And so for the kids, what I want them to do is just to be really proud of being Hmong—that, that being Hmong is not, like, a burden. 'Cuz I felt like it was burden to me as a child. 'Cuz I didn't have a lot growing up and I thought that it was because I was Hmong. But it's not, it's just our situations. And so, I just want the students to be proud and go to school, understanding that they are Hmong and teaching others that they are Hmong.

Mr. Thao argued that it is not enough to teach Hmong language; schools must also teach students that their culture and their people are valued: "It's not just to have Hmong kids speak Hmong or to read in Hmong. Like, I grew up not speaking Hmong and not reading and I think I do okay, right? . . . if I didn't speak Hmong, and, you know, I can still do okay in school, but not knowing who they are is what really causes that achievement gap." He advocated that any Hmong curriculum in school must teach students how to be "biliterate, bilingual, *and* bicultural." Mr. Thao continued by saying that curriculum must be "culturally relevant," a pedagogical approach advanced by Gloria Ladson-Billings (1995).

Ladson-Billings (1995) proposes "culturally relevant pedagogy" as a way for schools to create a curriculum that reflects the identities and knowledge that children of color bring with them into the classroom. She explains that that teaching must meet three criteria in order to be considered culturally relevant: "an ability to develop students academically, a willingness to nurture and support cultural competence, and the development of a sociopolitical or critical consciousness" (p. 483). Ladson-Billings argues, and Mr. Thao concurs, that through engaging in culturally relevant teaching, teachers can help students achieve academic success, helping to minimize racial disparities in education.

PROGRAM FUNDING AND SUPPORT

While the summer camp was the result of grassroots efforts led by Hmong leaders, Mr. Thao and Gao Moua leveraged their social capital with school district leaders, local businesses, and government officials to secure funding and support for the program. Mr. Thao explained that much of the funding for the program comes from him calling up his "donor friends" yearly to ask for donations. The program space was also donated to HMSC by the organization that Mr. Thao worked for at the time; the building was owned by the organization and is used as a neighborhood center as well as a public charter school during the school year.

In explaining his strategy for fundraising, Mr. Thao shared that he uses the disaggregated data from the district to say to funders, "Look, there's a real need here. When over 80% of students are not reading at grade level, we're doing a disservice to them." Secondly, Mr. Thao argues that, "unlike the Latino or the African American community, there is no nonprofit that helps the Hmong community here in Lakeview," which leads to his third point: that the city "historically and continually hasn't supported the Hmong communities. They give hundreds of thousands of dollars to the organization that serves the Black community, hundreds of thousands of dollars to the Boys' and Girls' Club, hundreds of thousands of dollars to the organization that serves that Latino community to help their respective community, but when it comes to the Hmong community, they might get—I think when I talked to the organization that serves Hmong elders, for example, they get ten thousand from the City, right? And so there's a little inequality there." Mr. Thao goes on to say that it helps that "I built a good relationship with these funders and a lot of these folks, so they know me well . . . I'm someone that is well respected and hold trust in the community, so when I do ask someone for money, they know it's going for a good cause as well as being used wisely and it's gonna do some good in the community."

In its third year of programming, the summer that Mai Neng observed the program, HMSC was listed as a summer enrichment program offered through the school district. As such, one of the HMSC teacher's part-time positions was funded by the district. This was a direct result of Mr. Thao's relationship with the district superintendent at the time. Gao Moua and Mr. Thao, along with others from HEA and parents of HMSC students, also organize a yearly spring gala to fundraise for the program. The gala consists of dinner, speakers, and testimonies (by parents and past participants), entertainment (performances by past HMSC participants and other youth and Hmong community members), and a silent auction with items donated from local artists and businesses. Past funders as well as potential funders from the founders' social networks are invited to attend the gala. Additionally, in the middle of the summer camp, the founders host an open house event where parents, community members, and funders are invited to learn more about the program and its impact on young people. The end-of-summer banquet, meant to celebrate the accomplishments of the young participants, also serves as another platform for inviting current and potential funders to learn more about the program. In explaining the purpose of these events, Gao Moua encouraged Stacey to tell her university colleagues:

> So yeah, and come and encourage your colleagues to tell them and yeah. That way you get to meet some of the Hmong people. I mean, the purpose is really to network between Hmong parents and professions to broaden up the communication.

As part of the desire to help cultivate a positive ethnic identity, among students but also within the larger Lakeview community (and especially with funders), staff would communicate positive messages about Hmong people. In some ways, some of the staff took up and embraced the language of the model minority stereotype as a way to push back on racialized deficit discourses about Hmong people. An example of one of these instances occurred during the program's open house event when funders and potential funders (the majority of whom were White) were invited to visit the HMSC space. In telling the guests about what the program hoped to do, Gao Moua explained that Hmong adults want their children to carry the legacy of what their grandparents did to get to the United States by fully participating in and contributing to society. Becoming assets to society is carrying on this legacy. In her interview with Mai Neng, Gao Moua explained more about what this "legacy" was, saying that it is "that *peb tsis yog ib co neeg tub nkeeg, peb tsis yog ib co neeg phem, peb yog ib co neeg zoo.*"[2] The legacy that she describes is the very discourse that upholds and perpetuates the model minority stereotype. It would be simple to condemn Gao Moua for embracing this racialized discourse. However, we must recognize that Hmong Americans' responses to racialized discourses are complicated by the fact that as racialized individuals, we cannot escape racialized discourses. We live in a society wherein our experiences as well as the access we have to resources and opportunities are all shaped by racialized discourses. Gao Moua recognizes that in the dominant imagination, based on racialized discourses, Hmong Americans are seen as criminals and dependent on welfare. Because of this, she knows that unless she uses the language of the model minority to appeal to her audience, it will be incredibly difficult for her to gain funding and support for the program.

---

2. *Translation:* "that we are not lazy people, we are not bad people, we are good people."

Furthermore, during these fundraising opportunities and events, the founders make sure to include performances and presentations of Hmongness and Hmong culture to funders and stakeholders. Their representations of Hmongness and Hmong culture appear to reflect a practice of *strategic essentialism*, a concept forwarded by postcolonial scholar Gayatri Spivak (1985). Though contested as a theory, strategic essentialism is often used as a (temporary) political strategy by members of minoritized communities (Ngo, 2013), wherein differences within a community are minimized in favor of a homogenous and static representation of the group, risking perpetuating stereotypical or essentialist understandings of the group. Strategic essentialism is not only employed during the camp's performances for a majority White audience, it is also reflected in the HMSC curriculum. While there are opportunities to provide nuanced narratives of Hmong history during the HMSC programming, the instructors are asked to teach the oft-told narrative of the Hmong participation in the "secret war" as U.S. allies, crossing the Mekong River and becoming refugees of war before being resettled in the United States. Another example: Although the majority of students in the program identify as Christians, when teaching about Hmong religious practices, the program only teaches about traditional Shamanic practices. One parent shared this as a point of concern:

> I think there's one thing that's a little lacking that I didn't see, that I think is very crucial to the program as well, is maybe incorporating the history of the Hmong Christians into that as well, because that is a part of our history as well and there are thousands of Hmong people in the States and in Southeast Asia who are believers as well.

The decision to focus on Shamanism, and to gloss over the fact that many Hmong Americans identify as Christian, appears to be a strategy aimed at cultural maintenance. In other words, in the face of an assimilationist curriculum in schools, the camp essentializes Hmongness in order to teach youth what it means to be Hmong, who gets to claim Hmongness and to foster ethnic pride.

YOUTH VOICES

For youth in the Hmong Meskas Summer Camp, learning about their culture, history, and language encouraged a sense of ethnic pride. Many youth expressed their frustrations about their non-Hmong friends and teachers not knowing who the Hmong are. Chaia, a 4th-grader, told Mai Neng, "People—a lot of my friends don't know about, like, Hmong people so I want, like, the world to know about [us]." Many students commented on a lack of Hmong curriculum in their schools. The ones that said that there was curricular inclusion in their school said that the material presented was often surface-level and any unit on Hmong culture or history was brief. When Mai Neng asked Pachee, a 5th-grader, if there was anything in her school curriculum about Hmong culture, history or language, Pachee said that "In schools, [Hmong] isn't important. They probably don't even know who we are." Not seeing herself and her experiences reflected in the curriculum has led Pachee to conclude that Hmong people and their experiences are not valued in school spaces. We argue that because of this exclusion from the curriculum, students end up with the unfair burden of feeling that they have to explain and educate their peers and teachers about who they are.

Many students expressed that they appreciated the HMSC for teaching them about their people so they are better able to articulate who the Hmong are. See, a 7th-grader, explained, "Well, I guess it has inspired me a lot to, like, spread awareness of the Hmong culture and stuff like that, so like I said before, there's no ignorance. And so then people can understand what the Hmong people really went through, instead of just kind of like, 'Oh just another Asian coming from Asia.'" In this response, it is clear that See feels that her identity, people, and history have been rendered invisible. See wants people to know about Hmong struggles so that people won't be "ignorant like I said before"—what See "said before" was that if people weren't ignorant, there would be less racism. See seems to recognize that when Hmong are racialized as Asians, it homogenizes the experiences of various Asian groups, and she is calling for recognition of Hmong Americans' unique experiences.

Not only was HMSC a space to learn about Hmong language, history, and culture, it also nurtured young people's sense of community and belonging. Chou, a 9th-grader, shared that although his parents "forced" him to come the previous year, he chose to come back because "it was fun and I wanted to see everyone again." This seemed to be a common occurrence among the older students with many of them and their parents sharing similar sentiments. Staff also expressed that it was important for them to help build a safe, validating, and caring community. Houa explained his desire to students, telling them that in order to be a community, they must think of one another as family:

> We want you guys to feel like a community, a family, you know. And that's why I feel like that the Hmong theory, you know, we are one big family, you know. This one's your aunt, this one's your cousin, you know, there's always a connection. Hopefully in the future, at least you guys will help one another. And that's something you should not lose in this competitive, you know, community that we are kind of thrown into where it kind of is like, every man for himself. You know, just remember, compete as hard as you can, but don't forget to help everyone else.

Houa is reminding students that we live in a tough world where competition and individualism are valued, but that students can rely on their family (each other) to help them navigate through this society. Caring for one another and supporting one another was stressed throughout the program. The community fostered in the HMSC space was evident time and time again. The last night of the program, Mai Neng documented this in her fieldnotes:

> After the closing ceremony, all the students wanted to stay around and spend more time together. One student in particular was having a hard time saying goodbye so the whole [zaub paj] class walked her out to her brother's

car, all of them crying and reassuring one another that they will see each
other again.

Mai Neng's fieldnotes, July 31, 2015

This example suggests that students developed such close relationships that it was
difficult for them to say goodbye to one another at the end of the program.

CONCLUSION

Chapter 4 has focused on the perspectives, strategies, and educational advocacy of middle-class professional Hmong leaders and parents. We've argued that
Hmong middle-class leaders embrace formal education as the route to social mobility, incorporation into the larger society, and productive citizenship for their
community. These leaders have successfully used formal education to gain social
mobility and believe that schooling is the best path forward for Hmong youth;
they fear that the educational challenges and invisibility facing Hmong students
will lead to continuing economic inequalities for the community. In addition to
their instrumental ideas regarding the value of education, middle-class leaders are
profoundly concerned with the preservation and maintenance of Hmong culture
and language and want schools to play a role in achieving these goals.

In the face of educational barriers, including invisibility, middle-class professional leaders have organized and positioned themselves as the voice of the Hmong
community in Lakeview. Through the formation of HEA, they sought to increase
the visibility of the Hmong community, and to serve as a bridge between Hmong
families and educational leaders at the K–16 level. By building relationships with
institutional leaders, they have pressed the Lakeview School District for culturally
relevant pedagogy, bilingual education, disaggregated data on Hmong students, and
the hiring of Hmong staff. Their efforts led to the disaggregating of Hmong data
and contributed to the approval of the Hmong development bilingual education
program at one elementary school in the Lakeview District. Additionally, middle
class advocates created a community-based educational summer program to serve
Hmong elementary and middle school children.

Our research shows that Hmong middle-class leaders have embraced market-
based assumptions about the purposes of education, adopted neoliberal rhetoric
in their educational advocacy, and attempted to work with and within the school
system for change. Neoliberalism is a theory of political economy that centers the
value of individual entrepreneurial freedom supported by private property rights,
free trade, and free markets (Harvey, 2007). Neoliberal thinking has permeated
social relations, institutions and policies, including education policies and practices. Neoliberalism assumes that the central purpose and value of education is economic, both the economic advancement of the individual and the assumed benefits
of individual economic gain for society. Neoliberalism has fostered the formation
of an educational marketplace where parents/individuals are positioned as consumers who make educational choices for their children based on the quality of the

schools available. Within neoliberal logics, the quality or performance of schools is assumed to be demonstrated by students' performance on standardized tests, which parents can use to evaluate schools (Au, 2010; Hursch, 2007; Lipman, 2013).

Advocates of market-based education reform assume that parents will make educational choices based on school performance data, thereby holding schools accountable for adequately serving students (Chubb & Moe, 1990). As Hill and Scott (2017) note, neoliberal education policies marked the shift from a focus on educational equity to a focus on excellence, standards, and accountability. Furthermore, within the context of shrinking school budgets and neoliberal assumptions regarding parent engagement, parents have been tasked with fundraising to fill budgetary gaps (Posey-Maddox, 2013, 2016). By emphasizing individual choice and action, neoliberal discourses and reforms have encouraged the idea that education is a private good rather than a public good (Labaree, 1997). This perspective on education encourages fierce individualism, competition, and a scarcity mindset while it simultaneously discourages the values of community and equity. The ideal neoliberal parent/consumer uses performance data to evaluate, make choices and be involved in their children's schools, including raising funds to support programming that benefits their own children.

While neoliberal frameworks position parents as consumers competing to promote the interests of their own children, a growing body of scholarship has pointed to the growth in parent activism aimed at resisting neoliberal education policies (Lipman, 2017; Pappas, 2012). This scholarship demonstrates that parents and communities have "participated in a wide and diverse array of engaged and collective actions, many of which have challenged the expansion of neoliberal education policies, particularly in the realms of privatization, charter school expansion, school closures, and high-stakes testing" (Rubin, Good, & Fine, 2020, p. 12). These parent and community activists are actively resisting the growing race and class inequalities in education that have been the result of neoliberal educational reforms. In contrast to the individualistic actions encouraged and imagined by proponents of neoliberal educational policies, these activists are fighting for group or collective rights in the name of equity.

Our argument is that middle-class Hmong advocates simultaneously *adopt* and *challenge* narrow neoliberal ideas regarding education in their fight for educational equity and recognition for Hmong students. In other words, they share similarities with both the ideal neoliberal parent as consumer and the activist parent who fights for collective rights. Sociocultural approaches to the study of policy, including the anthropology of policy, call attention to the complex ways that policies link people across locations and positions. Parents and community members at the local level encounter, interpret, and embrace or reject policies created by experts, thereby engaging in what Levinson, Sutton, and Winstead (2009) refer to as policy appropriation. Drawing on these perspectives on policy, we argue that middle-class advocates are policy actors who are embracing and contesting definitions of educational problems and solutions (Levinson, Sutton & Winstead, 2009).

Signaling a neoliberal perspective regarding the economic purposes of education, middle-class leaders argued that the Hmong achievement gap threatens the ability of Hmong youth to become "productive citizens," which they equated with economic self-sufficiency. In embracing the idea of "productive citizenship," middle-class advocates take up an idea of the "American Dream," which educational theorist J. E. Rhee (2013) argues is essentially capitalistic and requires proof of economic worthiness for "admission to become American" (p. 578). As such, middle-class advocates are focused on getting Hmong youth into college and/or job training programs as routes to economic self-sufficiency. In the spirt of neoliberal entrepreneurship, middle-class leaders involved in HEA and the summer camp actively engaged in fundraising to support programming and scholarships for Hmong youth.

Significantly, middle-class advocates used school district data as proof that the schools were failing Hmong youth and to hold the schools accountable. They understood that data had been central to highlighting the educational obstacles facing the Black community and were eager to use data to get attention for Hmong students too. Reflecting neoliberal reliance on data, they fought to disaggregate the data on Hmong students from the larger Asian American category and used the disaggregated data as evidence of a district-wide achievement gap between Hmong and White students, and to raise concerns about the policies for English learners. While proponents of neoliberalism view parents as consumers who will exercise their choice to leave a school that fails their children, middle-class Hmong advocates used the data to demand recognition, but they did not threaten to exit the schools. A large body of scholarship highlights the ways race and class constrain choice and the ability to exit public schools. Most members of the Lakeview Hmong community do not have the resources to leave the Lakeview public schools, and middle-class leaders were committed to advancing change within the public schools (Hill & Scott, 2017; Lubienski, 2005). Thus, we are arguing that while middle-class leaders used neoliberal educational discourses of data and accountability in their advocacy, they were not only concerned with their own children but for Hmong children at large, reflecting a collective stance. It is worth noting, however, that their collective stance did not extend to other Southeast Asians or other racial groups.

The middle-class leaders' case for multiculturalism also reflected a strategic use of neoliberal logics. In their arguments for bilingual education, culturally relevant pedagogy for Hmong people, and greater representation of Hmong teachers and staff in the schools, middle-class advocates blended aspects of more progressive forms of multiculturalism that emphasize cultural preservation, equity, and inclusion with a neoliberal multiculturalism, which views culture as a commodity useful for exchange (Melamed, 2006). Critical scholars have argued that neoliberalism has shifted ideas regarding the purpose and value of multiculturalism from the idea of cultural pluralism as an intrinsic good that should be fostered for the good of the public, to a more strategic understanding that views multiculturalism as only valuable insofar as it is linked to economic gains (Kymlicka, 2013; Mitchell, 2003). Neoliberal appropriations of multiculturalism rely on the principles of self-reliance and capital accumulation to argue for cultural recognition and maintenance.

Our interviews with middle-class advocates suggested that they sincerely believed in the inherent value of maintaining Hmong language and culture, reflecting more progressive ideas regarding multiculturalism. The curriculum of the summer camp clearly demonstrates a commitment to cultural and linguistic preservation and maintenance. Furthermore, they spoke about the value of understanding other cultures as part of living in the United States. Gao Moua's story about trying to get the PTO to address diversity, for example, reflects the goals of cross-cultural understanding and inclusion. In their educational advocacy with the Lakeview School District, however, middle-class leaders emphasized the link between cultural preservation, self-respect, academic success, and economic self-sufficiency. Thus, echoing the tenets of neoliberal multiculturalism, middle-class Hmong professionals frame culture as a commodity that can enhance academic success for economic purposes. The community-based summer program's cultural performance for the larger Lakeview community reflected a commodified notion of culture. Our data suggests that their embrace of neoliberal multiculturalism is largely a strategic move to gain access to resources in a neoliberal educational context. In other words, their neoliberal multicultural rhetoric was part of their effort to work within the dominant system to gain recognition for the larger Hmong community. While it represents consent to the hegemony of neoliberalism in the 21st century, our argument is that this consent is strategic.

Relatedly, middle-class advocates intentionally cultivated dominant forms of social capital through association with institutional leaders, most of whom were White. Middle-class leaders embraced and perpetuated aspects of the model minority discourse, particularly those regarding "good" Asian family values, in their rhetoric regarding why the Hmong community deserved recognition. While they acknowledged that Hmong youth did not exhibit the high academic achievement associated with the model minority image, they emphasized that Hmong youth were well behaved because, as Gao Moua explained, "We teach our kids to be respectful." Middle-class leaders were proud of the fact that school district data supported the idea that Hmong children and youth are "respectful," and they held model minority aspirations for their youth, including high academic achievement and enrollment in higher education. Although middle-class leaders were careful not to name other racial groups when pointing to the "good" behavior of Hmong youth, their descriptions were implicitly comparative. Indeed, there can be no model minority without a problematic minority, and since the civil rights era, when the model minority stereotype came to prominence, the image of Asian Americans as model citizens has relied on and perpetuated anti-Black ideologies.

In arguing for Hmong inclusion and recognition, middle-class leaders also advanced ideas of the good and deserving refugee figure who fought for the United States in the Vietnam War and was subsequently forced to migrate to the United States. Here, the discourse is one of the United States owing Hmong refugees for their sacrifices, and is most clearly demonstrated in the fight for expanding the definition of *veteran* to include Hmong refugees who fought with and for the United States in the Vietnam War (Xiong, 2016). In short, middle-class leaders argued that the Hmong community has demonstrated that they are deserving of inclusion and recognition through the sacrifice of the older generation during the war and their efforts to raise obedient children who they hope will grow up to be productive citizens.

CHAPTER 5

Solidarity Holds Our Unity Together (SHOUT): Education for Liberation

Stacey J. Lee and Choua Xiong

It affected me a lot when I joined SHOUT. I was really failing and struggling in high school and middle school, and they [SHOUT] were my supporters.

Parker, UHS senior and SHOUT youth leader, 2016

We met Parker at SHOUT (Solidarity Holds Our Unity Together) prior to starting our fieldwork at University Heights High School, and at the time Parker was a senior at UHS and an active youth leader at SHOUT. A grassroots, community-based, nonprofit organization, SHOUT serves some of the most economically and socially marginalized members of the Hmong, Khmer (Khmer are the largest ethnic group in Cambodia and SHOUT members preferred this term over Cambodian), and Black communities in the greater Lakeview area. SHOUT's community-based educational programming addressed the needs of Southeast Asian and Black youth facing intersecting forms of marginalization. Parker explained that prior to becoming involved with SHOUT he had been a "troublemaker" and was adrift. Having endured racist bullying when he was younger, Parker struggled academically and socially at UHS, and was without any direction until his aunt introduced him to SHOUT. As he explained in an interview, SHOUT gave him an emotional support system and a language for understanding the race, class, and gender hierarchies that shaped his life. In contrast to his experiences at UHS, where he felt unseen and lost among the crowd, Parker said that at SHOUT he found a home with supportive adult mentors.

SHOUT was founded by Pa Zao, a Hmong woman who grew up and attended local schools in Lakeview. Pa Zao and Bo, a Black gender-nonconforming person who grew up in Milwaukee, codirect SHOUT. Pa Zao is known throughout Southeast Asian American progressive circles across the nation for her nearly 3 decades of political organizing. Pa Zao's earliest political organizing focused on issues affecting Hmong women, particularly domestic violence, and she continues to do this work today. Pa Zao explained that she decided to address issues concerning girls and women because the Hmong Mutual Assistance Associations were dominated by men and focused almost exclusively on men's perspectives. As she illuminated in the following quotation, SHOUT's work evolved to include the needs of Hmong boys who were struggling with marginalization in the schools and in the city.

> I really just wanted to focus on Hmong women, girls, and youth. And so, it [programming for boys] was never a primary focus. But what we learned was that when we help Hmong girls, the Hmong boys wanted to come. They also wanted a place to go. And so, it was like really early on when we started to do Hmong girls-specific programming that Hmong boys were like, We want a place too. But one of the things that I've always made sure of the boys that come there was that they understood that we were a gender-justices agency—that we were, the leadership would always be femme.

As this quote suggests, challenging patriarchy and gendered violence have remained central to SHOUT's mission.

In addition to its work against gender-based violence, SHOUT is focused on addressing the harm posed by the intersections of racism and poverty in Black and Southeast Asian communities. In our very first meeting, Pa Zao emphasized that the Hmong and other Southeast Asians served by SHOUT were "extremely poor, you know, and working poor" and different from the more middle-class and professional families served by other organizations. Finally, SHOUT is deeply devoted to fostering cross-racial solidarity between low-income Southeast Asian American (SEAA) and low-income Black communities. All of SHOUT's staff/youth workers are SEAA or Black, and their commitment to SEAA and Black solidarity is expressed at all levels of the organization. For SHOUT leaders and youth workers, solidarity is expressed through SEAA support of Black-led movements and Black support for SEAA-led movements. Each ethnic/racial group is seen as responsible for taking the lead in identifying and addressing issues central to their racial/ethnic community.

SHOUT is committed to fighting for gender justice, queer justice, and Black and Southeast Asian liberation through an anticolonial lens, and they recognize the way issues of race and gender intersect with poverty. They view themselves as addressing the multitude of issues facing the most overlooked and invisible members of Lakeview's low-income Black and Southeast Asian communities. In fact, both Pa Zao and Bo noted that SHOUT gets involved in any issue that affects their community and is therefore "not issue-based but people-based." For example, in response to SEA elders' desire to grow their own food, SHOUT successfully campaigned for a large community garden where elders grow vegetables to feed themselves and their families. SHOUT's portfolio of activities includes affordable housing, access to healthcare, K–12 education reform, police accountability, domestic violence services, and citizenship attainment. SHOUT provides direct services to community members, is active in political organizing for various social justice issues, and also provides culturally relevant political education for youth. SHOUT also sponsors various community events, such as an annual sports tournament and a 5K run to promote health and wellness in SEAA and Black communities. SHOUT is part of a larger network of politically progressive Southeast Asian American organizations that share information and strategies in the fight against social injustices that face their communities.

Although SHOUT enjoys a national reputation among SEAA progressive organizers, its members are not acknowledged as Hmong or Southeast Asian American leaders by the Lakeview School District. Interestingly, the Lakeview School District recognizes the Black side of SHOUT but associates the SEAA side of SHOUT with the Waterway Foundation where SHOUT rented office space for over 15 years. The Waterway Foundation provides Section 8 housing and various services to many low-income residents of Lakeview, including many SEAAs. The Waterway Foundation funded some of the early stages of SHOUT and is home to many of SHOUT's clients and members. Although the Lakeview School District and the general public associate SHOUT with the Waterway Foundation, SHOUT leadership is clear that they do not share the political perspective of the Waterway Foundation. In particular, SHOUT leaders criticize the Waterway Foundation for embracing a "multiculturalism" that elides issues of power.

While SHOUT's work touches people of all ages in their communities through programming, our research focused on the community-based education for Southeast Asian and Black youth. Youth at SHOUT all experienced intersecting forms of inequality that rendered them among the most vulnerable residents of Lakeview. As Pa Zao proudly asserted, SHOUT fights for those most oppressed. The majority of the data for this chapter was collected between November of 2015 and June 2017 with additional follow-up research through 2018. Choua took primary responsibility for data collection at SHOUT, regularly attending youth programming and youth organizing events. Our experiences gaining research access to SHOUT highlight issues of researcher positionality and the political nature of research. The following field note snippet comes from our second meeting with Pa Zao.

> Pa Zao made it a point to tell me that she rarely allows university researchers or students into SHOUT because: (1) the community doesn't ever get anything in return for their time, and (2) it takes so much time to introduce/integrate even student volunteers or researchers into the community. She said that her attitude toward university researchers was cemented when an elder asked her what they/the community members got for allowing university folks into their lives. She then looked at Mai Neng and Choua and said that it was only because she knew them that she agreed to let us do the research at SHOUT.
>
> Stacey's fieldnotes, Nov. 15, 2015

Pa Zao made it abundantly clear that she didn't trust university researchers and had little interest in exposing her community to potential harm, reflecting her understanding that research with/on minoritized communities has too often been an act of dehumanization and colonization (Paris & Winn, 2013). While HEA members were interested in developing social capital with people from dominant institutions and viewed participation in our research as being potentially beneficial to the Hmong community, Pa Zao and the members of SHOUT have a healthy suspicion of dominant institutions and the people who represent those institutions. Pa Zao's trust in Mai Neng and Choua opened the doors for us, and we worked to build trust through reciprocity that reflected our commitment to research *with* rather than simply *on* communities (Irizary & Brown, 2013. Our research team agreed to run workshops for the youth on issues such as anti-Asian racism and understanding research as a form of reciprocity. More importantly, Choua and Mai Neng have remained connected to SHOUT even after completing our formal research.

COMMUNITY-BASED EDUCATION AT SHOUT

The adults in SHOUT were cognizant of the racialized achievement gap in Lakeview schools, but their criticism of the schools went beyond academic outcomes. SHOUT leaders and youth workers viewed the achievement gap as being secondary to other problems in local schools, and they were critical of middle-class Hmong professionals' sole focus on academic achievement. During one of our first meetings, for example, Pa Zao noted that the Hmong, other SEAA, and Black people served by SHOUT faced challenges related to healthcare, housing, and food insecurity and said, "If families don't have access to food, they don't have time to think about education." While the middle-class professional Hmong Americans discussed in the previous chapter viewed formal education as the route to social mobility and the American Dream, SHOUT leaders viewed the American Dream as a fiction that masked systemic inequalities. SHOUT youth workers described formal education as engines of racial and class reproduction in ways that echoed social reproduction theorists (e.g., Bowles & Gintis, 1976; Willis, 1977). While there are important differences among social reproduction theorists, all agree that schools reflect and reinforce social and cultural inequalities (Collins, 2009). Although Pa Zao and other members of SHOUT's leadership are college-educated and they support youth workers' and youth participants' pursuit of higher education, they reject the idea that schooling should be primarily about preparation for the workforce and social mobility. They characterize schools as hostile institutions that perpetuate racial and class-based harm and reproduce the status quo, including existing inequalities. While SHOUT is involved in the fight to change schools, they reject school-centric perspectives that view schools as the only legitimate spaces for learning and therefore devote significant attention to their own community-based educational programming. SHOUT's approach to community-based education privileges the deep pedagogical work in families and communities (Baldridge, 2020).

SHOUT leadership and youth workers argued that Lakeview schools harmed Black, brown, and Southeast Asian youth, leaving them physically, emotionally, and intellectually vulnerable. Specifically, they asserted that school policies regarding discipline were racist and that the curriculum was Eurocentric. Pa Zao explained in an interview that the underlying motivation for their political education programming was to fill in the cultural and political gaps left unaddressed by the school system.

> We believe that some of these things, they will never learn in school, right? How do Hmong kids learn about Black Lives Matter? How do African American kids learn about Hmong kids? And so, this is like ongoing. They also learn about issues of gender-based violence and learn about, like, racial profiling in school.

As Pa Zao's quote illustrates, SHOUT's educational programming fosters community self-determination and liberation through a critical understanding of patriarchy, capitalism, and racism. It supports youth in understanding the gendered, classed, and race-based injustices they face and encourages critical citizenship skills. SHOUT's youth programming includes separate culturally relevant programming for Hmong, Khmer/Cambodian (inactive during our fieldwork) and Black youth in recognition of the historical and cultural differences between Blacks and Southeast Asians. The goals of the culturally specific programming are for youth to learn and process their respective cultural and racial experiences, including their group traumas. SHOUT also brings together SEAA and Black youth in a cross-racial/cross-ethnic youth group that focuses on political education.

During our fieldwork two of the Hmong programs focused on dance. Each included 30 minutes of political discussion and 2 hours of dance practice. The dance groups were gender-segregated, with the girls' group focusing on Hmong dancing and building sisterhood to challenge gender-based violence, and the boys' group focusing on breakdancing and social justice education. The Hmong youth workers also aspired to offer gender-segregated discussion-based groups for girls and boys based on the assumption that gender-segregated spaces would encourage youth to interrogate the role of patriarchy in their own lives. The Hmong girls' discussion group was active throughout our fieldwork, but the group for Hmong boys struggled to get off the ground. The cross-racial youth group, Youth Leader Team (YLT), focused on building cross-racial solidarity and direct political education for youth and included four Hmong and two Black youth during our fieldwork. YLT meetings provided Black and Hmong American youth a space to update one another on individual programs, provide emotional support, and organize their political campaigns. During our fieldwork, SHOUT tried to bring Khmer youth into YLT, with limited success because most of the Khmer community lived outside of Lakeview in neighboring towns. SHOUT used the terms Southeast Asian and Hmong interchangeably, reflecting their aspirations to grow Khmer programming.

CHALLENGING ANTI-BLACKNESS

SHOUT leaders and youth workers view anti-Blackness as the central and foundational expression of racism in the United States, and their commitment to resisting anti-Black racism is at the core of their cross-racial solidarity and anti-racist education (Lee, Xiong, Pheng, & Vang, 2020). Scholars writing on anti-Blackness assert that anti-Black racism has shaped the United States from slavery to Jim Crow to mass incarceration. Scholars representing a range of academic disciplines have highlighted the foundational, pervasive, and persistent nature of anti-Black racism throughout American institutions, laws, and culture (Feagin, 2013; Melamed, 2006; Sexton, 2010; Wilderson, 2010). Anti-Blackness construes Blackness as the ultimate racial threat to the white nation and white supremacy, and requires Black bodies to be feared, controlled, and disciplined (Feagin, 2013; Sexton, 2010). Scholars writing about anti-Black racism argue that anti-Blackness has been and continues to be central to various social policies. including various educational policies that view the Black child as a problem (Dumas 2014, 2016; Wun, 2014).

Resistance to anti-Blackness and the fight for Black liberation is at the core of the Black Lives Matter (BLM) Movement. Mirroring the scholarship on anti-Blackness, the BLM Movement highlights the central and foundational nature of anti-Blackness. Calling out police violence, particularly through efforts to defund the police, has been at the core of BLM. Furthermore, the BLM Movement asserts that freedom for Black people will lead to freedom for all oppressed groups (Garza, 2014). SHOUT leaders are active in the national and local BLM Movement, and regularly advocate for SEAA support for BLM, including by participating in protests against police violence against Black bodies. At a public event in 2016, for example, Pa Zao critiqued the mostly Hmong audience for their lack of support of the Black community and urged Hmong people to be "Asians for Black lives, not Asians for Asians" (Lee, Xiong, Pheng, & Neng Vang, 2020). In an interview uploaded to SHOUT's website, Pa Zao explained that the root of racism is devaluing Black bodies and Black people and that fighting against racism requires being pro-Black.

Shared Experiences with Poverty

In their youth educational programming, youth workers regularly asserted that the fight against anti-Blackness will lead to liberation for Black people and Southeast Asian people. They asserted that the challenges faced by Hmong and Cambodians make them more like Black people than East Asians. Pa Zao identified the history of refugee resettlement, including policies regarding refugee employment and resettlement in low-income Black communities, as being at the root of Black and SEAA shared experiences and common struggle. In one of her social media posts, Pa Zao wrote, "40 years ago Southeast Asians were placed in some of the poorest communities throughout the United States. Nobody thought that one day Southeast Asians and Black folks would talk to each other and actually figure out we have a lot in common." Pa Zao regularly asserted that SEAA communities and Black communities had similar experiences with poverty and racism that were rooted in institutional neglect and the larger system of capitalism.

Reflecting the perspective of scholars in critical refugee studies, Pa Zao implicated resettlement policies in the ongoing economic struggles faced by many Southeast Asian refugees. Hegemonic narratives typically depict refugees, including Southeast Asian refugees as desperate victims in need of rescue and position the United States as the generous savior. In contrast to these narratives, scholars in critical refugee studies point to the role of the United States in creating refugee crises, including the Southeast Asian refugee crises. Furthermore, this scholarship implicates refugee resettlement policies, capitalism, and the broader forces of racialization for the ongoing marginalization of many Southeast Asian refugees (Dao, 2020; Espiritu, 2006; Nguyen, 2019; Schlund-Vials, 2016; Vue, 2021). Critical refugee scholar Yen Le Espiritu, for example, asserted that dominant scholarship on Vietnamese refugees paints Vietnamese refugees as grateful for low-paid labor, thereby erasing "questions about U.S. power structures that continue to consign a significant number of Vietnamese Americans to unstable, minimum-wage employment, welfare dependency, and participation in the informal economy" (Espiritu, 2006, p. 414).

An examination of refugee resettlement policies for Southeast Asians reveals that the priority was immediate economic self-sufficiency rather than education, job training, mental health services, or opportunities to adjust to life in the United States. Language acquisition focused on rudimentary and survival English for entry-level jobs. Authors of one of the early studies on Hmong resettlement argued that while individuals who quickly found low-skill jobs appeared to have achieved self-sufficiency, the "success" was only temporary (Reder, 1984). The 1980 Refugee Act, for example, had an explicit goal to encourage immediate economic self-sufficiency and discourage cash assistance (Office of Refugee Resettlement, 2012). Initially the 1980 Refugee Act provided cash assistance to refugees for up to 36 months; after 1982, this changed to only 18 months of assistance. As a result, many Southeast Asians got stuck in low-wage jobs without health insurance or other forms of security. Resettlement policies reflected the "compassion fatigue" regarding refugees that was exacerbated by the economic recession and concerns regarding welfare dependence and economic competition from immigrants (Ong, 1996). Within the logic of refugee resettlement policies, reliance on public assistance was viewed as a violation of the social agreement.

As Pa Zao pointed out, many Hmong and other Southeast Asian refugees were resettled in low-income Black communities where Black people struggled with multigenerational poverty because of systemic racism and insufficient infrastructure. In Pa Zao's words, Hmong people were "the new kid in town" struggling alongside poor Black people to survive. Resettlement in Black and brown urban communities was often surrounded by a dominant narrative that framed Southeast Asian refugees as being among the temporary poor who would soon achieve the immigrant dream of success (Jew, 2014; Tang, 2015). Immigration scholars framed SEAA poverty and reliance on public assistance as a developmental stage that would be quickly overcome (e.g., Rumbaut & Ima, 1988). In other words, SEAA refugees were positioned as potential model minorities who were different from the Black and brown communities who lived in multigenerational poverty in these communities. Some of this scholarship even suggested that avoiding the supposedly negative influence of urban youth of color was key to healthy assimilation and achievement (Caplan et al., 1991; Zhou & Bankston, 1998).

In addition to relying on and reproducing anti-Black attitudes and attempting to pit SEAA refugees against Black communities, much of this earlier scholarship failed to fully recognize that refugee policies that encouraged quick self-sufficiency set many refugees up for economic failure. A recent report by SEARAC states that 2.5 million SEAA live in the United States and 1.1 million are low income, including 460,000 who live in poverty (SEARAC, 2020). In other words, today many SEAA refugees live in a constant state of economic precarity alongside their low-income Black neighbors. Many of the Hmong and Cambodian/Khmer community members served by SHOUT have experienced one or more hardships (e.g., death of a primary wage earner, disability, divorce) and remain trapped in poverty. Through his research on Cambodian refugees in the Bronx hyperghetto, Eric Tang (2015) demonstrates that refugee resettlement in the hyperghetto is a continuation of U.S. imperialism and White supremacy in Southeast Asia. Pa Zao noted that poverty among Hmong and Cambodian communities may be missed because it differs from standard portraits of poverty. As she explained,

> What we've learned is that poverty plays and looks very different now. So, in the past, poverty looks like everybody in low-income housing. But now, what poverty looks like is that we have a four-bedroom and there are like 15 people living there. That's what poverty looks like and it's very different.

Adults in SHOUT view poverty as a product of racism and capitalism and their political education for youth centers these ideas.

The belief that freedom for Black people will lead to freedom for SEAAs was uniformly expressed by youth workers and other staff at SHOUT and was a core part of the political education. Riley, a Hmong youth worker, explains that in fighting for Black liberation they are simultaneously fighting for Hmong liberation, as the two are tied together.

> Black freedom, Black liberation is like freedom for everybody, right? Freedom for Black people is like freedom for all people because of, like, because of anti-Blackness, right? You see that like Black people are treated the worst in your community. Like Hmong people face, Hmong people go through what Black people go through but it's not, that bad, right? . . . I would like to think that like, when Black people are free, everybody is free.

According to Riley and other SHOUT youth workers, the differences between the racism experienced by SEAAs and that experienced by Black people are differences of degree, whereby Black people experience a greater level of racism.

Hmong youth workers explained that anti-Blackness within the larger Hmong community was something they had to address directly with Hmong youth in order to build racial solidarity between SEAA and Black communities. Indeed, the prevalence of anti-Blackness in the larger Hmong community can be traced to refugee resettlement policies that settled Hmong and other SEAA in predominately Black

low-income communities where the groups were forced to fight over limited resources without a common language for communication. Riley, a Hmong youth
worker at SHOUT, explained that many Hmong parents and elders don't understand the support for Black Lives Matter, which makes it difficult for the youth.

> I think for the Southeast Asian youth specifically, I think they're scared. Because, you
> know, I think it's such a high profile when you put yourself out there and you say,
> "Black Lives Matter," right. And like, because again, there's so much like backlash
> from your own families and the community and like, "Why the hell are you doing
> this, right? Like, why is it, why does it even affect you?"

Tracy, a Hmong staff member and former youth worker, believed that many
Hmong elders develop a fear of the Black community because of the negative media representations of Black people. Tracy recalled that her own assumptions regarding the Black community only changed after Pa Zao challenged her by asking:
"If you hate Black people so much then why do you listen to R&B, why do you
listen to rap, why do you listen to blues? Why do you wear their types of clothes?
You know?" As Tracy explained, Pa Zao's questions forced her to grapple with
her own anti-Black racism.

In the YLT group Hmong and Black youth workers make efforts to acknowledge and value differences between SEAA and Black communities and also to recognize similarities between the groups. There was, for example, an openness to
Hmong youth speaking Hmong and/or Hmonglish during YLT meetings. Like
SHOUT leadership, Hmong youth workers asserted that a shared experience with
poverty made Black and SEAA people vulnerable to the same social injustices in
Lakeview and in the larger national context. Mee, a Hmong youth worker who
identifies as femme, explained that "at SHOUT we are, we always joke about this,
but we are like the Blacks of like the Asian community." Here, Mee was referring
to the fact that dominant perceptions of immigrants and refugees are shaped by a
group's economic standing, and by the bipolar White/Black paradigm of race. As
such, economically successful immigrants and refugees are ideologically whitened,
and those who suffer from poverty are ideologically blackened in the dominant
imagination (Lee, 2005; Ong, 2013; Vaught, 2012). As Mee suggested in her joke,
high rates of poverty within Hmong communities have led to their ideological
blackening (DePouw, 2012; Lee, 2005). While some segments of the Hmong community have resisted the association with the Black community, SHOUT leaders
and youth workers embrace the Black community as important allies in the fight
for racial liberation.

The fact that many SEAA people and Black people share a common experience with poverty was a regular theme in YLT meetings. In the fieldnote below, we
see Mee work with the YLT youth in filling out an application to attend a training
for political organizing in California.

> Mee asks the group, "Who wants to go to Oakland?" A group is holding
> a training for organizing in Oakland May 24–26. The youth all responded

positively & Mee hands out applications and tells them all to start filling them out. The application asks for basic demographic and one of the Black youth asks what to put down for income. Mee laughs and says, "You can put low-income or poor. I usually put poor!" This comment led Riley and the others to laugh and all the youth put down "poor."

Stacey's fieldnotes, March 31, 2016

Mee's naming of the "poor" category lifts the silence and shame that surrounds the mundane conditions of poverty. Her use of humor here erases the shame surrounding poverty and simultaneously serves to emphasize a shared experience with poverty. While the dominant society too often blames people who live in poverty for their economic situations, SHOUT teaches the youth that poverty is the result of systemic inequality. By discussing poverty as a condition created by unequal distribution inherent to capitalism, SHOUT youth workers challenge frameworks that position low-income SEAA and Black communities as burdens or threats. Furthermore, by claiming their identities as "poor" people SHOUT is critiquing capitalism and racism.

Anti-Blackness in Schools

During our fieldwork, a central educational issue addressed in YLT concerned the relationship between anti-Blackness and the police state. Discussions regarding the harm caused by Lakeview's policy of having police inside schools occurred in the weekly YLT programming and was the focus of SHOUT's Freedom School in April of 2017. Inspired by the Freedom School of the civil rights movement, SHOUT's Freedom School provides youth leaders an opportunity to expand on the conversations in YLT groups and workshops. As in the Freedom Schools during the civil rights movement, SHOUT's focus is on fostering discussion related to racial (in)justice (Perlstein, 1990). Freedom School 2017 focused on building capacity for SHOUT's fight alongside the Movement for Black Lives and Asian Americans for Black Lives. SHOUT gathered Black and Hmong American youth together at a rental house where the youth spent the whole weekend together. The participants spent the weekend engaging in several activities where they ate, slept, and bonded together. While building these intimate relationships and trust amongst one another, the main objective of Freedom School 2017 was to learn about the history of SHOUT as an organization, build youth power and organizing, and plan their Police Out of School campaign. In preparation for their campaign, the participants were taught about the history of policing, the relationship between anti-Blackness and policy, and the history and role of police in schools and in Black communities. They engaged in discussions about historical movements and contemporary challenges and strategized ways to resist school disciplinary and policing policies and practices that criminalize Black youth.

Our fieldwork confirmed that youth participants at SHOUT have all come to understand that anti-Blackness is the primary form of racism in schools and in the nation. In response to Choua's question about why it was important for them to learn about Black Lives Matter, Gao Sheng quickly responded, "Knowing that their lives are the same as our lives. So, if they die, knowing that they die for no reason, then that means that we are going to die for no reason too. So, I think that it's just important for us to know that we might die from just killing, by police killing us." As Gao Sheng spoke, Kendall nodded in agreement and added that "Black people and Southeast Asians, we're kind of like brothers and sisters, but with different skin color. Because we're targeted by White people." Like the Hmong youth workers, Hmong youth argue that while the Black and SEAA communities share experiences with racism, the Black community suffers more because of anti-Blackness and colorism.

Youth workers regularly encouraged Hmong youth to reflect on the racism they experience and observe in schools and in the city of Lakeview. Discussions included concerns with teachers, school-based police, and police in their neighborhoods. In an interview with Parker, we hear an example of how the youth make sense of the similarities and differences between Hmong and Black communities:

> We always see the statistics of Hmong high school dropouts and Black high school dropouts and it's really . . . the results are really similar. When we see that, we already know why they are failing youth and it's all connected to the school to jail pipeline. It all connects to the juvenile system, the prison system, and the jail system. And like, they wanna lock us up because of poverty and because we're poor we have nowhere to go and of course we're gonna steal because we gotta survive. We support [Black Lives Matter] as allies or Asian allies. It's not Asian but we know that our liberation is bounded [bonded] with one another, which you know, is powerful.

As Parker's quotation suggests, Hmong youth understood the relationship between anti-Black racism, police in schools, and the incarceration of Black people. Parker's explanation of the similarities between SEAA and Black communities emphasizes the shared experiences with poverty and marginalization at school. These comparisons help Parker feel less alone, and therefore more hopeful about "winning this fight." Furthermore, in pointing to the dropout rate among Hmong students, Parker is implicitly distinguishing the educational experiences of Hmong students from those of East Asian Americans who are generally characterized as high achieving model minorities (Lee, 2009).

CULTURALLY SPECIFIC PROGRAMMING

Every time we attended SHOUT events, it was no secret that this was a Hmong and Black space. The political and cultural artworks displayed on the walls, the type of music in the background, the languages that were used, and the ways that people greeted each other revealed the deep radical healing that happens at SHOUT (Ginwright 2007, 2010). The culturally specific programs at SHOUT seek to counter the exclusion Hmong youth encounter at school. SHOUT provides a space for youth to be themselves, which includes the right to express themselves in their own languages, including Hmonglish. As noted earlier, all Hmong members of the SHOUT community engaged in code-meshing (Hmonglish) and/or code-switching when interacting at SHOUT and in public (Canagarajah, 2011; Young et al., 2014). Although SHOUT staff and youth did not explicitly discuss their language use or linguistic choices, there was an automatic sense of belonging that happened when young people entered SHOUT's space and they could speak without being othered. The following is an excerpt from an interview that Choua conducted with two youth members of SHOUT.

> *Choua:* Okay, so at SHOUT, what do you guys feel like . . . what is the language that you guys usually use to communicate?
> *Gao Sheng:* Um, English and Hmong. . . . Or Hmonglish
> *Kendall:* (laughing) Yeah, Hmonglish.
> *Choua:* And you guys said that it's important. So, at school, what about at school? What language do you use most?
> *Both:* English.
> *Kendall:* Well, if I'm around a lot of like my friends, oh like her, I would speak Hmong, Hmonglish. (laughing)
> *Choua:* Do you guys feel more comfortable using English or Hmonglish?
> *Gao Sheng:* Hmonglish.
> *Kendall:* Hmonglish.

As Kendall and Gao Sheng explained (using Hmonglish) in the interview, the use of Hmonglish allowed them to speak freely and authentically without worrying about finding English words for Hmong concepts.

Kendall and Gao Sheng had been in the Hmong girls' dance group since elementary school and joined the discussion group in middle school. The girls' dance group is a space for girls of any age to learn traditional Hmong dance and to begin talking about social issues in their community while connecting to their culture. The girls' dance group is designed as a feeder into the girls' discussion group for middle- and high school-aged girls. Kendall and Gao Sheng explained that dance group meetings are primarily devoted to dancing and having fun, but the older girls also try to introduce discussion of the struggles that impact Hmong people. Kendall described the process of introducing political education to elementary-aged girls as slow and requiring patience because the girls "are really young, so they probably don't understand it much. But then we keep telling them and teaching them; probably soon or later or in the future, they will understand it more." As Kendall's quote suggests, SHOUT intentionally scaffolds discussions of complex social issues for younger students.

The weekly Hmong girls' discussion group, Ntxhais Hmoob (Hmong Sisterhood), was a space for adolescent girls to discuss issues related to gender, sexuality, race, and poverty. The girls were encouraged to share their personal experiences while connecting their experiences to larger structures and systems. Additionally, the gender-based discussion group was a space where concepts such as anti-Blackness were interrogated and where other issues facing the SEAA and

Black communities were discussed. The following is an excerpt from an interview where Gao Sheng and Kendall discuss the focus of the girls' group:

> *Gao Sheng:* So we just learn, so everybody learn about the struggles of every group that they have in SHOUT.
> *Interviewer:* So, what are the struggles of the Hmong group?
> *Kendall:* Patriarchy, domestic violence [pause]; immigration, yeah.

Gao Sheng and Kendall went on to explain that the girls' discussion group gives them an opportunity to discuss gender inequality in their families and the larger Hmong community, including the fact that boys have more privileges and freedoms and fewer responsibilities in the home.

A typical girls' discussion group meeting started with participants repeating their names, stating their preferred pronouns, and sharing personal updates, including their emotional states. Mee, the youth worker responsible for the girls' discussion group, generally gave the girls an update on issues in the community and then introduced an activity.

> Today's activity was for the girls to write or draw their vision board. One girl asked why they had to do this vision board, and Mee answered that it was to flush out our visions for our future. Mee stressed that it is important to have a vision about our future and draw out our pictures because Hmong girls are not given a chance to think about their vision. Mee shared a piece from her own vision board and said that it is important to put dates and times to indicate when you will like to accomplish your goals. The goals can be long term and short term. Mee points out that it is important to have dreams, but also to be realistic. Additionally, Mee urged the girls to find out how they are and when they will be achieving these goals. After about 15 minutes Mee asked the girls to take turns sharing using the popcorn style where one girl started sharing and then called on someone else. Eventually we made our way to everyone. Some of the kids shared that they wanted to travel. They wanted to become smarter at school. Some said they wanted to learn Hmong and others said they want to become better readers.
>
> Choua's fieldnotes, Feb. 24, 2016

This activity reflects SHOUT's commitment to fostering Hmong girls' aspirations and self-determination. As Mee's statement that "Hmong girls are not given a chance to think about their vision" suggests, the Hmong girls' discussion group was a counterhegemonic, culturally specific space.

On some days the girls' discussion group focused more directly on discussions of patriarchy and gender-based violence in their communities. These discussions gave opportunities for the girls to connect their individual experiences and observations with larger social, cultural, and political contexts. The girls drew on all of their linguistic repertoires in tackling these complex subjects. In the following fieldnote, youth participants and youth workers used Hmonglish to discuss sexual violence.

> The girls at Ntxhais Hmoob, the Hmong girls' discussion group, were discussing the differences between sexual violence and sexual abuse during a lesson about April as Sexual Assault Awareness Month. Mee shared that the group is talking about this topic because SHOUT wanted the girls to know the differences between the legal definition and the everyday acts that are also sexual assaults. Kendall then added that "We should not con, con, condone?" She looked at Mee to see if she pronounced the word "condone" correctly. Mee helped Kendall by repeating the word "condone." Kendall then nodded and finished her sentence, "We should not condone rape culture." Kendall continued and asked, "Do you know what rape means?"

> Kabao, one of the active youth at Ntxhais Hmoob, answered, "I know what rape means. Rape means *mos* [Hmong word for rape]. It's like you don't even like them." Mee agreed and she added in Hmonglish that these acts are acts committed by *neeg phem* [bad, evil people] and these are acts are often out of malicious intent. Kabao interrupted and asked, "*es*, malicious *yog dabtsi* [what does malicious mean?]" Mee tried to describe the Hmong expression for "malicious intentions" but said the wrong tone. As Kabao recognized the expression Mee was trying to convey, she chuckled and tried to help Mee pronounce it. Kabao made a distinction between the vowel "i" and "w," saying that the correct word should be "*lim hiav*" and not "*lwm hiav*" like how Mee originally said. They all laughed, and Mee thanked Kabao for helping her speak better Hmong. Then, Mee courageously tried to repeat the word in the correct tone as she continued to explain rape culture using Hmonglish.

> Choua's fieldnotes, Apr. 6, 2016

As is evident in this fieldnote, youth workers like Mee supported the development of English language skills while simultaneously taking the risk to relearn Hmong vocabulary. Mee gave the word "condone" to Kendall, but Mee also opened herself to learning the word "lim hiav" from Kabao. Through this, Mee provided the social justice language she knew using English, and she modeled what it means to confront her own trauma of not knowing enough Hmong.

The ways Hmonglish was embraced at SHOUT reflected the organization's compassion for Hmong youth, who struggled to learn dominant American English and retain Hmong. Rather than being positioned as failed English learners and/or unauthentic Hmong kids, they used Hmonglish as an opportunity to freely exist and embrace their displacement as racialized Southeast Asian refugees. At SHOUT, Hmong youth can be Hmong and American without being subjected to racialized linguistic scrutiny and lessen a sense of loss of the Hmong language. In other words, SHOUT embraces who the youth are and the languages they use.

Baldridge (2019) describes the "come as you are" culture of community-based spaces as "one of the many characteristics that sets these spaces apart from traditional school settings" (p. 69). Lakeview schools, including UHS, where Gao Sheng and Kendall were students, were *de facto* English-only spaces. While school policies and practices resulted in a kind of language surveillance that silenced many Hmong youth, language practices at SHOUT fostered a sense of community. The simple act of being able to speak Hmonglish allowed Hmong youth at SHOUT to develop a stronger community connection in their reclamation of loss as displaced refugees. Using Hmonglish is in fact a confrontation with White supremacy, colonialism, and capitalism (Bucholtz et al., 2017; Rosa & Flores 2017).

In addition to being introduced to political issues by the youth workers, the girls were encouraged to identify and explore topics for discussion. This attention to youth-led discussion has been identified as a common feature of community-based education (Ventura, 2017). Kendall had recently assumed a new role as a youth leader when we began our research at SHOUT. Like other youth leaders, Kendall had been an active participant in SHOUT's youth programming for years, and during our fieldwork she was being mentored into a new role where she would play a larger role in facilitating discussions and planning political organizing. During one meeting of Ntxhais Hmoob (Hmong Sisterhood), for example, Kendall planned a discussion on self-esteem, self-confidence, and beauty standards.

> Kendall wrote the following on the board and then read the questions out loud in English and then she explained in Hmong. The girls were then instructed to write their ideas down on pieces of paper that Kendall had passed out, and then the girls were asked to share out loud: "What do you like about yourself?" "What do you not like about yourself?" "What is something you wish you could change about yourself?" In response to the first question, Kendall started by saying, "I see an ugly stupid girl." After Kendall spoke, another girl immediately added that she was also dissatisfied with her appearance, particularly her eyebrows.
>
> Stacey's fieldnotes, April 27, 2016

Mee explained that she had suggested that the group discuss the situation surrounding the deportation of Southeast Asians on this day, but Kendall asked to talk about self-esteem. Like other youth, Kendall participated in social media (Facebook, Instagram) and consumed various forms of youth culture (K-pop) where idealized images of beauty were rampant. The girls all noted that the "perfect girl" had to look a certain way: skinny, straight teeth, long hair, big butt, "boobs," light skin, nice clothes, make-up, wearing high heels. During the discussion Mee encouraged the youth to consider the role that colorism and anti-Blackness play in definitions of beauty. Specifically, Mee attempted to connect ideas of colorism (i.e., the preference for lighter skin toned individuals within a group) to anti-Blackness (Norwood, 2015).

The Hmong boys' dance group focused on breakdancing and was the result of Parker's passion for breakdancing. When Parker became a more active youth leader at SHOUT, he asked the Hmong youth workers about the possibility of organizing a new program that centered breakdancing. In the spirit of youth-initiated activities, SHOUT youth workers collaborated with Parker to imagine how the group might combine opportunities for boys to learn dance moves and advance social justice. Parker's passion for breakdancing came from his personal experiences. In the following interview segment, he explained that a friend introduced him to breakdancing in middle school, and he used this new hobby to move away from the school bullies and violence.

> I was just trying new moves . . . because I felt really good when I did it. I don't know. It just heals me. What I think about it is like finding enlightenment. It was really good for me, because I think I found, and I chose the right path. I was out of trouble, out of the streets with my friends. You never know what I could have done.

Parker's original goal for the program was to combine breakdancing and racial justice, including discussions of Asian American cultural appropriation of a Black art form. Because the breakdancing group was a boys' space, and we did not have any masculine/male-identified people on our research team, we did not regularly conduct fieldwork on the group.

During our fieldwork, SHOUT attempted to restart a discussion-based group for Hmong boys that would address issues of patriarchy in the Hmong community. As the oldest and most involved Hmong boy in SHOUT, Parker was identified by the Hmong youth workers to be the youth leader for the Hmong boys' discussion group. Mee, one of the Hmong youth workers, worked with Parker to set goals for the boys' discussion group, which she hoped would extend from the breakdancing group he led. In the following fieldnote, Mee pushed Parker to work with Riley, a Hmong youth worker, to reflect on how he might interrogate traditional gender norms and patriarchy with the male youth in his programs.

> Mee insisted that Parker continue to work with Riley, the trans Hmong youth worker, to conceptualize and plan his youth programs. Parker looked at Riley, then back at Mee, and nodded in agreement. Mee continued to describe the spiral activity that talked about gender expectations and the prevalence of patriarchy in the Hmong community. She then turned to Parker and asked him to think about these questions. "What does it mean to be a Hmong man? What are the consequences to be born a woman? What about LGBTQ?" Mee suggested that Parker talk about these things with "your boys" before the hip-hop group starts their activities in tomorrow's training.
>
> Choua's fieldnotes, March 14, 2017

As one of the more experienced Hmong youth workers, Mee was often overwhelmed with various tasks at SHOUT, and in this interaction she was pushing the masculine/male-identified people in SHOUT to step up and take responsibility for the programming for Hmong boys. In an interview, Parker explained that he understood that the goal of the boys' discussion group was to use "male privilege to support his sisters." Despite Parker's interest, SHOUT struggled throughout our fieldwork to form a boys' group; eventually Parker reached a compromise where he used his breakdancing group to address issues related to gender.

As these examples illustrate, SHOUT's culturally specific programming is distinctive both for its centering of Hmong culture and for its commitment to interrogating patriarchy in that culture. Their discussions revealed an understanding that cultural traditions should not be viewed as excuses for patriarchy and misogyny. For SHOUT leadership and youth workers, loving the Hmong culture requires confronting issues within the culture and community. SHOUT's embrace of Hmonglish also reflected their fluid understanding of language and culture. As an organization that served the children and grandchildren of Hmong refugees, SHOUT recognized that the youths' language reflected their complex histories, experiences and identities.

CRITICAL APPROACHES AND RADICAL HEALING

SHOUT's political education reflects and builds on the central tenets of critical pedagogy and the concept of radical healing (Freire, 1996; Ginwright, 2007, 2010). In the spirit of critical pedagogy, SHOUT's programming fosters a critical awareness of the social, cultural, racial, and economic structures that shape the lives of the youth and their communities (Apple & Au, 2009). SHOUT's youth workers and leaders regularly talked about education for "freedom" and "liberation," echoing the discourse's critical pedagogy. SHOUT's youth workers help youth put their individual experiences and observations of injustice into a larger political context (Baldridge, 2019). Through critical discussions and political organizing, SHOUT aims to transform youth into active agents of social change for liberation (Freire, 1996; Macedo, 2009). For SHOUT, "freedom" and "liberation" are political states and emotional states as well (Ginwright, 2007, 2010).

SHOUT's youth groups center the Freirean concepts of dialogue (active discussion about issues affecting their lives), critique (analysis of self and society) and praxis (applying the knowledge to make change) (Braa & Callero, 2006). At SHOUT this means that Southeast Asian and Black youth are pressed to identify and break down the world of oppression and to take action that transforms this world. This involves ongoing discussions about anti-Blackness, class inequality, and patriarchy and misogyny. Youth are encouraged to share and make sense of their own experiences with oppression(s) and are offered a language for understanding how these oppressions are rooted in contemporary and historical policies and laws. Finally, they are introduced to various forms of political participation, including voting, talking with political officials, facilitating political debates within the community, and exercising their rights to petition.

Alongside the political education, SHOUT provides youth members with a caring and welcoming space. In fact, an important piece of critical pedagogy includes the role of caring adults and educators who foster safe spaces that help young people heal from their traumatic past and violence. As Parker expressed in the quote that opens this chapter, SHOUT provided important emotional support to him during a time in his life when he was struggling at home and at school. Riley explained the culture at SHOUT and how youth workers foster a caring and safe space:

> It [SHOUT] feels more like a family. And these are my kids, you know, and I'm like an adult that they can trust. And also [pause] also just always remind the kids that this is a safe space. I think that makes them feel good. If you feel unsafe in this space, we will figure something out. Whatever that is hurting you, we will address it. So, safe space, and building relationships.

Bianca Baldridge (2018) has described Black youth workers as "educators, counselors, cultural workers, mediators, and negotiators who assist youth of color as they construct their identities in a racially hostile society . . . [they] don many hats: teacher, counselor, curriculum developer, janitor, disciplinarian, mentor, party planner, trainer, tutor, grant writer, or marketing strategist" (p. 3). Similarly, SHOUT youth workers serve multiple roles in the youths' lives.

SHOUT youth workers, leaders, and youth come from the same communities, share cultural backgrounds, and struggle with some of the same forms of oppression. As noted earlier, Hmong folks at SHOUT regularly spoke in Hmong and Hmonglish in ways that fostered community and belonging. Adults at SHOUT consciously choose to mentor and uplift the stories of the most marginalized youth in the neighborhoods, including youth from single-mother or no-parent families, low- to no-income households, and youth who identify as queer, trans, or gendernonconforming. Indeed, many active youth participants are ostracized at school and within the Hmong community.

In addition to speaking the same language(s) and sharing an ethnic culture, many of the youth workers came through SHOUT as youth members and leaders. Riley explained that participating in SHOUT as a youth helped him understand racism and that one of his goals as a youth worker was to help the next generation develop a critical understanding of racism and other oppressions so that they know "we aren't alone." In his role as a youth worker, Riley uses personal stories to encourage youth to share.

> The way I challenge youth, I would, I kind of like to guide them with questions or like, I find it [is] hard for like the Southeast Asian youth, it's hard for them to share what they feel, or they just, sometimes, they know a lot, but they don't talk. So, I like to share stories about myself, like if I were teaching them about racism or homophobia, like I would give them an examples of the times that I've witness that and I would ask them, like, "Hey, is there a time you've ever felt like someone was discriminate or prejudices or racist towards you?"

By sharing stories and expressing their own vulnerabilities, youth workers built trusting relationships with the youth. Remarking on the bond among the SHOUT community, Riley proudly asserted "All of us come together, and I think everybody is a survivor that comes through SHOUT and even me, and as we're learning about all these intersecting isms that affect us."

Many of the adults at SHOUT were once youth participants who grew up in the programs created by Pa Zao and have stayed at SHOUT to continue the work of fighting for liberation. Tracy, a SHOUT staff member, has been involved with SHOUT for over 15 years. Tracy identifies as gender nonbinary, low-income, and Hmong. Tracy explains in the following segment from an interview with Stacey that Pa Zao mentored them and a few other Hmong girls who had dropped out of high school and were simply hanging out.

> T: We were all high school dropouts, all young girls, high school
>   dropouts . . . Then led to where Pa Zao would just take us places like
>   here on Apple Street. Cause we hadn't really been around here cause
>   we're always I want to say locked up in the neighborhood, or we didn't
>   know where else to go, right? So she'll take us to different places. She
>   had her little black book and I thinks it was like her Journal book, but
>   she doodles a lot too; it looks like she's doodling, but she's taking notes
>   and then she'll ask us, like, what is our goal. And some of us would be
>   like, "I wanna pay off all my driving tickets" or "I wanna get back into
>   school" or "I wanna get my GED, I wanna go to college," or "I wanna
>   get a home pretty much I wanna get off the streets." And then within
>   a year I remember Pa Zao opened her book again and: This is what
>   all y'all said last year all through this season and all of you guys have
>   proven we could all reach our goal. Like for me it was to get through
>   high school; some of them it was like pretty to much get off the streets,
>   or not be homeless you know, get an apartment, go to school or so
>   forth, right? We all reached our goals, and it led to we're like
> S: (So cool)
> T: Yeah, yeah and then she's like, "You guys wanna organize?" and we're
>   like "What?" [laughs] We're like, "Organize your office?"

Tracy credits Pa Zao for encouraging them to complete her high school diploma and finding a focus for her life. As Tracy explained, Pa Zao spent a significant amount of time building relationships with Tracy and Pa Zao introduced Tracy and others to social justice issues while building trusting connections. Furthermore, Pa Zao guided Tracy to identify individual and collective goals.

Ginwright (2010) refers to this as the process of "radical healing" that "contributes to individual well-being, community health and broader social justice where young people can act on behalf of others with hope, joy and a sense of possibility" (p. 85). Radical healing recognizes the emotional, material, and cultural aspects of youths' everyday lives and builds on these to seek political justice. Tracy embodies radical healing and mentors the current generation of youth through their healing. While Tracy continues to work through their health issues and everyday struggles with access to health care and social services, they remain present when interacting with young people at SHOUT. Tracy was hired to support the elder and gender programs, but always attends youth programming as the caretaker: taking everyone's photos, offering counseling and advice, and transporting youth to and from programming. Tracy's willingness to be a resource for the youth workers and youth leaders acts as a visible model for SHOUT youth. Specifically, Tracy's position as the generation between Pa Zao and the youth further fosters a sense of community commitment to radical healing. The young people at SHOUT participate in radical healing when SHOUT staff like Tracy offer their service with love and possibility. Finally, youth at SHOUT witness the deep and caring bond between Pa Zao and Tracy and the link between this care and the continued fight for political justice.

Not Like School

Hmong and Black youth regularly noted that they appreciated that SHOUT was different from school, and that being at SHOUT made them feel like part of a community. SHOUT provides a space for youth to be themselves, which includes the right to express themselves in their own languages, including Hmonglish. As noted earlier, all Hmong members of the SHOUT community engaged in code-meshing (Hmonglish) and/or code-switching when interacting at SHOUT and in public, and Hmong youth identified the freedom to use Hmonglish as key to their sense of belonging at SHOUT. Lakeview schools were *de facto* English-only spaces. While school policies and practices resulted in a kind of language surveillance that silenced many Hmong youth, language practices at SHOUT fostered a sense of community. Throughout our fieldwork we heard Hmong youth and youth workers speaking Hmonglish, whether they were talking about complex political issues or joking around. We argue that the right to use their own language(s) is central to the radical healing that happens at SHOUT.

SHOUT's political education addresses issues that matter to their communities and are relevant to the youths' lives (Ladson-Billings, 1995). Several Hmong youth asserted that SHOUT teaches about issues of race and racism while schools ignore or downplay these issues. Kendall explained: "Well, at SHOUT, they teach you the stuff that, like, school doesn't teach. Or like they talk about the things that school doesn't talk about." Youth also regularly commented on the fact that adults at SHOUT "understand your problems." As Gao Sheng stated, "We have a bond with SHOUT and then for school we don't really have a bond. . . . Because SHOUT's like family to me. So, it would be easier to replace school with them. Because they're like a bond to me, and school is not a bond to me."

CONCLUSION

Our data illustrates that SHOUT is a counterhegemonic space that offers Hmong youth opportunities for critical and culturally specific education that is healing. SHOUT argues that education should be aimed toward freedom and liberation for oppressed groups rather than toward participation in the economy. Unlike the middle-class professionals in HEA, SHOUT rejects neoliberal assumptions about the economic purposes of education for individuals. SHOUT leaders and youth workers want to transform educational institutions, not participate within the current education system. While HEA focuses on the achievement gap, SHOUT's critique centers on the persistent physical, emotional, and intellectual harm done to Black and Southeast Asian students. As leaders and youth workers in SHOUT repeatedly stressed, SHOUT is focused on the often-invisible suffering of the most oppressed members of the SEAA and Black communities in Lakeview, and their educational organizing focuses on the concerns of these communities. They identified anti-Blackness as the central form of racism in the United States and in public schools, and their commitment to fighting anti-Blackness is at the core of their political education and their educational organizing.

SHOUT leadership and youth workers embrace a cross-racial solidarity between SEAA and Black people, and they argue that SEAA and Black communities are vulnerable to the same social injustices. Their assumption is that freedom for Black communities will lead to freedom for SEAA communities. Through participation in SHOUT's youth programming, Hmong youth learned to recognize and criticize anti-Blackness in their schools, the dominant society, and their co-ethnic communities. In discussion groups, we observed Hmong and Black youth learning about their shared challenges with poverty and teaching each other about their cultures and histories. The focus on challenging anti-Blackness provided Hmong youth a larger political and historical framework for understanding racism and helped them to feel less alone in their struggle. Hmong youth demonstrated consistent support for their Black peers and for the BLM movement, and the respect that Hmong youth demonstrated for their Black peers was mutual. SHOUT's focus on challenging anti-Blackness and the cross-racial solidarity between SEAA and Black communities is among the organization's greatest strengths, but the relative absence of discussion regarding anti-Asian racism limited Hmong youths' understanding of the anti-Asian racism they faced.

While Hmong youth are encouraged to view themselves as part of a larger Southeast Asian community, they resist a pan-Asian identification with East Asians. In fact, SHOUT members generally viewed Chinese Americans and other East Asians as being high achieving and wealthy model minorities who were almost like White people. The assumption that all East Asian Americans are model minorities may be due to the fact that many East Asian American students at UHS appeared to be doing well and many East Asian Americans in the larger community, including Stacey, are affiliated with the university. While there are important cultural and historical differences between SEAA communities and East Asian American communities, Asian Americans across various ethnic groups are subjected to similar processes of racialization in the United States.

During the workshop we led on Asian American racialization, we found that Hmong and Black youth were comfortable articulating the way Black people have been racialized in the dominant society but struggled to articulate the racism specific to Hmong and SEAA communities. In fact, the youth simply laughed and said that SEAAs were stereotyped the way Black people are. Our data confirmed that

SEAA have been ideologically blackened in the dominant imagination, but our data also revealed that Hmong youth are vulnerable to specific anti-Asian racism. In interviews, for example, Hmong youth talked about being subjected to specifically Asian stereotypes including the ideas that "Asian people eat cats" or "Asians know how to do math." Furthermore, all reported having been taunted by fake Asian accents, but the youth didn't have a larger historical or social context for making sense of specifically anti-Asian racism. It is important to point out that Hmong adults in SHOUT recognize that Hmong and other SEAA youth need more education on the racialization of Asians and the relationship between anti-Asian racism and anti-Black racism.

With limited staffing and resources, SHOUT, like many community-based organizations, can't do everything (Baldridge, 2019). As an organization dedicated to serving oppressed communities and fighting for social justice for their communities, SHOUT's work is evolving in response to issues in its communities. In the time since we finished our data collection SHOUT has grown to include a section devoted to civic engagement, including efforts to get community members to vote. SHOUT has also returned to a focus on fighting against the deportation of SEAA in response to the increased attention to deportation between 2017 and 2018. During the COVID-19 pandemic and the rise in anti-Asian racism, SHOUT worked to address the various needs of their communities, including leading discussions on how to make sense of and resist anti-Asian racism.

During our fieldwork, SHOUT's primary educational organizing focused on getting police out of Lakeview Schools. After we completed our formal fieldwork, SHOUT continued to organize and hold public events in support of police-free schools, and one month after George Floyd was murdered by Derek Chauvin the Lakeview School District severed its contract with the local police department. Although SHOUT's educational organizing focused on police-free schooling during and after our fieldwork, Pa Zao expressed critical opinions about ESL. In an interview with Choua, Pa Zao rhetorically asked, "If ESL is so good and is supposed to help these Hmong kids . . . then it would be good for the White kid who doesn't also speak English well, yeah?" Like the middle-class Hmong professionals profiled in the previous chapter, Pa Zao and Hmong youth workers recognized that ESL had been necessary for earlier cohorts of Hmong youth, but they worried that the English learner label was stigmatizing and tracking today's Hmong youth. Although SHOUT expressed concerns about ESL, they did not play a significant role in educational advocacy regarding ESL and bilingual education, leaving this largely to middle-class professionals. Again, SHOUT's decision to focus on one issue for their educational organizing likely reflects the fact that they are a small organization with limited staff and resources.

SHOUT also provided culturally specific programming for Hmong youth, including gender-specific discussion groups and a Hmong dance group. SHOUT's culturally relevant programming challenged gender-based violence by building "sisterhood" and fought against patriarchy, homophobia, racism, and classism through the use of Hmong arts. By directly resisting patriarchy and homophobia within the Hmong community, SHOUT is questioning traditional gender norms and calling for cultural change. While SHOUT has gender-specific groups, they embrace gender-nonbinary people in the organization and gender-nonconforming people have led the boys' discussion group. Their understanding of culture reflects an understanding that cultures are always fluid, in motion, and multidimensional. SHOUT's instantiation of culturally specific programming is therefore quite different from HEA's conceptualization of culturally relevant pedagogy, which privileges the preservation of tradition.

SHOUT's centering of Hmonglish reflects the privileging of youths' dynamic linguistic and cultural forms that are at the heart of culturally sustaining pedagogy (Paris & Alim, 2017). As we described in this chapter, Hmong adults and youth regularly employed a range of linguistic repertoires including code-meshing and code-switching. The opportunity to speak uncensored in their own languages freed youth to express themselves emotionally and intellectually. It allowed youth to tackle complicated social issues related to race, class, gender, sexuality, and immigration. Furthermore, the shared linguistic repertoires fostered a sense of belonging and community among the participants. As the youth noted, the unregulated speech at SHOUT stood in stark contrast to the highly regulated speech demanded by schools, including UHS.

Finally, SHOUT provided a space for the most marginalized SEAA and Black youth in Lakeview to be seen and heard, and to heal. Hmong youth participants in SHOUT came from families that struggled with poverty, health issues, and other traumas. Some of the youth identified as queer, trans, or gender nonconforming, and some of the girls had experienced gender-based violence. Ginwright (2010) points to the social, economic, and political conditions that lead to emotional and physical trauma for urban residents by arguing that violence and poverty in urban communities are social toxins that contribute to despair, hopelessness, anger, and fear. Radical healing involves a process of detoxification where youth name social toxins, shift the blame from an individual level to the system, and engage collective struggle to challenge systemic conditions that create the toxins. In this vein, Hmong youth at SHOUT learn that the everyday violence they experience is rooted in the system. As a multigenerational organization, SHOUT provides Hmong youth with loving mentoring and models for resistance to the everyday violence they face. Naming poverty, the use of Hmonglish, interrogating anti-Blackness, naming and challenging gender-based violence are all ways that SHOUT engages in radical healing.

By connecting to the youths' cultural identities, fostering critical consciousness, and encouraging active social agency, SHOUT is practicing a culturally relevant and culturally sustaining pedagogy that is all too rare in our schools (Ladson-Billings 1995, 2014; Paris, 2012). As a community-based space, SHOUT provides an alternative to traditional schools, one dedicated to challenging "inequality within schools and communities, while fostering spaces for youth of color to build, connect, and thrive" (Baldridge et al., 2017, p. 382). In short, SHOUT offered both critical social capital and radical healing through the formation of a community devoted to the fight for liberation (Ginwright, 2007).

CHAPTER 6

Disrupting Invisibility

The story of Lakeview's Hmong community illustrates the harm of misrecognition—invisibility and hypervisibility—to Hmong youth, and the resilience and agency of the Hmong community in the face of that misrecognition. We began our research just over 10 years after the last large group of Hmong refugees was resettled in the United States, but many educators and non-Hmong students knew very little about Hmong people or how they came to live in the United States. The "secret war" that turned Hmong people into refugees in the United States was treated like old news and it seemed many educators had forgotten about Hmong students. Indeed, some scholars have suggested that the secrecy surrounding the war has contributed to the misrecognition surrounding Hmong refugees (Vang, 2021). Hmong youth were also rendered largely invisible by the predominately Black-and-White racial paradigm in Lakeview that left little space for the racial in-betweenness occupied by Hmong and other Asian American students (Bow, 2010). The Asian American racial category blurred cultural and historical differences among Asian groups, further obscuring Hmong youth. A culture of whiteness dominated UHS and the larger Lakeview community setting the standards for social and academic belonging. Like most students of color, Hmong youth were viewed through the lens of Whiteness and deemed lacking by these standards. Hmong youth were also judged by the standards of the model minority stereotype that expects Asian American students to be high achieving and uncomplaining. Both the culture of Whiteness and the model minority stereotype contributed to deficit-based ideas about Hmong people as unsuccessful Asians, stigmatizing the Hmong identity. Invisibility and hypervisibility drove most Hmong youth to the margins of University Heights High and to the margins of the city.

UHS and other schools in Lakeview have made efforts to be more inclusive and to address racial inequities, and there is some evidence that educators are generally more aware of disparities in opportunities and experiences faced by students of color. Like other school districts across the country, however, Lakeview has defined racial equity in narrow terms, represented by such actions as raising test scores. The fixation on raising achievement has failed to address issues of power, culture, or structure, and our research demonstrates that accountability efforts have exacerbated academic inequalities and feelings of exclusion for Hmong youth (Au, 2010; Lipman, 2017; Turner, 2020). Indeed, the focus on the achievement gap and Lakeview's culture of "niceness" work together to re-center Whiteness (Castagno,

2014, 2019). Neoliberal educational policies regarding the testing of English learners reflect the White gaze (Paris & Alim, 2017) that too often views the language used by youth of color as "unacademic," "improper," "wrong, "ungrammatical," and in need of fixing (Bucholtz et al., 2017).

The most marginalized Hmong students at UHS were long-term English learners who experienced multiple forms of vulnerability, including poverty. These students suffered from a lack of belonging in the school that contributed to feelings that they didn't belong in the larger society. Their status as long-term English learners marked them as academically challenged and as problematic exceptions to the stereotype of Asian Americans as high-achieving model minorities. In other words, Hmong youth at UHS who were long-term English learners were rendered hypervisible as failed model minorities. Given these realities, it is not surprising that many Hmong youth struggled with internalized racism and shame regarding their ethnic backgrounds.

Far from being silent or passive victims, Hmong youth and adults in Lakeview are actively fighting back against inequality through educational advocacy and the formation of community-based educational spaces. Defying dominant assumptions about being a monolithic group, Lakeview's Hmong community represents different political perspectives, priorities, and strategies for resistance. HEA and other middle-class Hmong professionals worked with the Lakeview School District for educational inclusion and equity. As we argued in Chapter 4, middle-class leaders' rhetoric displayed a neoliberal perspective regarding the economic purposes of education whereby the Hmong achievement gap was understood to be a threat to Hmong youths' productive citizenship. Led by HEA, middle-class Hmong professionals were successful in getting the district to recognize the importance of disaggregating data on Hmong students and have been instrumental in advocating for cultural and linguistic representation in schools, including the development of the new Hmong–English bilingual program at one Lakeview elementary school. The goals and aspirations regarding cultural preservation, educational success, and economic mobility expressed by middle-class advocates mirror the expressed goals of mainstream national Hmong organizations. One of the first national Hmong organizations, Hmong National Development (HND), for example, states that their goals are to achieve "prosperity and equality" for Hmong people in the United States through education, policy, and advocacy. HND's politics and those expressed by Lakeview's middle-class Hmong community focus on the politics of recognition and inclusion, which can be seen in Hmong Americans' fight for public recognition of Hmong sacrifices in the "secret war" in Laos and for recognition of Hmong culture in U.S. schools (Xiong, 2022).

In stark contrast, members of SHOUT's community directly identified racial capitalism and imperialism as being endemic to U.S. policies and to the inequalities that Hmong people face in the United States (Melamed, 2015; Vang, 2021). Rejecting the idea that formal education leads to social mobility, SHOUT asserted that racialized economic inequality is pervasive in U.S. capitalism. As our data demonstrates, SHOUT identified anti-Blackness as the foundational and central form of racism in the United States, and the organization is focused on fighting anti-Blackness, including the anti-Blackness reflected in the district's disciplinary policies and use of police in schools. The political differences between the two groups led to some tensions within Lakeview's Hmong community when members of SHOUT accused many in Lakeview's Hmong community, including HEA leaders, of failing to address anti-Black racism. On the other hand, HEA members and many in the larger Hmong community alleged that SHOUT did not focus enough on the issues that affected the Hmong community.

Critical refugee scholar Loan Dao (2020) has observed similar divisions within Southeast Asian American community organizers on a national level, arguing that the differences represent a generational divide in which younger activists are embracing the politics of intersectionality and an explicit critique of U.S. imperialism. We certainly observed that SHOUT leaders advanced the knowledge and leadership of youth in ways that distinguished SHOUT from HEA. Our research also reveals that differences in class position and class aspirations shaped Lakeview's Hmong community leaders' politics, goals, and strategies. In other words, the intersections of race and class along with other identities shape perspectives, priorities, and strategies. Specifically, our research demonstrates that strategies for resistance reflect racial politics, which are connected to class aspirations. Although the Hmong community in Lakeview does not speak with a single voice, the middle-class Hmong professionals are the ones recognized by the school district as being "the community" and "the Hmong leaders." Indeed, who gets to speak for whom among immigrant and diasporic communities is highly contested (Lukose, 2007). As our data clearly shows, minoritized communities do not speak with a singular or monolithic voice and school districts need to be attuned to diversity within communities.

Although HEA and SHOUT represent two very different approaches to resistance, both groups turned to community-based education as way to achieve educational self-determination for Hmong students in Lakeview. Both groups shared a concern regarding the relative lack of culturally and linguistically responsive programming in the schools and emphasized the importance of Hmong culture and arts in their respective community-based educational programming. As illustrated in Chapters 4 and 5, HEA and SHOUT developed very different educational programming that reflected their respective political commitments. While HEA emphasized more traditional Hmong arts, SHOUT included both traditional arts and more hybrid forms of art embraced by youth. While HEA emphasized academic achievement, SHOUT emphasized political education for resistance. Like other nonprofit community-based educational spaces, SHOUT and HEA had to negotiate the nonprofit industrial complex to access funding to support youth programming (Baldridge, 2019). As we mentioned in Chapter 5, for example, SHOUT's relationship with the foundation that funded their initial work was fraught with political tension.

Interestingly, both HEA and SHOUT largely rejected an identification with the pan-Asian racial category. During the 1960s, Asian American activists coined the term "Asian American" to stress common experiences with marginalization and colonization, and to call for global solidarity with Asian ethnic groups (Espiritu, 1992). From its inception, however, the Asian American racial category has been unstable, and the growing diversity among Asian Americans after the influx of post-1965 Asian immigrants and post-1975 Southeast Asian refugees has further challenged the relevance of the category. Both HEA and SHOUT criticized the Asian American category for failing to recognize the unique history, culture, and experiences of Hmong people in the United States. HEA members occasionally used the terms Southeast Asian or Asian American, but worked primarily to maintain and preserve a distinct Hmong identity. Their stance is that of the majority of Hmong American leaders across the country. For example, during their fight against federal welfare reform in the 1990s, Hmong Americans in California joined with pan-Asian organizations but resisted an Asian identity (Xiong, 2022). SHOUT members were openly resistant to a pan-Asian identity, arguing that they shared more in common with the Black community. In fact, SHOUT members stereotyped East Asian Americans as model minorities, assuming that Chinese American and other East Asian American students were all high-achieving students from relatively wealthy families. At UHS, the Hmong student leaders of Asian Club attempted to build a pan-Asian group in order to increase club membership and the visibility of the group, but had little success. East Asian students were reluctant to embrace panethnic identification with Hmong students and thought of the Asian Club as a Hmong group. The responses of adults and youth to Asian American panethnicity raise questions about the ongoing usefulness of the category for political action and solidarity.

Some readers may be tempted to characterize the stories told in this book as being narrowly focused on one small group in one community, but we argue that our data demonstrates the relationship between particular/local/micro level issues and broader/macro level issues (Bartlett & Vavrus, 2017; Weis & Fine, 2012). The Hmong youth and adults in our study negotiate their lives within larger social, economic, political, and historical contexts. The challenges both HEA and SHOUT faced getting funding for their programs demonstrate the interconnected webs between ethnic communities and the larger society. Hmong youths' academic experiences and opportunities in schools are shaped by district, state, and national-level policies and assumptions regarding testing and accountability. Our research also shows that the broader social context influenced Hmong leaders' educational advocacy, including their strategies and the outcomes. As discussed in Chapter 4, HEA used neoliberal discourses regarding the links between cultural preservation, academic success, and economic self-sufficiency in their educational advocacy. Although the middle-class Hmong professionals have had their share of victories, they have also encountered some setbacks. For example, they wanted the district to develop Hmong dual immersion programs like the Spanish dual immersion programs in the school district but were offered a Hmong developmental bilingual education (DBE) program at one elementary school. Many Hmong people feared that the DBE program was second-class, and others suspected that the district didn't support a Hmong dual immersion program because they assumed that non-Hmong parents wouldn't be interested in having their children learn Hmong, evidence that Hmong language and culture were not valued by the dominant group.

Lakeview's Hmong youth and community leaders must contend with both the dominant Black-and-White racial paradigm that shapes conversations about race and racism in Lakeview and across the nation, and the Asian American panethnic category that erases diversity among those assigned to the Asian American group. School-level understandings about race are influenced by the dominant Black-and-White paradigm of race, and so focus primarily on the racialized achievement gap between Black and White students. As we discussed in Chapter 4, middle-class Hmong leaders critiqued dominant racial discourses that framed educational equity in Black-and-White terms and worked to create a space for the Hmong community, but their strategies for resisting assimilation and demanding recognition leave the racial hierarchy largely intact. In contrast, our profile of SHOUT in Chapter 5 revealed that their racial politics centered around resisting anti-Blackness. While we agree that attention to anti-Blackness is long overdue, our research illustrates the importance of recognizing race and racism beyond Black and White. Hmong youth and other Asian American youth need a historical and political context for understanding anti-Asian taunts like "Go back to your country." Finally, like other Hmong American communities across the United States, Lakeview's Hmong American community continues to grapple with their refugee experience (e.g., resettlement policies) and the war that forced their migration to the United States. SHOUT leaders and other progressive Southeast Asian American organizers have highlighted the way resettlement policies left many Southeast Asian American refugees vulnerable to intergenerational poverty, racism, and exclusion.

DISRUPTING INVISIBILITY THROUGH CULTURALLY SUSTAINING PEDAGOGY

We believe that by conducting fieldwork with/on Hmong youth in both formal and informal educational spaces we gained a fuller understanding of Hmong youths' concerns, strengths, resources, interests, and aspirations. Although public schools and community-based educational spaces have different missions and are accountable to different people, we suggest that the knowledge we gained from observing youth in CBES and talking to Hmong community leaders and youth workers in CBES offer insights into how schools might better serve Hmong youth. Our data from both the Hmong Meskas Summer Camp and SHOUT's youth programming points to the link between cultural recognition and a sense of belonging. Both community-based educational spaces engaged in culturally relevant educational programming that established a culture of belonging among the youth, and, in turn, this fostered participation, engagement, and learning.

How can schools foster a sense of belonging for Hmong youth? We argue that culturally sustaining pedagogy offers promising insights for how schools might support and recognize Hmong youth and create a sense of belonging. The idea of culturally sustaining pedagogy has been advanced by Paris and Alim (Alim & Paris, 2017; Paris, 2012; Paris & Alim, 2014) and extends the scholarship on asset-based approaches to pedagogy such as culturally relevant pedagogy (Ladson-Billings, 1995). Culturally sustaining pedagogy "seeks to perpetuate and foster—to sustain—linguistic, literate, and cultural pluralism as part of schooling for positive social transformation" (Alim & Paris, 2017, p. 1). Although neither of the community-based educational spaces in our study described their pedagogy as being influenced by culturally sustaining pedagogy (CSP), both programs reflected aspects of CSP's central tenets, including a connection to Hmong culture, history, and arts. HEA's summer camp focused on teaching more traditional elements of culture and arts, while SHOUT included both traditional arts and youth culture. Schools can support and sustain culture and arts through both the formal curriculum and in cocurricular activities.

Our suggestions for a culturally sustaining pedagogy for Hmong and other SEAA youth also build off the earlier work that Stacey did with Daniel Walsh on culturally sustaining pedagogy for immigrant youth. There they argued that a socially just, culturally sustaining pedagogy for immigrant youth should recognize and respect students' evolving and hybrid identities, foster a justice-oriented citizenship, and encourage critical dialogues around race and racism (Lee & Walsh, 2017). Research has demonstrated that becoming a racialized subject is central to immigrant youths' incorporation into the United States (Deaux, 2006; Lee, 2005, 2009). Youth from immigrant and refugee backgrounds cannot escape the racial context of this country, and therefore culturally sustaining pedagogy for immigrant and refugee youth must provide students with opportunities for deep and critical conversations about race, racialization, and racism. These discussions should include chances to critically reflect on their own racial positioning and the larger racial context. For the Hmong youth in our study, this would require attention to the racialization of Asian Americans, Southeast Asian Americans, and Hmong people, and opportunities to critically reflect on anti-Blackness and other expressions of racism. Attention to these issues in the schools would reflect some of what SHOUT members want from them.

Conversations about race, racialization, and racism should be linked to discussions of immigration, including refugee policies. How have issues related to race been implicated in debates about immigration throughout U.S. history? What are the similarities and differences between people categorized as immigrants and those categorized as refugees? The children and grandchildren of Hmong and other Southeast Asian refugees need access to their specific refugee history in order to make sense of the conditions of their lives. For our Hmong youth participants, this would mean support to examine the conditions that led to the migration of their families, including the war and refugee resettlement policies. All students, not just those from refugee backgrounds, would benefit from understanding the political context that creates refugees. In fact, the scholarship on civic education has long argued that opportunities to discuss complex and controversial issues, such as policies regarding immigration and refugees, are essential to supporting all students in developing skills to be engaged citizens (Hess, 2009; Zimmerman & Robertson, 2017). Our data shows that both HEA and SHOUT want youth to understand their refugee backgrounds. Furthermore, our data strongly suggests that both groups want Hmong youth to become civically engaged.

The recent surge in anti-Asian racism has fueled a movement to mandate the teaching of Asian American history in K–12 education. Illinois and New Jersey have successfully passed such legislation and New York has a bill pending that would require the teaching of Asian American content (Liu, 2022). As we mentioned in Chapter 4, there is an ongoing effort in Wisconsin to pass legislation to require teaching about Hmong Americans and other Asian Americans, Pacific Islanders, and South Asian Americans/Desi Americans. Middle-class Hmong American leaders in Lakeview have long supported this type of legislation, and we have learned that SHOUT has also been involved in supporting these bills in the last 2 years. We agree that legislation requiring the teaching of Asian American history in K–12 schools would be an important step in signaling support for Asian American communities. A culturally sustaining pedagogy that challenges the misrecognition of Asian Americans, however, will require more than just legislation. Schools need access to Asian American curriculum and teachers need meaningful training on how to address Asian American issues. Community-based organizations like HEA and SHOUT can serve as important resources for school districts that are working to incorporate Asian American content. Importantly, we argue that youth should be encouraged and supported in being active agents in their education by identifying and exploring topics of relevance to them. Research has demonstrated that youth participatory action research (YPAR) has the potential to foster intellectual curiosity, academic skills, and civic engagement, empowerment, and belonging (Cammarota & Fine, 2008; Dyrness & Sepulveda, 2020; Rubin, Ayala, & Zaal, 2017; Walsh, 2018). Daniel Walsh (2018) argues that "YPAR offers young people the opportunity to identify heartfelt and real issues in their lives and engages them in the design and implementation of sophisticated social science research projects" (p. 128). A recent PAR study with Hmong college students found that student-led PAR provided an opportunity to engage in "counter-invisibility" work through the creation of counter-narratives (Smolarek et al., 2021).

As discussed in Chapters 3 and 5, many Hmong youth in Lakeview are most comfortable speaking Hmonglish, and a culturally sustaining approach to language encourages educators to embrace Hmonglish rather than seeing it as a sign of deficiency. As many critical language scholars have argued, even asset-based language policies privilege standard forms of language and emphasize language separation (García & Lin, 2017). Drawing on the scholarship on code-meshing and translanguaging, culturally sustaining pedagogy demands that we recognize the strength and linguistic flexibility embodied in Hmonglish (Alim & Paris, 2017; Bucholtz et al, 2017; Rosa & Flores, 2017). As Bucholtz and colleagues (2017) explain, a culturally sustaining approach to language recognizes that youth from "economically, racially, and/or linguistically marginalized communities, are in fact innovative, flexible, and sophisticated language users" (p. 44). Opportunities to engage in rigorous academic classes and conversations should not be limited to those who master and perform standard English. Our fieldwork at SHOUT demonstrates clearly that speakers of Hmonglish are critical and creative thinkers capable of grappling with complex issues surrounding race, class, gender identity, and refugee status, among other issues. Once again, the arts can play an important role in fostering Hmong youths' linguistic flexibility. There is a wealth of Hmong

American poetry, fiction, and spoken word that could be drawn on and students could also be encouraged to write their own stories using their own languages.

We recognize that our suggestions for culturally sustaining pedagogy may sound overwhelming, particularly in the current political context of 2022 when many conservatives are calling for a ban on the teaching of race issues and racial history. Those who engage in these attacks wrongly assert that critical conversations about race encourage divisiveness. Silence and denial of racism, including anti-Asian racism, only serves to perpetuate racism. As we have argued throughout this book, lack of recognition and invisibility are forms of exclusion and status inequality that harm Hmong American youth. Erasing the histories and experiences of Hmong Americans threatens belonging. A culturally sustaining pedagogy for Hmong and other Southeast Asian American youth has the potential to foster a sense of belonging and critical citizenship while simultaneously supporting academic skills among Hmong and other Southeast Asian American students.

While our book has focused on the harm of invisibility/hypervisibility done to Hmong youth, we will conclude by arguing that misrecognition also hurts the broader society. The story of how Hmong refugees came to the United States is not just a Hmong story. It is a quintessentially American story. The fact that many in the dominant society don't know who Hmong people are or how they came to live in the United States reflects a collective amnesia that harms us all. The experiences of Hmong and other Southeast Asian American refugees have much to teach us about how refugees are created by political conditions. As critical Hmong scholar Ma Vang (2021) writes, "The refugee, therefore, is a critical subject for understanding the human impact of our global order or unending wars and ongoing state repression" (p. 10). Hmong and other Southeast Asian American refugees were created by U.S. foreign policy and uncritical assumptions about American exceptionalism. All students, including Hmong and other Southeast Asian Americans, need to learn this history. Hmong and all other students need opportunities to consider why and how Hmong refugees have been rendered invisible, and to examine the consequences of the silence and secrecy that perpetuates this invisibility. Critical understandings of their history, migration, and issues related to power and inequality are crucial to the development of critical and engaged citizenship for Hmong and non-Hmong students (Dyrness & Abu El-Haj, 2019; Fabricant & Fine, 2013, Hursh & Martina, 2003; Jaffe-Walter et al., 2019; Taylor, 2021).

References

Alba, R. (2004). *Language assimilation today: Bilingualism persists more than in the past, but English still dominates* (Working Paper No.11). Center for Comparative Immigration Studies, University of California–San Diego.

Alim, H. S., & Paris, D. (2017). What is culturally sustaining pedagogy and why does it matter? In D. Paris & H. S Alim (Eds.), *Culturally sustaining pedagogies: Teaching and learning for justice in a changing world* (pp. 1–21). Teachers College Press.

Alim, H. S., & Smitherman, G. (2012). *Articulate while Black: Barack Obama, language, and race in the U.S.* Oxford University Press.

Apple, M. W. (2004). Creating difference: Neo-liberalism, neo-conservatism and the politics of educational reform. *Educational Policy, 18*(1), 12–44.

Apple, M. W., & Au, W. (2009). Politics, theory, and reality in critical pedagogy. In R. Cowen & A. M. Kazamias (Eds.), *International handbook of comparative education* (pp. 991–1007). Springer.

Au, W. (2010). *Unequal by design: High-stakes testing and the standardization of inequality.* Routledge.

Au, W. (2016). Meritocracy 2.0: High-stakes, standardized testing as a racial project of neoliberal multiculturalism. *Educational Policy, 30*(1), 39–62.

Baldridge, B. J. (2014). Relocating the deficit: Reimagining Black youth in neoliberal times. *American Educational Research Journal, 51*(3), 440–472.

Baldridge, B. J. (2018). On educational advocacy and cultural work: Situating community-based youth work[ers] in broader educational discourse. *Teachers College Record, 120*(2), 1–28.

Baldridge, B. J. (2019). *Reclaiming community: Race and the uncertain future of youth work.* Stanford University Press.

Baldridge, B. J. (2020). The youthwork paradox: A case for studying the complexity of community-based youth work in education research. *Educational Researcher, 49*(8), 618–625.

Baldridge, B. J., Beck, N., Medina, J. C., & Reeves, M. A. (2017). Toward a new understanding of community-based education: The role of community-based educational spaces in disrupting inequality for minoritized youth. *Review of Research in Education, 41*(1), 381–402.

Bartlett, L., & Vavrus, F. (2017). *Rethinking case study research: A comparative approach.* Routledge.

Bernhardt, P. E. (2013). The Advancement Via Individual Determination (AVID) program: Providing cultural capital and college access to low-income students. *School Community Journal, 23*(1), 203–222.

Birks, M., Chapman, Y., & Francis, K. (2008). Memoing in qualitative research: Probing data and processes. *Journal of Research in Nursing, 13*(1), 68–75.

Bonilla-Silva, E., & Dietrich, D. R. (2009). The Latin Americanization of U.S. race relations. In E. N. Glenn (Ed.), *Shades of difference* (pp. 40–60). Stanford University Press.

Bourdieu, P. (1991). *Language and symbolic power.* Harvard University Press.

Bow, L. (2010). *Partly colored: Asian Americans and racial anomaly in the segregated south.* NYU Press.

Bowles, S., & Gintis, H. (1976). *Schooling in capitalist America: Educational reform and the contradictions of economic life.* Haymarket Books.

Braa, D., & Callero, P. (2006). Critical pedagogy and classroom praxis. *Teaching Sociology, 34*(4), 357–369.

Brown, A. L., & Donnor, J. K. (2011). Toward a new narrative on Black males, education, and public policy. *Race Ethnicity and Education, 14*(1), 17–32.

Bucholtz, M., Casillas, D. I., & Lee, J. S. (2017). Language and culture as sustenance. In H. S. Alim & D. Paris (Eds.), *Culturally sustaining pedagogies: Teaching and learning for justice in a changing world* (pp. 43–59). Teachers College Press.

Budiman, A., & Ruiz, N. G. (2021, April 29). *Key facts about Asian Americans, a diverse and growing population.* Pew Research Center. https://www.pewresearch.org/fact-tank/2017/09/08/key-facts-about-asian-americans

Burawoy, M. (1998). The extended case method. *Sociological Theory, 16*(1), 4–33.

Callahan, R. (2005). Tracking and high school English learners: Limiting opportunity to learn. *American Educational Research Journal, 42*(2), 305–328.

Callahan, R., Wilkinson, L., Muller, C., & Frisco, M. (2009). ESL placement and schools: Effects on immigrant achievement. *Educational Policy, 23*(2), 355–384.

Callahan, R., Wilkinson, L., & Muller, C. (2010). Academic achievement and course taking among language minority youth in US schools: Effects of ESL placement. *Educational Evaluation and Policy Analysis, 32*(1), 84–117.

Cammarota, J., & Fine, M. (2008). *Revolutionizing education: Youth participatory action research in motion.* Routledge.

Canagarajah, S. (2011). Codemeshing in academic writing: Identifying teachable strategies of translanguaging. *The Modern Language Journal, 95*(3), 401–417. https://doi.org/10.1111/j.1540-4781.2011.01207.x

Caplan, N. (1985). Southeast Asian refugee self-sufficiency study. Office of Refugee Resettlement, U.S. Department of Health and Human Services.

Caplan, N., Choy, M. H., & Whitmore, J. K. (1991). *Children of the boat people: A study of educational success.* University of Michigan Press.

Castagno, A. E. (2014). *Educated in whiteness: Good intentions and diversity in schools.* University of Minnesota Press.

Castagno, A. E. (Ed.). (2019). *The price of nice: How good intentions maintain educational inequity.* University of Minnesota Press.

Chanbonpin, K. D. (2015). Between Black and White: The coloring of Asian Americans. *Washington University Global Studies Law Review, 14*(4), 637–663. https://openscholarship.wustl.edu/law_globalstudies/vol14/iss4/10

Chhuon, V., & Hudley, C. (2010). Asian American ethnic options: How Cambodian students negotiate ethnic identities in a U.S. urban school. *Anthropology & Education Quarterly, 41*(4), 341–359.

Chubb, J. E., & Moe, T. M. (1990). *Politics, markets, and America's schools.* Brookings Institution Press.

Collins, J. (2009). Social reproduction in classrooms and schools. *Annual Review of Anthropology, 38*, 33–48.

Conchas, G. Q., & Perez, C. C. (2003). Surfing the "model minority" wave of success: How the school context shapes distinct experiences among Vietnamese youth. *New Directions for Youth Development, 2003*(100), 41–56.

Cramer, K. J. (2016). *The politics of resentment: Rural consciousness in Wisconsin and the rise of Scott Walker.* University of Chicago Press.

Creese, A., Bhatt, A., Bhojani, N., & Martin, P. (2008). Fieldnotes in team ethnography: Researching complementary schools. *Qualitative Research, 8*(2), 197–215.

Cucchiara, M. (2008). Re-branding urban schools: Urban revitalization, social status, and marketing public schools to the upper middle class. *Journal of Education Policy, 23*(2), 165–179.

Cummins, J. (1979). *Cognitive/academic language proficiency, linguistic interdependence, the optimum age question and some other matters* (Working Papers on Bilingualism, No. 19). Ontario Institute for Studies in Education.

Cushing, I. (2020). 'Say it like the Queen': The standard language ideology and language policy making in English primary schools. *Language, Culture and Curriculum, 34*(3), 1–16.

Dao, L. T. (2020). *Generation Rising: A new politics of Southeast Asian American activism.* Eastwind Books of Berkeley.

Deaux, K. (2006). *To be an immigrant.* Russell Sage Foundation.

Delgado-Gaitan, C. (2004). *Involving Latino families in schools: Raising student achievement through home-school partnerships.* Corwin Press.

DePouw, C. (2012). When culture implies deficit: Placing race at the center of Hmong American education. *Race Ethnicity and Education, 15*(2), 223–239.

Desimone, L. (1999). Linking parent involvement with student achievement: Do race and income matter? *The Journal of Educational Research, 93*(1), 11–30.

DeWalt, K., & DeWalt, B. R. (2010). *Participant observation: A guide for fieldworkers.* Rowman Altamira.

Dhingra, P. (2020). *Hyper education: Why good schools, good grades, and good behavior are not enough.* NYU Press.

DiCerbo, P. A., Anstrom, K. A., Baker, L. L., & Rivera, C. (2014). A review of the literature on teaching academic English to English language learners. *Review of Educational Research, 84*(3), 446–482.

Dixon, A. R., & Telles, E. E. (2017). Skin color and colorism: Global research, concepts, and measurement. *Annual Review of Sociology, 43*, 405–424.

Dumas, M. J. (2014). 'Losing an arm': Schooling as a site of black suffering. *Race Ethnicity and Education, 17*(1), 1–29.

Dumas, M. J. (2016). Against the dark: Antiblackness in education policy and discourse. *Theory Into Practice, 55*(1), 11–19.

Dyrness, A., & Abu El-Haj, T. R. (2020). Reflections on the field: The democratic citizenship formation of transnational youth. *Anthropology & Education Quarterly, 51*(2), 165–177.

Dyrness, A., & Sepúlveda, E., III. (2020). *Border thinking: Latinx youth decolonizing citizenship.* University of Minnesota Press.

Eckert, P. (1989). *Jocks and burnouts: Social categories and identity in the high school.* Teachers College Press.

Emerson, R. M., Fretz, R. I., & Shaw, L. L. (2011). *Writing ethnographic fieldnotes.* University of Chicago Press.

Espiritu, Y. L. (1992). *Asian American panethnicity: Bridging institutions and identities* (Vol. 231). Temple University Press.

Espiritu, Y. L. (2006). Toward a critical refugee study: The Vietnamese refugee subject in U.S. scholarship. *Journal of Vietnamese Studies, 1*(1–2), 410–433.

Fabricant, M., & Fine, M. (2013). The changing politics of education: Privatization and the dispossessed lives left behind. Paradigm.

Falk, T. (2022). Wisconsin school boards support Asians and Native American students. *Wisconsin Examiner.* https://wisconsinexaminer.com/2022/02/01/wisconsin-school -boards-support-asians-and-native-american-students/

Fanon, F. (2008). *Black skins, white masks.* Grove Press.

Feagin, J. (2013). *Systemic racism: A theory of oppression.* Routledge.

Ferguson, A. A. (2000). *Bad boys: Public schools in the making of black masculinity.* University of Michigan Press.

Fishman, J. A. (2014). Three hundred-plus years of heritage language education in the United States. In T. G. Wiley, J. K. Peyton, D. Christian, S. C. K. Moore, & N. Liu (Eds.), *Handbook of heritage, community, and Native American languages in the United States* (pp. 50–58). Routledge.

Flanagan, C. A., & Christens, B. D. (2011). Youth civic development: Historical context and emerging issues. *New Directions for Child and Adolescent Development, 2011*(134), 1–9.

Flores, N. (2016). A tale of two visions: Hegemonic whiteness and bilingual education. *Educational Policy, 30*(1), 13–38.

Flores, N. (2019). Translanguaging into raciolinguistic ideologies: A personal reflection on the legacy of Ofelia García. *Journal of Multilingual Education Research, 9*(1), 5, 45–60.

Flores, N. (2020). From academic language to language architecture: Challenging raciolinguistic ideologies in research and practice. *Theory Into Practice, 59*(1), 22–31.

Flores, N., & Beardsmore, H. B. (2015). Programs and structures in bilingual and multilingual education. In W. E. Wright, S. Boun, & O. García (Eds.), *Handbook of bilingual and multilingual education* (pp. 205–222). Wiley.

Flores, N., Kleyn, T., & Menken, K. (2015). Looking holistically in a climate of partiality: Identities of students labeled long-term English language learners. *Journal of Language, Identity & Education, 14*(2), 113–132.

Flowers, K. S. (2019). Resisting and rewriting English-only policies: Navigating multilingual, raciolinguistic, and translingual approaches to language advocacy. *Literacy in Composition Studies, 7*(1).

Fraser, N. (2009). *Scales of justice: Reimagining political space in a globalizing world* (Vol. 31). Columbia University Press.

Fraser, N., Honneth, A., & Golb, J. (2003). *Redistribution or recognition?: A political-philosophical exchange.* Verso.

Freire, P. (1994). *Pedagogy of hope.* New York: Continuum.

Freire, P. (1996). *Pedagogy of the oppressed* (rev. ed.). Continuum.

García, O. (2009a). Education, multilingualism and translanguaging in the 21st century. In T. Skutnabb-Kangas, R. Phillipson, A. K. Mohanty, & M. Panda (Eds.), *Social justice through multilingual education* (pp. 140–158). Multilingual Matters.

García, O. (2009b). Emergent bilinguals and TESOL: What's in a name? *Tesol Quarterly, 43*(2), 322–326.

García, O. (2011). *Bilingual education in the 21st century: A global perspective.* John Wiley & Sons.

García, O., & Kleifgen, J. A. (2010). *Educating emergent bilinguals: Policies, programs, and practices for English language learners.* Teachers College Press.

García, O., & Lin, A. M. (2017). Translanguaging in bilingual education. In O. García, A. Lin, & S. May, *Bilingual and multilingual education* (3rd ed., pp. 117–130). Springer.

García, O., & Solorza, C. R. (2020). Academic language and the minoritization of US bilingual Latinx students. *Language and Education, 35*(6), 505–521.

Garza, A. (2014). A herstory of the # BlackLivesMatter movement. https://thefeministwire .com/2014/10/blacklivesmatter-2/

Ginwright, S. A. (2007). Black youth activism and the role of critical social capital in Black community organizations. *American Behavioral Scientist, 51*(3), 403–418.

Ginwright, S. A. (2010). Peace out to revolution! Activism among African American youth: An argument for radical healing. *Young, 18*(1), 77–96.

Ginwright, S. A., & Cammarota, J. (2007). Youth activism in the urban community: Learning critical civic praxis within community organizations. *International Journal of Qualitative Studies in Education, 20*(6), 693–710.

Gonzales, R. G. (2015). *Lives in limbo.* University of California Press.

Goto, S. G., Gee, G. C., & Takeuchi, D. T. (2002). Strangers still? The experience of discrimination among Chinese Americans. *Journal of Community Psychology, 30*(2), 211–224.

Haines, D. W. (1982). Southeast Asian refugees in the United States: The interaction of kinship and public policy. *Anthropological Quarterly, 55*(3), 170–181.

Harvey, D. (2007). *A brief history of neoliberalism.* Oxford University Press.

Heath, S. B. (1983). Ways with words: Language, life, and work in communities and classrooms. Cambridge University Press.

Hess, D. E. (2009). *Controversy in the classroom: The democratic power of discussion.* Routledge.

Hill, K., & Scott, J. (2017). A critical look at parental choice. *The Wiley handbook of school choice.* John Wiley.

Hing, B. O. (2012). *Defining America: Through immigration policy.* Temple University Press.

Hunter, M. (2007). The persistent problem of colorism: Skin tone, status, and inequality. *Sociology Compass, 1*(1), 237–254.

Hursh, D. (2007). Assessing No Child Left Behind and the rise of neoliberal education policies. *American Educational Research Journal, 44*(3), 493–518.

Hursh, D., & Martina, C. A. (2003). Neoliberalism and schooling in the U.S.: How state and federal government education policies perpetuate inequality. *Journal for Critical Education Policy Studies, 1*(2), 1–13.

Irizarry, J. G., & Brown, T. M. (2014). Humanizing research in dehumanizing spaces: The challenges and opportunities of conducting participatory action research with youth in schools. In D. Paris & M. T. Winn (Eds.), *Humanizing research: Decolonizing qualitative inquiry with youth and communities* (pp. 63–80). Sage.

Jaffe-Walter, R., Miranda, C. P., & Lee, S. J. (2019). From protest to protection: Navigating politics with immigrant students in uncertain times. *Harvard Educational Review, 89*(2), 251–276.

Jalao, L. C. (2010). Looking *Gran Torino* in the eye: A review. *Journal of Southeast Asian American Education and Advancement, 5*(1), 15.

Jew, V. (2014). "It falls into 'Who are they?'": The cultural interface of Southeast Asian refugee policy making, 1975–1980. *Asian American Policy Review, 25*, 10.

Kanno, Y., & Harklau, L. (Eds.). (2012). *Linguistic minority students go to college: Preparation, access, and persistence.* Routledge.

Katz, M. B. (2013). *The undeserving poor: America's enduring confrontation with poverty: Fully updated and revised.* Oxford University Press.

Keddie, A. (2012). Schooling and social justice through the lenses of Nancy Fraser. *Critical Studies in Education, 53*(3), 263–279.

Kim, C. J. (2000). *Bitter fruit: The politics of Black-Korean conflict in New York City.* Yale University Press.

Kim, C. J. (2018). Are Asians the new Blacks? Affirmative action, anti-blackness, and the 'sociometry' of race. *Du Bois Review: Social Science Research on Race, 15*(2), 217–244.

Kim, S. Y., Wang, Y., Deng, S., Alvarez, R., & Li, J. (2011). Accent, perpetual foreigner stereotype, and perceived discrimination as indirect links between English proficiency and depressive symptoms in Chinese American adolescents. *Developmental Psychology, 47*(1), 289.

Kirshner, B. (2007). Introduction: Youth activism as a context for learning and development. *American Behavioral Scientist, 51*(3), 367–379.

Koyama, J. P. (2011). Generating, comparing, manipulating, categorizing: Reporting, and sometimes fabricating data to comply with No Child Left Behind mandates. *Journal of Education Policy, 26*(5), 701–720.

Koyama, J. P., & Menken, K. (2013). Emergent bilinguals: Framing students as statistical data? *Bilingual Research Journal, 36*(1), 82–99.

Kwon, S. A. (2013). *Uncivil youth.* Duke University Press.

Kymlicka, W. (1995). *Multicultural citizenship: A liberal theory of minority rights.* Clarendon.

Kymlicka, W. (2013). Neoliberal multiculturalism? In P. Hall & M. Lamont (Eds.), *Social resilience in the neoliberal era* (pp. 99–126). Cambridge University Press.

Labaree, D. F. (1997). Public goods, private goods: The American struggle over educational goals. *American Educational Research Journal, 34*(1), 39–81.

Ladson-Billings, G. (1995). Toward a theory of culturally relevant pedagogy. *American Educational Research Journal, 32*(3), 465–491.

Ladson-Billings, G. (1998). Just what is critical race theory and what's it doing in a nice field like education? *International Journal of Qualitative Studies in Education, 11*(1), 7–24.

Ladson-Billings, G. (2012). Through a glass darkly: The persistence of race in education research & scholarship. *Educational Researcher, 41*(4), 115–120.

Ladson-Billings, G. (2014). *Culturally relevant pedagogy 2.0: aka the remix. Harvard Educational Review, 84*(1), 74–84.

La Gorce, T. (2020, April 5). Chinese-Americans, facing abuse, unite to aid hospitals in coronavirus battle. *The New York Times.* https://www.nytimes.com/2020/04/05/nyregion/coronavirus-chinese-americans-supplies.html

Lareau, A. (2000). *Home advantage: Social class and parental intervention in elementary education.* Rowman & Littlefield.

Lareau, A. (2011). *Unequal childhoods.* University of California Press.

Lee, E. (2003). *At America's gates: Chinese immigration during the exclusion era, 1882–1943.* University of North Carolina Press.

Lee, G. Y., & Tapp, N. (2010). *Culture and customs of the Hmong.* ABC-CLIO.

Lee, J., & Zhou, M. (2015). *The Asian American achievement paradox.* Russell Sage Foundation.

Lee, R. G. (1999). *Orientals: Asian Americans in popular culture.* Temple University Press.

Lee, S. J. (2005). *Up against Whiteness: Race, school, and immigrant youth.* Teachers College Press.

Lee, S. J. (2009). *Unraveling the "model minority" stereotype: Listening to Asian American youth.* Teachers College Press.

Lee, S. J. (2015). Immigrant stories: The how, when, and where of representation. In K. Bhopal (Ed.), *Researching marginalized groups.* Routledge.

Lee, S. J. (2017). The (in)flexibility of racial policies: Chinese Americans in the Jim Crow South. In A. Castagno & T. McCarty (Eds.), *The anthropology of education policy: Ethnographic inquiries into policy as sociocultural process* (pp. 125–138). Routledge.

Lee, S. J., & Hong, J. J. (2020). Model minorities and perpetual foreigners: Stereotypes of Asian Americans. In J. T. Nadler & E. C. Voyles (Eds.), *Stereotypes: The incidence and impacts of bias* (pp. 165–174). Praeger.

Lee, S. J. & Kumashiro, K. (2005). *A report on the status of Asian Americans and Pacific Islanders in education: Beyond the "model minority" stereotype.* National Education Association.

Lee, S. J., Park, E., & Wong, J. H. S. (2017). Racialization, schooling, and becoming American: Asian American experiences. *Educational Studies, 53*(5), 492–510.

Lee, S. J., & Walsh, D. (2017). Socially just, culturally sustaining pedagogy for diverse immigrant youth. In D. Paris & H. S. Alim (Eds.), *Culturally sustaining pedagogies: Teaching and learning for justice in a changing world* (pp. 191–206). Teachers College Press.

Lee, S. J., Xiong, C. P., Pheng, L. M., & Neng Vang, M. (2020). "Asians for Black lives, not Asians for Asians": Building Southeast Asian American and Black solidarity. *Anthropology & Education Quarterly, 51*(4), 405–421.

Leonardo, Z. (2002). The souls of white folk: Critical pedagogy, whiteness studies, and globalization discourse. *Race ethnicity and education, 5*(1), 29–50.

Levinson, B. A., Sutton, M., & Winstead, T. (2009). Education policy as a practice of power: Theoretical tools, ethnographic methods, democratic options. *Educational Policy, 23*(6), 767–795.

Lewis, A. E., & Diamond, J. B. (2015). *Despite the best intentions: How racial inequality thrives in good schools.* Oxford University Press.

Lipman, P. (2013). *The new political economy of urban education: Neoliberalism, race, and the right to the city.* Routledge.

Lipman, P. (2017). The landscape of education "Reform" in Chicago: Neoliberalism meets a grassroots movement. *Education Policy Analysis Archives, 25*(54).

Lippi-Green, R. (2012). *English with an accent: Language, ideology and discrimination in the United States.* Routledge.

Liu, M.C-M. (2022). States are mandating Asian American history lessons to stop bigotry. *Washington Post.* https://www.washingtonpost.com/education/2022/05/20/asian-american-history-schools-aapi/

Lo, B. (2017). Gender, culture, and the educational choices of second generation Hmong American girls. *Journal of Southeast Asian American Education and Advancement, 12*(1), 4.

Loewen, J. W. (1988). *The Mississippi Chinese: Between black and white.* Waveland Press.

Lopez, G., Ruiz, N. G., & Patten, E. (2017). *Key facts about Asian Americans, a diverse and growing population.* Pew Research Center.

Lorenzo, M. K., Frost, A. K., & Reinherz, H. Z. (2000). Social and emotional functioning of older Asian American adolescents. *Child and Adolescent Social Work Journal, 17*(4), 289–304.

Louie, V. S. (2004). *Compelled to excel: Immigration, education, and opportunity among Chinese Americans*. Stanford University Press.

Lubienski, C. (2005). Public schools in marketized environments: Shifting incentives and unintended consequences of competition-based educational reforms. *American Journal of Education, 111*(4), 464–486.

Lukose, R. A. (2007). The difference that diaspora makes: Thinking through the anthropology of immigrant education in the United States. *Anthropology & Education Quarterly, 38*(4), 405–418.

Macedo, D. S. (2009). Foreword. In Sheila L. Macrine (Ed.), *Critical Pedagogy in Uncertain Times: Hope and possibilities*. Palgrave Macmillan.

Maeda, D. J. (2005). Black panthers, red guards, and Chinamen: Constructing Asian American identity through performing blackness, 1969-1972. *American Quarterly, 57*(4), 1079–1103.

Masuoka, N., & Junn, J. (2013). *The politics of belonging: Race, public opinion, and immigration*. University of Chicago Press.

Mathews, J. (2015). *Question everything: The rise of AVID as America's largest college readiness program*. John Wiley & Sons.

Matias, C. E. (2013). Check yo'self before you wreck yo'self and our kids: Counterstories from culturally responsive White teachers? . . . to culturally responsive White teachers! *Interdisciplinary Journal of Teaching and Learning, 3*(2), 68–81.

Melamed, J. (2006). The spirit of neoliberalism: From racial liberalism to neoliberal multiculturalism. *Social text, 24*(4), 1–24.

Melamed, J. (2015). Racial capitalism. *Critical Ethnic Studies, 1*(1), 76–85.

Menken, K., Kleyn, T., & Chae, N. (2012). Spotlight on "long-term English language learners": Characteristics and prior schooling experiences of an invisible population. *International Multilingual Research Journal, 6*(2), 121–142.

Mitchell, K. (2003). Educating the national citizen in neoliberal times: from the multicultural self to the strategic cosmopolitan. *Transactions of the Institute of British Geographers, 28*(4), 387–403.

Molina, N. (2010). In a race all their own: The quest to make Mexicans ineligible for U.S. citizenship. *Pacific Historical Review, 79*(2), 167–201.

Molina, N. (2018). Understanding race as a relational concept. *Modern American History, 1*(1), 101–105.

Morales, P. Z., & Maravilla, J. V. (2019). The problems and possibilities of interest convergence in a dual language school. *Theory Into Practice, 58*(2), 145–153.

Morris, M. (2016). *Pushout: The criminalization of Black girls in schools*. New Press.

Moses, M. S., Maeda, D. J., & Paguyo, C. H. (2019). Racial politics, resentment, and affirmative action: Asian Americans as "model" college applicants. *The Journal of Higher Education, 90*(1), 1–26.

Mouttapa, M., Valente, T., Gallaher, P., Rohrbach, L. A., & Unger, J. B. (2004). Social network predictors of bullying and victimization. *Adolescence, 39*(154).

Museus, S. D., & Chang, M. J. (2009). Rising to the challenge of conducting research on Asian Americans in higher education. *New Directions for Institutional Research, 142*, 95–105.

Museus, S. D., & Kiang, P. N. (2009). Deconstructing the model minority myth and how it contributes to the invisible minority reality in higher education research. *New Directions for Institutional Research, 2009*(142), 5–15.

Ng, J., Pak, Y., & Hernandez, X. (2016). Beyond the perpetual foreigner and model minority stereotypes: A critical examination of how Asian Americans are framed.

In M. Zhou & A. C. Ocampo (Eds.), *Contemporary Asian America: A multidisciplinary reader* (pp. 576–599). NYU Press.

Ngai, M. M. (2004). *Impossible subjects*. Princeton University Press.

Ngo, B. (2013). Culture consciousness among Hmong immigrant leaders: Beyond the dichotomy of cultural essentialism and cultural hybridity. *American Educational Research Journal, 50*(5), 958–990.

Ngo, B. (2015). Hmong culture club as a place of belonging: The cultivation of Hmong students' cultural and political identities. *Journal of Southeast Asian American Education and Advancement, 10*(2), 2.

Ngo, B. (2017a). The costs of "living the dream" for Hmong immigrants: The impact of subtractive schooling on family and community. *Educational Studies, 53*(5), 450–467.

Ngo, B. (2017b). Naming their world in a culturally responsive space: Experiences of Hmong adolescents in an after-school theatre program. *Journal of Adolescent Research, 32*(1), 37–63.

Ngo, B., & Lee, S. J. (2007). Complicating the image of model minority success: A review of Southeast Asian American education. *Review of Educational Research, 77*(4), 415–453.

Nguyen, N. (2019). *Suspect communities: Anti-Muslim racism and the domestic war on terror*. University of Minnesota Press.

Nguyen, V. (2019). Refugeetude: When does a refugee stop being a refugee? *Social Text, 37*(2), 109–131.

Norwood, K. J. (2015). If you is White, you's alright: Stories about colorism in America. *Washington University Global Studies Law Review, 14*, 585.

Ochoa, G. L. (2013). *Academic profiling: Latinos, Asian Americans, and the achievement gap*. University of Minnesota Press.

Office of Refugee Resettlement (2012). *The Refugee Act*. http://www.acf.hhs.gov/programs/orr/resource/the-refugee-act

Olneck, M. R. (2009). What have immigrants wanted from American schools? What do they want now? Historical and contemporary perspectives on immigrants, language, and American schooling. *American Journal of Education, 115*(3), 379–406.

Olsen, L. (2014). Meeting the unique needs of long term English language learners. *National Education Association, 1*(1), 1–36.

Omi, M., & Winant, H. (2014). *Racial formation in the United States* (3rd ed.). Routledge.

Ong, A.(1996). Cultural citizenship as subject-making: Immigrants negotiate racial and cultural boundaries in the United States [and comments and reply]. *Current Anthropology, 37*(5), 737–762.

Ong, A. (1999). *Flexible citizenship: The cultural logics of transnationality*. Duke University Press.

Ong, A. (2003). *Buddha is hiding*. University of California Press.

Ong, A. (2013). Cultural citizenship as subject-making. In S. Lazar (Ed.), *The anthropology of citizenship: A reader* (pp. 79–92). Wiley.

Paik, S. J., Rahman, Z., Kula, S. M., Saito, L. E., & Witenstein, M. A. (2017). Ethnic afterschool programs and language schools in diverse Asian American communities: Varying resources, opportunities, and educational experiences (Part 2: How They Differ). *School Community Journal, 27*(2), 67–97.

Pappas, L. N. (2012). School closings and parent engagement. *Peace and Conflict: Journal of Peace Psychology, 18*(2), 165.

Paris, D. (2012). Culturally sustaining pedagogy: A needed change in stance, terminology, and practice. *Educational Researcher, 41*(3), 93–97.

Paris, D., & Alim, H. S. (2014). What are we seeking to sustain through culturally sustaining pedagogy? A loving critique forward. *Harvard Educational Review, 84*(1), 85–100.

Paris, D., & Alim, H. S. (Eds.). (2017). *Culturally sustaining pedagogies: Teaching and learning for justice in a changing world.* Teachers College Press.

Paris, D., & Winn, M. T. (Eds.). (2013). *Humanizing research: Decolonizing qualitative inquiry with youth and communities.* Sage.

Park, E. (2020). Asian Americans in the suburbs: Race, class, and Korean immigrant parental engagement. *Equity & Excellence in Education, 53*(1–2), 30–49.

Park, J. J., & Liu, A. (2014). Interest convergence or divergence? A critical race analysis of Asian Americans, meritocracy, and critical mass in the affirmative action debate. *The Journal of Higher Education, 85*(1), 36–64.

Perlstein, D. (1990). Teaching freedom: SNCC and the creation of the Mississippi freedom schools. *History of Education Quarterly, 30*(3), 297–324.

Pfeifer, M. E., Sullivan, J., Yang, K., & Yang, W. (2012). Hmong population and demographic trends in the 2010 Census and 2010 American Community Survey. *Hmong Studies Journal, 13*(2), 1–31.

Pheng, L. (n.d.). Refugees take root: Refugitude in Southeast Asian community-based educational spaces [Unpublished manuscript].

Poon, O. A., Dizon, J. P. M., & Squire, D. (2017). Count me in! Ethnic data disaggregation advocacy, racial mattering, and lessons for racial justice coalitions. *Journal Committed to Social Change on Race and Ethnicity, 3*(1), 91–124.

Poon, O. A., Squire, D., Kodama, C., Byrd, A., Chan, J., Manzano, L., Furr, S., & Bishundat, D. (2016). A critical review of the model minority myth in selected literature on Asian Americans and Pacific Islanders in higher education. *Review of Educational Research, 86*(2), 469–502.

Portes, A., & Rumbaut, R. G. (2001). *Legacies: The story of the immigrant second generation.* University of California Press.

Posey-Maddox, L. (2013). Professionalizing the PTO: Race, class, and shifting norms of parental engagement in a city public school. *American Journal of Education, 119*(2), 235–260.

Posey-Maddox, L. (2016). Beyond the consumer: Parents, privatization, and fundraising in U.S. urban public schooling. *Journal of Education Policy, 31*(2), 178–197.

Prashad, V. (2002). *Everybody was Kung Fu fighting: Afro-Asian connections and the myth of cultural purity.* Beacon Press.

Quan, R. S. (1982). *Lotus among the magnolias: The Mississippi Chinese.* University Press of Mississippi.

Reder, S. (1984). A study of English language training for refugees. Public Report. https://www.academia.edu/65862081/A_Study_of_English_Language_Training_for_Refugees_Public_Report

Reyes, A. (2005). Appropriation of African American slang by Asian American youth. *Journal of Sociolinguistics 9*(4), 509–532.

Reyes, A. (2007). *Language, identity, and stereotype among Southeast Asian American youth: The other Asian.* Lawrence Erlbaum.

Reyes, A. (2016). The voicing of Asian American figures. In H S. Alim, J. R. Rickford & A. F. Ball (Eds.), *Raciolinguistics: How language shapes our ideas about race* (pp. 309–326). Oxford University Press.

Rhee, J. E. (2013). The neoliberal racial project: The tiger mother and governmentality. *Educational Theory, 63*(6), 561–580.

Riessman, C. K. (2008). *Narrative methods for the human sciences*. Sage.

Rondilla, J. L. (2009). 4 Filipinos and the Color Complex. In E. N. Glenn (Ed.), *Shades of difference* (pp. 61–80). Stanford University Press.

Rondilla, J. L., & Spickard, P. R. (2007). *Is lighter better?: Skin-tone discrimination among Asian Americans*. Rowman & Littlefield.

Rosa, J., & Flores, N. (2017). Unsettling race and language: Toward a raciolinguistic perspective. *Language in Society, 46*(5), 621–647.

Rubin, B. C., Ayala, J., & Zaal, M. (2017). Authenticity, aims, and authority: Navigating youth participatory action research in the classroom. *Curriculum Inquiry, 47*(2), 175–194.

Rubin, J. S., Good, R. M., & Fine, M. (2020). Parental action and neoliberal education reform: Crafting a research agenda. *Journal of Urban Affairs, 42*(4), 492–510.

Rumbaut, R. G., & Ima, K. (1988). *The adaptation of Southeast Asian refugee youth: A comparative study*. U.S. Department of Health and Human Services, Family Support Administration, Office of Refugee Resettlement.

Schlund-Vials, C. J. (2016). The subjects of 1975: Delineating the necessity of critical refugee studies. *MELUS: Multi-Ethnic Literature of the United States, 41*(3), 199–203.

SEARAC (2020). National snapshot. https://www.searac.org/wp-content/uploads/2020/02/SEARAC_NationalSnapshot_PrinterFriendly.pdf

Sexton, J. (2010). People-of-color-blindness: Notes on the afterlife of slavery. *Social Text 28*(2), 31–56.

Sherwood, E. (2018). Providing equity or creating marginalization? ACCESS for English Language Learners and its potential effects on the educational outcomes for some of America's most vulnerable students. *The TFLTA Journal, 7* (43–49).

Shohamy, E., & Menken, K. (2015). Language assessment: Past to present misuses and future possibilities. *The handbook of bilingual and multilingual education*, 253–269.

Smith, J. B., Elder, E. C., & Stevens, K. (2014). Evaluation of a college readiness program: Advancement via individual determination (AVID). *Review of Higher Education & Self-Learning, 7*(25).

Smolarek, B. B., Vang, M., & Wolfgram, M. (2019). *HMoob American undergraduate students at University of Wisconsin's 4-Year comprehensive colleges—Background, enrollment statistics, and graduation trends*. Center for Research on College-Workforce Transitions, UW–Madison.

Smolarek, B. B., Wolfgram, M., Vang, M. N., Xiong, C. P., Lee, L., Lee, P., Thao, M., Vang, K., Xiong, P. K., Xiong, O., & Xiong, P. (2021). Our HMoob American College: Student-engaged community-based participatory action research (CBPAR) as counter-invisibility work. *International Journal of Qualitative Studies in Education*, 1–21.

Spivak, G. (1985). Subaltern studies: Deconstructing historiography. In D. Landry & G. MacLean (Eds.), *The Spivak reader* (pp. 203–235). Routledge.

Sue, D. W., Bucceri, J., Lin, A. I., Nadal, K. L., & Torino, G. C. (2016). Racial microaggressions and the Asian American experience. In M. Zhou & A. C. Ocampo (Eds.), *Contemporary Asian America: A multidisciplinary reader* (3rd ed.; pp. 464–484). NYU Press.

Takaki, R. (2008). *A different mirror: A history of multicultural America* (revised ed.). Little, Brown & Company.

Tang, E. (2015). *Unsettled: Cambodian refugees in the New York City hyperghetto* (Vol. 204). Temple University Press.

Taylor, C. (1994). The politics of recognition. In A. Gutman (Ed.), *Multiculturalism: Examining the politics of recognition*. Princeton University Press.

Taylor, C. (2021). The politics of recognition. In *Campus wars* (pp. 249–263). Routledge.

Taylor, C., & Gutmann, A. (1997). The politics of recognition. In A. Heble, D. P. Pennee, & J. R. Struthers (Eds.), *New contexts of Canadian criticism* (pp. 25–73). Broadview Press.

Teranishi, R. T. (2010). *Asians in the ivory tower: Dilemmas of racial inequality in American higher education*. Teachers College Press.

Thao, Yer J. (2003). Empowering Mong students: Home and school factors. *The Urban Review, 35*(1), 25–42

Truong-Vu, K.-P. (2022). On the margins of hyperinvisibility and hypervisibility: The paradox of being an Asian-American during the COVID-19 pandemic. In M. Heath, A. Darkwah, J. Beoku-Betts, & B. Purkayastha (Eds.), *Global feminist autoethnographies during COVID-19* (pp. 199–210). Routledge.

Tuck, E. (2009). Suspending damage: A letter to communities. *Harvard Educational Review, 79*(3), 409–428.

Tuck, E., & Yang, W. (2014). R-words: Refusing research. In D. Paris. & T. Winn (Eds.), *Humanizing research: Decolonizing qualitative inquiry with youth and communities* (pp. 223–248). Sage.

Turner, E. O. (2020). *Suddenly diverse*. University of Chicago Press.

Turney, K., & Kao, G. (2009). Barriers to school involvement: Are immigrant parents disadvantaged? *The Journal of Educational Research, 102*(4), 257–271.

Tyson, K. (2011). *Integration interrupted: Tracking, Black students, and acting White after Brown*. Oxford University Press.

Um, K. (2003). *A dream denied: Educational experiences of Southeast Asian American youth: Issues and recommendations*. Southeast Asia Resource Action Center.

Umansky, I. M., & Dumont, H. (2021). English Learner labeling: How English Learner classification in kindergarten shapes teacher perceptions of student skills and the moderating role of bilingual instructional settings. *American Educational Research Journal, 58*(5), 993–1031.

Valenzuela, A. (1999). *Subtractive schooling: U.S.–Mexican youth and the politics of caring*. SUNY Press.

Valdés, G. (1997). Dual-language immersion programs: A cautionary note concerning the education of language-minority students. *Harvard Educational Review, 67*(3), 391–430.

Valdez, V. E., Freire, J. A., & Delavan, M. G. (2016). The gentrification of dual language education. *The Urban Review, 48*(4), 601–627.

Vang, M. (2021) *History on the run: Secrecy, fugitivity, and Hmong refugee epistemologies*. Duke University Press.

Vaught, S. E. (2012). 'They might as well be Black': the racialization of Sa'moan high school students. *International Journal of Qualitative Studies in Education, 25*(5), 557–582.

Vaught, S. E. (2017). *Compulsory: Education and the dispossession of youth in a prison school*. University of Minnesota Press.

Ventura, J. (2017). "We created that space with everybody": Constructing a community-based space of belonging and familia in a Latina/o youth group. *Association of Mexican American Educators Journal, 11*(1), 23–37.

Vue, R. (2021). Trauma and resilience in the lives and education of Hmong American students: Forging pedagogies of remembrance with critical refugee discourse. *Race Ethnicity and Education, 24*(2), 282–301.

Walsh, D. (2018). Youth participatory action research as culturally sustaining pedagogy. *Theory Into Practice, 57*(2), 127–136.

Wang, J., Leu, J., & Shoda, Y. (2011). When the seemingly innocuous "stings": Racial microaggressions and their emotional consequences. *Personality and Social Psychology Bulletin, 37*(12), 1666–1678.

Watt, K. M., Huerta, J. J., & Alkan, E. (2011). Identifying predictors of college success through an examination of AVID graduates' college preparatory achievements. *Journal of Hispanic Higher Education, 10*(2), 120–133.

Weis, L., & Fine, M. (2012). Critical bifocality and circuits of privilege: Expanding critical ethnographic theory and design. *Harvard Educational Review, 82*(2), 173–201.

Wilderson III, F. B. (2010). *Red, white & black*. Duke University Press.

Willis, P. (1977). *Learning to labour: How working class kids get working class jobs*. Routledge.

Wisconsin Policy Forum. (2019, March.) *Another alarming achievement gap*. https://wispolicyforum.org/research/another-alarming-achievement-gap

Wong, N. W. A. (2010). "Cuz they care about the people who goes there": The multiple roles of a community-based youth center in providing "youth (comm) unity" for low-income Chinese American youth. *Urban Education, 45*(5), 708–739.

Wortham, S. (2008). Linguistic anthropology of education. *Annual Review of Anthropology, 37*(1), 37–51. doi:10.1146/ annurev.anthro.36.081406.094401

Wu, E. D. (2014). *The color of success*. Princeton University Press.

Wun, C. (2014). The anti-black order of No Child Left Behind: Using Lacanian psychoanalysis and critical race theory to examine NCLB. *Educational Philosophy and Theory, 46*(5), 462–474.

Wun, C. (2016). Unaccounted foundations: Black girls, anti-Black racism, and punishment in schools. *Critical Sociology, 42*(4–5), 737–750.

Xiong, C. (2021). *HMoob-making lessons: Politics of belonging, home-making and education* (Unpublished doctoral dissertation).

Xiong, Y. S. (2012). Hmong Americans' educational attainment: Recent changes and remaining challenges. *Hmong Studies Journal, 13*(2), 1–18.

Xiong, Y. S. (2016). The centrality of ethnic community and the military service master frame in Hmong Americans' protest events and cycles of protest, 1980–2010. *Hmong Studies Journal, 17*, 1–33.

Xiong, Y. S. (2021). *Home-making in a neoliberal nationalist Thai school* (Unpublished doctoral dissertation). University of Wisconsin–Madison.

Xiong, Y. S. (2022). *Immigrant agency: Hmong American movements and the politics of racialized incorporation*. Rutgers University Press.

Xiong, Y. S., & Xiong, N. (2011). *The prevalence of English monolingualism and its association with generational status among Hmong Americans, 2005–2009*. Hmong Studies Journal, 12.

Yang, A. (2020, April 1). We Asian Americans are not the virus, but we can be part of the cure. *The Washington Post*. https://www.washingtonpost.com/opinions/2020/04/01/andrew-yang-coronavirus-discrimination/

Young, V. A., Barrett, R., & Lovejoy, K. B. (2014). *Other people's English: Code-meshing, code-switching, and African American literacy*. Teachers College Press.

Zhou, M., & Bankston, C. (1998). *Growing up American: How Vietnamese children adapt to life in the United States*. Russell Sage Foundation.

Zhou, M., & Kim, S. (2006). Community forces, social capital, and educational achievement: The case of supplementary education in the Chinese and Korean immigrant communities. *Harvard Educational Review, 76*(1), 1–29.

Zhou, M., & Li, X. Y. (2003). Ethnic language schools and the development of supplementary education in the immigrant Chinese community in the United States. *New Directions for Youth Development, 2003*(100), 57–73.

Zimmerman, J., & Robertson, E. (2017). *The case for contention: Teaching controversial issues in American schools.* University of Chicago Press.

Index

Abu El-Haj, T. R., 114
Academic English, 37
  emergent bilinguals and, 39
  LTELLs and, 36–37
Academic levels, Hmong Meskas Summer
  Camp, 75
"Academic middle" grouping, 17
Achievement gap, racialized, 17, 41–45,
  107–108
  Asian American students and, 9, 43
  Black–White, 2, 16, 61, 111
  HEA focus on, 73, 75–76, 104
  Hmong students and, 71, 75–76, 81–82
  persistent, 31, 41–42
  productive citizenship and, 108
  SHOUT and, 87
Adoptees, Asian, 33
Advancement via Individual Determination
  (AVID) classes/program, 33–34, 42–45,
  55
  fieldnotes on, 41, 43, 44, 55
African American vernacular (AAVE), 39, 40
Alba, R., 69
Alim, H. S., 40, 106, 108, 111–113
Alkan, E., 42
Alvarez, R., 8
"American Dream," 82, 87
Anstrom, K. A., 37
Anti-Asian racism, resisting
  model minority politics and, 8–10
  panethnicity/cross-racial coalitions, 10–12
Anti-Blackness
  as route to freedom, 4
  in schools, 93–94
  SHOUT's challenges to, 88–94
Anti-Hmong sentiment, 57–58
Apple, M. W., 100
"Asian"
  as panethnic category, 51, 54
  use of term, 33

Asian American(s)
  ethnic data disaggregation and, 62
  ethnicity/misethnicization of, 16, 46–55
  origin/history of term, 109–110
  as panethnic category, 11, 54
  racialization of, 40
  stereotyping of, 2–3, 4, 8, 10, 40, 46, 48,
    51–52, 68, 104–105, 108
Asian Club, 47–55
  fieldnote on, 45
  members of, 23–24
Au, W., 17, 62, 81, 100, 107
Ayala, J., 113

Baker, L. L., 37
Baldridge, B. J., 12–13, 87, 98, 100–101, 106,
  109
Bankston, C., 90
Barrett, R., 39, 40, 95
Bartlett, L., 19, 110
Beardsmore, H. B., 39
Beauty, colorism and, 98
Beck, N., 12, 13, 106
Bernhardt, P. E., 42
Bhatt, A., 18
Bhojani, N., 18
Bilingual resource specialists (BRS), 34–36,
  38–39
Birks, M., 19
Bishundat, D., 63
Black communities
  colorism within, 94, 98
  SEAA solidarity with, 85–94, 104
  SHOUT and, 85, 86
Black Lives Matter (BLM) Movement, 89,
  92–94, 104
Bonilla-Silva, E., 49
Bourdieu, P., 32
Bow, L., 107
Bowles, S., 87

Braa, D., 100
Breakdancing, 98–99
Brown, A. L., 4
Brown, T. M., 87
Bucceri, J., 46
Bucholtz, M., 98, 108, 113
Budiman, A., 11
Burawoy, M., 19
Byrd, A., 63

Callahan, R., 55, 68
Callero, P., 100
Cambodian refugees, 91
Cambodian students, 52
Cammarota, J., 13, 113
Canagarajah, S., 39, 41, 95
Caplan, N., 65, 90
Casillas, D. I., 98, 108, 113
Castagno, A. E., 15, 107–108
Chae, N., 36
Chan, J., 63
Chanbonpin, K. D., 48–49
Chang, M. J., 62
Chapman, Y., 19
Chhuon, V., 52
Chinese students, 47
Choy, M. H., 90
Christens, B. D., 13
Chubb, J. E., 81
Code-meshing, 39
    among Hmong students, 40
    code-switching vs., 39–40
Code-switching, 39
    code-meshing vs., 39–40
Collaborative research project, 22, 29–55
    community characteristics, 15–17
    methodology, 19–20, 30–31
    participant anonymity, 20
    research period, 29, 30
    student demographics, 30
College readiness programs, 41–45
Collins, J., 87
Colorism, 48
    in Asian American communities, 49
    beauty and, 98
    in Black communities, 94
Community-based education spaces (CBES),
        12–13. See also Hmong Meskas Summer
        Camp (HMSC)
    SHOUT involvement in, 87–88, 100–101
Conchas, G. Q., 9
Cramer, K. J., 15–16

Creese, A., 18
Critical pedagogy, 100–103
Critical refugee studies/scholars, 89–93, 109
Cross-racial coalitions, 10–12
Cucchiara, M., 59
Cultural pluralism, 58–59
Culturally relevant pedagogy, 76
Culturally sustaining pedagogy (CSP), 14
    HEA call for, 70–73, 82
    for invisibility disruption, 111–114
Cummins, J., 36
Cushing, I., 39

Dao, L. T., 11, 90, 109
Data desegregation, 61–66, 82
Deaux, K., 112
Deficit perspective
    emergent bilinguals, 39
    Hmonglish/Hmong language, 39–40
    stereotyping contributing to, 66
Delavan, M. G., 69
Delgado-Gaitan, C., 59
Deng, S., 8
DePouw, C., 40, 63, 92
Desimone, L., 57
Developmental bilingual education (DBE),
        69–70, 110
DeWalt, B. R., 18
Dewalt, K., 18
Dhingra, P., 9, 12, 54
Diamond, J. B., 17, 54–55
DiCerbo, P. A., 37
Dietrich, D. R., 49
Disabled Hmong, 66
Disrespect, shown by White students, 32
Dixon, A. R., 49
Dizon, J. P. M., 63
Donnor, J. K., 4
Dual language immersion (DLI), 69–70
Dumas, M. J., 4, 89
Dumont, H., 55
Dyrness, A., 13, 113–114

Eckert, P., 32
Elder, E. C., 42
Elderly Hmong, 66
Emergent bilinguals, 34–35, 39
Emerson, R. M., 19
English as a Second Language (ESL) program, 34
    HEA concerns regarding, 66–70
    teachers/bilingual resource specialists for,
        35–36

English learners (ELs)/English language learners
(ELLs), 17, 18
    academic status, 55
    definitions and limitations, 34
    "emergent bilingual" vs., 34–35
    language support/services for, 36, 38
    long-term, 36
    as stigmatized label, 34
    WIDA ACCESS exams for, 35, 37
English proficiency, 35
Espiritu, Y. L., 10, 11, 51, 89–90, 109–110
Ethical concerns, in ethnographic research, 21
Ethnic misidentification
    invisibility and, 46
    researcher's experience, 24
Ethnographic research
    political and ethical concerns in, 20–21
    positionality statements of researchers,
        21–28
    team approach to, 18–20

Fabricant, M., 114
Family values, in model minority discourse, 83
Fanon, F., 5
Feagin, J., 5, 89
Ferguson, A. A., 4
Fine, M., 19, 81, 110, 113–114
Fishman, J. A., 12
Flanagan, C. A., 13
Flores, N., 37–40, 68, 98, 113
Flowers, K. S., 68
Francis, K., 19
Fraser, N., 5, 53
Freedom
    BLM movement and, 89
    critical pedagogy and, 100
    entrepreneurial, 80
    gender inequality and, 96
    Hmonglish use and, 103
    for marginalized/minoritized groups, 4–5, 91
Freedom School, 93
Freire, J. A., 69
Freire, P., 100
Fretz, R. I., 19
Frost, A. K., 8

Gallaher, P., 8
García, O., 34, 39–40, 113
Garza, A., 89
Gee, G. C., 7–8
Gender injustice, SHOUT and, 85
Gifted education/grouping, 17

Gintis, H., 87
Ginwright, S. A., 13, 94, 100, 102, 106
Golb, J., 5, 53
Gonzales, R. G., 13
Good, R. M., 81
Goto, S. G., 7–8
Gran Torino (movie), 63
Gutmann, A., 4, 5, 70

Haines, D. W., 65
Harklau, L., 68
Harvey, D., 80
Heath, S. B., 32
Hernandez, X., 46
Hess, D. E., 112
High school
    invisibility/hypervisibility in, 13
    racialized achievement/opportunity gaps in,
        17, 41–45
    research project at, 22, 30–55. See also
        Collaborative research project
High school students
    political activism of, 29
    socialization among, 45
Hill, K., 81, 82
Hing, B. O., 7
Hmong American community
    middle-class professionals in, 56–59, 82–83.
        See also Hmong Education Advocates
        (HEA)
    recognition pursued by, 13, 83
    resilience, 12–13, 107
    stereotyping of, 58, 63
    subgroups among, 20
    traditional/refugee leaders in, 57
Hmong culture and history
    commodification of, 83
    inclusion in curriculum, 72–73
Hmong Education Advocates (HEA), 22,
    59–61
    on achievement gap, 73, 75–76, 104
    data desegregation and, 61–66, 82
    fundraising by, 76–80, 77n2
    goals, 72–73
    rejection of "Asian American" racial
        category, 109–110
Hmong Meskas Summer Camp (HMSC), 21,
    73–76
    academic levels, 75
    curriculum at, 75–76, 78, 82–83
    funding and support for, 76–80, 77n2
    program goals, 74–75, 74n1

Hmong Mutual Assistance Association, 84
Hmong National Development (HND), 108
Hmong parents
    frustrations, 58–59
    sacrifice/self-sufficiency and, 64–65
Hmong refugees, 24, 27, 40, 53–54, 73,
        113–114
    as community leaders, 57
    "good refugee" image, 66
    from "secret war," 78, 107, 108
    from Vietnam War, 2, 11, 83
Hmong students
    academic status/world, 18, 31–34, 64
    achievement gap and, 71, 75–76, 81–82
    culturally sustaining pedagogy for, 14
    data disaggregation and, 61–66
    EL/ELL designation, 34, 35, 36, 38, 55
    high school demographics, 33
    Hmonglish identity and, 39
    model minority image and, 83
    racialized microaggressions and, 32, 45–46
    summer camp for. See Hmong Meskas
        Summer Camp (HMSC)
    testing data for, 18
Hmonglish, 21–22, 39
    deficit perspective regarding, 39, 40
    freedom to speak, 103
    Hmong attitudes to, 41
Hong, J. J., 46
Honneth, A., 5, 53
Hudley, C., 52
Huerta, J. J., 42
Hunter, M., 48
Hursh, D., 62, 81, 114
Hypervisibility, 13. See also Misrecognition
    harm caused by, 4–5, 107, 113–114
    HEA concerns about, 63

Ima, K., 90
Inclusion
    Hmong culture and history, as HEA goal,
        72–73, 83
    inadvertent inequality and, 17, 107–108
Inequality
    inclusion implementation and, 17, 107–108
    niceness/tolerance and, 15, 107–108
    parent/community activism and, 81
Institutions, dominant
    cultivating social capital with, 83, 86–87
    mistrust of, 87
Invisibility, 1–2, 13
    disruption strategies, 107–114

    harm caused by, 4–5, 107, 113–114
    HEA resistance efforts, 63–64
    misethnicization and, 46
Irizarry, J. G., 87
Isolation, invisibility and, 1–2

Jaffe-Walter, R., 114
Jalao, L. C., 63
Jew, V., 65, 90
Junn, J., 7, 10

Kanno, Y., 68
Kao, G., 57, 59
Katz, M. B., 66
Keddie, A., 5
Kendall (Hmong high school student), 1–2
Khmer refugees, 23
Kiang, P. N., 62
Kim, C. J., 7, 9
Kim, S., 12
Kim, S. Y., 8
Kirshner, B., 12–13
Kleifgen, J. A., 34
Kleyn, T., 36–38
Kodama, C., 63
Koyama, J. P., 38, 62
Kula, S. M., 13
Kumashiro, K., 62
Kwon, S. A., 12, 13
Kymlicka, W., 5, 60, 82

La Gorce, T., 8
Labaree, D. F., 81
Ladson-Billings, G., 15, 20, 44, 76, 103, 106
Language, White students correcting, 40–41
Lareau, A., 32, 57, 59
Lee, E., 7
Lee, G. Y., 20
Lee, J., 9
Lee, J. S., 98, 108, 113
Lee, L., 113
Lee, P., 113
Lee, R. G., 7
Lee, S. J., 29
    career activities, 137
    cited, 2, 4, 6, 9, 11, 20, 22, 28–29, 32–33,
        40, 46, 51–54, 57, 62–64, 71, 89, 92,
        94, 112, 114
    fieldnotes of, 29, 30, 86, 98
    positionality statement, 21–22
Leonardo, Z., 54
Leu, J., 46

Levinson, B. A., 81
Lewis, A. E., 17, 54–55
Li, J., 8
Li, X. Y., 12
Liberation. *See also* Freedom
  critical pedagogy and, 100
  SHOUT educational programming for,
    84–106
Limited English proficiency, 35
Lin, A. I., 46
Lin, A. M., 113
Linguistic repertoires, interweaving of, 39
Linguistic segregation, code-switching as, 40
Lipman, P., 62, 81, 107
Lippi-Green, R., 37, 39
Liu, A., 9
Lo, B., 53
Loewen, J. W., 8, 9
Long-term English language learners
    (LTELLs), 36
  academic English and, 36–37
  Hmong students, 1–2, 38
  labeling impact, 37–38
  WIDA ACCESS exams and, 37
Lopez, G., 7
Lorenzo, M. K., 8
Louie, V. S., 9
Lovejoy, K. B., 39–40, 95
Lubienski, C., 82
Lukose, R. A., 109

Macedo, D. S., 100
Maeda, D. J., 9–10
Mainstream American English (MAE), 39
Manzano, L., 63
Maravilla, J. V., 69
Marginalized/Minoritized groups
  freedom for, 4–5, 91
  misrecognition and, 4, 5, 24, 53, 70–71
  model minority. *See* Model minority
  research restrictions on, 86–87
Martin, P., 18
Martina, C. A., 114
Masuoka, N., 7, 10
Mathews, J., 42
Matias, C. E., 41
Medina, J. C., 12–13, 106
Melamed, J., 82, 89, 108
Menken, K., 36–38
Microaggressions, racialized, 32, 45–46
Miranda, C. P., 114
Misethnicization, invisibility and, 46

Misrecognition/Misidentification, 4, 5, 24
  harm caused by, 70–71, 107, 113–114
  Hmong Americans, 53, 55
Mitchell, K., 82
Model minority
  academic success, 64
  discourses, 64, 83
  Hmong students and, 83
  politics of, 5–10
  stereotyping, 6, 9, 40, 83
Moe, T. M., 81
Molina, N., 6, 7
Monoglossic language ideology, 39–40
Morales, P. Z., 69
Morris, M., 4
Moses, M. S., 9
Mouttapa, M., 8
Muller, C., 55
Multiculturalism, 58–59, 82–83
Museus, S. D., 62

Nadal, K. L., 46
Neoliberal educational policies, 17, 31, 53,
    56, 62
  Hmong community goals and, 64–65, 108
  Hmong educational advocates and, 80–82,
    89, 104
  multiculturalism and, 82–83
  parent activism against, 81
  SHOUT rejecting, 104
  testing of English learners, 108
Neoliberalism, defined, 80–81
Ng, J., 46
Ngai, M. M., 7
Ngo, B., 3, 39, 64, 70, 78
Nguyen, N., 4, 90
Niceness, inequality and, 15, 107–108
No Child Left Behind (NCLB) Act, 16, 35
Norwood, K. J., 98

Ochoa, G. L., 55
Office of Refugee Resettlement, 90
Olneck, M. R., 12
Olsen, L., 36
Omi, M., 6
1.5 generation, 56
Ong, A., 40, 65, 90, 92
Opportunity gap, 3, 9, 42

Paguyo, C. H., 9
Paik, S. J., 13
Pak, Y., 46

Panethnicity, 10–12
    "Asian" and, 33, 60
    Cambodian students and, 52
    erased diversity and, 111
    Hmong concerns and, 55, 62, 110
    identification difficulty and, 51
Pappas, L. N., 81
Parent activism, 81
Parent Teacher Organization (PTO), 58–59, 83
Paris, D., 21, 86, 106, 108, 111–113
Park, E., 4, 9, 12
Park, J. J., 9
Parker (high school senior/SHOUT youth
        leader), 46, 51, 84, 94, 98–101
Patten, E., 7
Pedagogy
    critical, 100–103
    culturally relevant, 76
    culturally sustaining, 14, 70–73, 82, 111–114
Pérez, C. C., 9
Perlstein, D., 93
Personal responsibility, as AVID theme, 44
Pfeifer, M. E., 20, 56
Pheng, L. M., 13
    career activities, 137
    cited, 28–29, 89
    fieldnotes, 33, 34, 41, 43, 45, 48, 50, 52
    positionality statement, 22–24
Political activism, of high school students, 29
Political education, critical pedagogy and, 100–103
Political perspectives
    of community where research conducted,
        15–16
    of ethnographic research, 21
    radical healing concepts and, 100–103
Poon, O. A., 63
Portes, A., 69
Posey-Maddox, L., 59, 81
Positionality statements, researchers, 21–28
Poverty
    Black/Hmong experiences of, 89–93
    racism intersection with, 85
    views on, 65, 66
Prashad, V., 10
Precollege programs, 41–45
Productive citizens
    achievement gap as threat to, 108
    as Hmong community goal, 64–65, 108
    neoliberal perspective on, 81–82

Quan, R. S., 9
Queer injustice, SHOUT and, 85

Racialized microaggressions, 32, 45–46
Raciolinguistics, 40
Racism
    anti-Asian. See Anti-Asian racism
    internalized, code-switching and, 40
    poverty intersection with, 85
Radical healing, 100–103
Rahman, Z., 13
Recognition, Hmong community pursuit of,
        13, 83
Reder, S., 90
Reeves, M. A., 12–13, 106
Refugees, Asian, 10–11, 49. See also Hmong
        refugees; Khmer refugees
    employment/resettlement issues, 89–91
    government policy toward, 65, 112, 114
    U.S. racial context and, 112
Reinherz, H. Z., 8
Researchers
    collaboration. See Collaborative research
        project
    fieldnotes. See under individually named
        researchers
    positionality statements of, 21–28
    SHOUT mistrust of, 28, 86–87
Resilience, of Hmong community, 12–13,
        107
Resistance, to Anti-Asian racism, 8–12
    in community-based education spaces,
        12–13
    model minority politics and, 5–8
    panethnicity/cross-racial coalitions, 10–12
    politics of, 14
Reyes, A., 12, 39–41
Rhee, J. E., 82
Riessman, C. K., 21
Rivera, C., 37
Robertson, E., 112
Rohrbach, L. A., 8
Rondilla, J. L., 48–49
Rosa, J., 40, 68, 98, 113
Rubin, B. C., 113
Rubin, J. S., 81
Ruiz, N. G., 7, 11
Rumbaut, R. G., 69, 90

Saito, L. E., 13
Schlund-Vials, C. J., 90
School. See High school
Scott, J., 81, 82
SEARAC (Southeast Asia Resource Action
        Center), 63, 91

"Secret war," 78, 107, 108
Self-determination, 88
Self-reliance/Self-sufficiency, 64–65, 110. *See also* Productive citizens
Sepúlveda, E., 13, 113
Sexton, J., 6, 89
Shaw, L. L., 19
Sherwood, E., 37
Shoda, Y., 46
SHOUT (Solidarity Holds Our Unity Together), 1, 59–61
  anti-Blackness challenged by, 88–94
  "Asian American" racial category and, 110–111
  culturally-specific programming, 94–100
  educational programming, 88
  founding/founders of, 84–85
  mission/activities of, 85–86
  political education by, radical healing and, 100–103
  racialized achievement gap and, 87, 104
  relationship with school district, 86
  trust issues and, 28, 86–87
  Xiong on, 27–28
Smith, J. B., 42
Smitherman, G., 40
Smolarek, B. B., 56, 113
Social capital, cultivating, 83, 86–87
Socialization, high school students, 45
Solidarity, Black-SEAA, 85–94, 104. *See also* SHOUT (Solidarity Holds Our Unity Together)
Solorza, C. R., 39
Southeast Asian American (SEAA) populations
  Black solidarity with, 85–94, 104
  SHOUT awareness among, 86
  socialization patterns among, 45
Southeast Asians (SEA)
  community elders, 85
  high school demographics, 30, 44
  marginalized, 53
  SHOUT and, 85
Spivak, G., 78
Squire, D., 63
Stereotype/Stereotyping
  of Asian Americans, 2–4, 8, 10, 40, 46, 48, 51–52, 68, 104–105, 108
  challenges to, 43–44
  cultural, 58
  data desegregation and, 61–66, 82
  of Hmong community, 58, 63

of model minority, 6, 9, 40, 83
  shared experiences, connecting with students through, 43
Stevens, K., 42
Stigma/ Stigmatization
  of EL label, 34, 55, 105
  of Hmong, 40, 53, 68, 107
Sue, D. W., 46
Sullivan, J., 20, 56
Sutton, M., 81

Takaki, R., 7
Takeuchi, D. T., 7–8
Tang, E., 90, 91
Tapp, N., 20
Taylor, C., 4, 5, 70, 114
Telles, E. E., 49
Teranishi, R. T., 62
Testing data
  Asian Americans and, 17–18
  Hmong data desegregation and, 61–66, 82
Thao, Yer J., 67
Tolerance, inequality and, 15
Torino, G. C., 46
Truong-Vu, K.-P., 4
Tuck, E., 20, 27
Turner, E. O., 17, 55, 107
Turney, K., 57, 59
Tyson, K., 55

Um, K., 64
Umansky, I. M., 55
Unger, J. B., 8
Unity. *See* SHOUT (Solidarity Holds Our Unity Together)
Up Against Whiteness: . . . (S.J. Lee)
  collaborative project based on, 22, 30–55. *See also* Collaborative research project
  data collection/fieldwork for, 16, 18
  Hmong community changes and, 56
Uplift (UP) program, 42

Valdés, G., 57, 69
Valdez, V. E., 69
Valente, T., 8
Valenzuela, A., 71
Vang, M. N.
  career activity, 137
  cited, 28, 56, 66, 89, 107–108, 113–114
  fieldnotes, 70, 79–80
  positionality statement, 24–27
Vaught, S. E., 4, 92

Vavrus, F., 19, 110
Ventura, J., 98
Vietnam War, 2, 11, 83
Violence
    gender-based, 84–85, 88, 96, 105–106
    police, 89
    symbolic, 13
Vue, R., 90

Walsh, D., 112–113
Wang, J., 46
Wang, Y., 8
Waterway Foundation, 86
Watt, K. M., 42
Weis, L., 19, 110
Welfare dependence, racialized stereotypes
        and, 66
White middle-class parents
    Asian adoptees and, 33
    concerns, 17
    Hmong voice and, 58–59
White saviorism, 41
White students
    classroom behavior patterns, 31–32,
        40–41
    social behavior, 45–46
Whiteness/White gaze, 107–108
Whitmore, J. K., 90
WIDA Consortium, 35
    ACCESS exams for ELs/ELLs, 35, 37
Wilderson III, F. B., 89
Wilkinson, L., 55
Willis, P., 87

Winant, H., 6
Winn, M. T., 21, 86
Winstead, T., 81
Wisconsin
    Hmong American community in, 20
    research location characteristics, 15–16
Wisconsin Policy Forum, 18
Witenstein, M. A., 13
Wolfgram, M., 56, 113
Wong, J. H. S., 4
Wong, N. W. A., 12
Wortham, S., 37
Wu, E. D., 8
Wun, C., 4, 89

Xiong, C., 28, 89, 113
    career activities, 137–138
    cited, 46, 56, 84
    fieldnotes, 96, 97, 99
    positionality statement, 27–28
Xiong, N., 69
Xiong, P., 113
Xiong, Y. S., 38, 46, 56, 66, 69, 83,
        108, 110

Yang, A., 8
Yang, K., 20, 56
Yang, W., 20, 56
Young, V. A., 39, 40, 95

Zaal, M., 113
Zhou, M., 9, 12, 90
Zimmerman, J., 112

About the Authors

Stacey J. Lee is the Frederick Erickson Professor of Educational Policy Studies at the University of Wisconsin–Madison and a faculty affiliate in Asian American Studies. Her research focuses on the role of education in the incorporation of immigrants into the United States. She is the author of *Unraveling the Model Minority Stereotype: Listening to Asian American Youth* and *Up Against Whiteness: Race, School, and Immigrant Youth*.

Linda M. Pheng is a PhD candidate in the Department of Educational Policy Studies at the University of Wisconsin–Madison. Linda's research lies at the intersection of critical race theory and pedagogy, anthropology and sociology of race and class in education, and displacement and belonging. Grounded in her identity as a daughter of Khmer refugees, Linda's academic praxis aims to empower students through a socially just curriculum and to recognize and respect the knowledge of multiply marginalized communities through community-engaged research practices. Her dissertation examines community-based pedagogical approaches for reclaiming and resisting deficit racialized discourses of Southeast Asian refugee identity, knowledge, and agency.

Mai Neng Vang (she/nws/they) is a PhD student in the Educational Policy Studies program at UW–Madison with a broad research interest in the educational experiences of minoritized students. More specifically, she explores how students and young people organize and respond to inequities and advocate for transformative changes. Mai Neng is currently a research mentor for the HMoob American College Paj Ntaub participatory action research team, working alongside two researchers at the Center for Research on College-Workforce Transitions and undergraduate student activists from the HMoob American Studies Committee.

Choua Xiong's research approach is informed by her activism as an educator in Southeast Asian community-based educational spaces, schools, and higher education. Choua led various collaborative and community-based participatory action research (CBPAR) projects that center the perspectives of minoritized youth and highlight the roles communities of color play in educating youth about schooling, political participation, belonging, historical trauma, and healing. Her dissertation, funded by the USED Fulbright-Hays Doctoral Dissertation Abroad 2019 and NAEd/Spencer Dissertation 2020 fellowships, examines how stateless people navigate exclusionary practices of citizenship and demand inclusive educational opportunities in northern Thailand. Her dissertation, titled "HMoob-Making Lessons: Stateless Belonging and Home-making in a Neoliberal Nationalist Thai School," reveals that HMoob people draw on their embodied knowledge as stateless, indigenous, and diasporic people to enact HMoob-making as everyday practices of home-making to counter neoliberal nationalistic schooling. Choua will be an Assistant Professor in the Education for Equity and Justice Department at the University of Wisconsin–Eau Claire starting in fall 2022.